Cities & the Sea

Cities & the Sea

Port City Planning in Early Modern Europe

JOSEF W. KONVITZ

THE JOHNS HOPKINS UNIVERSITY PRESS · BALTIMORE AND LONDON

This book has been brought to publication with the generous assistance of the Andrew W. Mellon Foundation.

The Johns Hopkins University Press, Baltimore, Maryland 21218
The Johns Hopkins Press Ltd., London

Library of Congress Catalog Number 77–12976
ISBN 0–8018–2038–3

Library of Congress Cataloging in Publication data
will be found on the last printed page of this book.

For Isa

Contents

PART III **THE DECLINE OF PORT CITY PLANNING**

Illustrations

From the hundreds of maps, prints, and drawings I examined in the course of research, I have selected this sample to illustrate *Cities and the Sea*. Many of the visual documents not reproduced are cited in notes and in the bibliography as primary historical sources, and the interested scholar can consult them in archives as he would any unpublished source. Historians of cartography must accept my apology for omitting the conventional data on size, scale, and methods of projection and manufacture; such information is too specialized to be included.

Figures

Tables

Preface

Cities appear as a constant in every civilization, but comparisons between urban cultures across time and space have rarely been attempted. Without them, the historical contours of urban development, even in such well-documented regions as Europe, can become distorted. Thus, because few studies focus upon themes in European urban history that straddle both the preindustrial and industrial eras, the importance of urban change and of new patterns of urban living are mistakenly assumed to be phenomena of industrialization alone. The realization has been slow in coming that early modern Europeans were able to mold city growth into a variety of social, political, economic, and spatial patterns, and that their capacity to make such connections probably facilitated industrialization.[1] This book, a study of how and why Europeans since the Renaissance have planned new port cities and rebuilt existing ones, demonstrates that a view of the European past and present can take preindustrial urbanization into account, that graphic documentation of spatial planning can illustrate the process of early modern urban growth, and that then and since, the pursuit of maritime affairs has played a neglected but critical role in the European urban world.

It is no accident that this study focuses upon port cities. Until the railroad reduced long-distance land transport costs, the needs of ten thousand or more city dwellers could only be met through waterborne commerce. In fact, any city with direct access to a navigable waterway had great growth potential: London had some three hundred thousand inhabitants at the end of the sixteenth century, and over eight hundred thousand at the end of the eighteenth century. The great Italian port cities were the first to develop the commercial system whereby the products of faraway places were transformed into the everyday necessities and occasional luxuries of urban living; this happened in the eleventh and twelfth centuries. But every coastal town did not become a city, nor did communities exist wherever there was a good harbor, nor did every port city have a good harbor: there are mysteries about why men have chosen to live in cities, to occupy certain sites, and to link their destinies to the movements of ships that cannot be entirely explained by economic, social, and political events.[2] By the seventeenth century the most prominent networks of port cities existed along rivers in Italy, Flanders, Germany, and France, and along the shorelines of the Baltic, Northern, and

Mediterranean Seas. These cities, and their commercial links connecting them to each other and to their rural hinterlands, represented a very large proportion of Europe's economic exchange. Until the end of the sixteenth century the maritime and commercial technologies that supported such urban growth would have been recognizable to a medieval Genoan or Flemish merchant. After that time, there were changes in the maritime world and in the ways cities were tied to it. In the early seventeenth century northern Europeans began to colonize North America and the Far East; they initiated commercial joint-stock trading companies; and they created permanent commercial and military fleets to replace the seasonal or temporary ones that had sufficed until then. The variety of products brought to and commonly available in cities increased, the volume of commerce multiplied, and maritime affairs took on more profound political and social implications than ever before. Turning to city planning techniques, Europeans tried to relate the expansion of commercial and military maritime affairs to changes in the number and appearance of their port cities.

The documents needed to reconstruct the meaning of early modern port city planning have survived. Thousands of plans, drawings, and maps in archives and in libraries have remained largely unexamined, certainly because historians have not been overly concerned about city planning, but also because these documents have usually been separated from any letters or memoirs to which they may once have been attached. Historians have been unwilling to work without written records in this case, and have left graphic documents for other specialists. Those few items relating to cities that have become known in historical works have been used as illustrations, and not as primary sources themselves, of interest for what they were made to do—translate ideas and ambitions into projective and symbolic physical and spatial forms.[3] Urban geographers have used these documents to classify the evolutionary morphology of city forms;[4] art historians have examined the fine-arts interests of planners from these maps and plans;[5] and, recently, students of semiotics have provided a descriptive method to study a society and its ideas from the signs that were maps and architecture.[6] All these approaches have relevance in this book. Maps, plans, and drawings of port cities reveal an important aspect of the seventeenth-century world. Just as written documents reflect the development of the vernacular language, of precision and clarity as ends in themselves, and of the confidence men had in their ability to think about and act upon the affairs of the day, just as statistical records illustrate a growing concern to quantify the material world, so graphic documents demonstrate to us the capacity of seventeenth-century Europeans to think in spatial terms. Graphic documents can be used as primary sources once the historian has recovered the autonomy and independence of visual language and has identified its place in an economy of knowledge. What remains central here, however, is not simply the question of how planning, and especially its visual, graphic, and spatial dimensions, was used in the seventeenth century, but what difference that sort of planning made to the conquest of the sea and to the creation of a new urban age.

That question has been at the center of my research since I began preparing a dissertation at Princeton University on the four new port cities established and nurtured by the government of Louis XIV.[7] Although the dissertation illustrated what such urban development indicates of Louis XIV's capabilities and ambitions and of his government's practices and innovations, it also highlighted the problems a rural-based administrative central government faced when it undertook as unlikely and important a venture as the establishment of maritime supremacy. By itself, however, the French record cannot illuminate the sources of port city planning and the reasons for its widespread diffusion in the seventeenth century and its diminished importance thereafter. Those topics, representing research undertaken since the dissertation, are covered in parts one and three of this book. The French material, making up part two, is considerably revised from its original presentation, and serves as a detailed, in-depth analysis of early modern Europe's port city planning and development.

Today the law of the sea and existing patterns of maritime exploitation are being reordered. This time the entire world, and not just the Western countries, stands at the start of a new maritime age, one likely to be as different in its economic, legal, political, and military characteristics from that which survived from 1600 to the present, as that age was from the one preceding it. Despite the importance of this turning point, specialists in urban affairs and those responsible for changing the legal, political, and military setting for maritime exploitation have few points of contact. Port cities contain larger urban communities than other cities, make specific demands on maritime resources, and support a wide variety of maritime activities. In turn, changes being brought to maritime affairs may have still-unforseen implications for urban development, and for the welfare of countries such as the United States, whose port cities are its most important ones. It should make a difference for us to know more about what impact the maritime age now drawing to a close has had on Europe's urban civilization.

It is a pleasure to recognize publicly the contributions of so many scholars to this work. The critical influence of one may have led me to omit an item, a phrase, or an idea, and the suggestions of another may have encouraged me to pursue a fact or a concept further, so that it has become impossible for me to attribute a particular quality of this book to a given individual. I hope that those who find themselves cited here, and my other friends and colleagues, who must forgive me for not mentioning them individually, will consider this book worthy of their time and devotion. Whatever faults remain are my own responsibility.

Theodore K. Rabb, as my advisor at Princeton University, directed the dissertation that serves as the base for part two. He graciously read this book in manuscript form, and his comments enabled me to make many important changes. His interest encouraged me to give the story of port city planning the widest possible dimension.

Emmanuel Le Roy Ladurie, of the Collège de France, introduced me to seventeenth-century studies, generously supervised my research in France, and prepared me in so many ways to join the community of scholars.

Edward W. Fox has been my counselor, teacher, and friend since my undergraduate years at Cornell University. He opened the study of urban history for me, and I have found his enthusiastic support of great value.

Horace M. Kallen, my godfather, always knew that this book was about why people wanted to do things and whether their efforts to change the shape of their world increased the well-being of individuals and societies. I regret that he did not live to see it completed.

Yves Bercé, David Bien, Charles Carrière, Guy Chaussinand-Nogaret, Natalie Davis, Jean Delumeau, Louis Dermigny, Daniel Dessert, Pierre Deyon, Christopher Friedrichs, François Furet, Helmut Koenigsberger, Steven Kramer, Marjorie Nicolson, Marc Perrichet, John Reps, Yves Tanguy, Charles Tilly, and Anthony Vidler, in varying degrees, offered useful advice, corrected errors, and introduced me to new frameworks for the maritime and urban history of Europe. The opportunity to include a study of Liverpool was made possible by Frances Hyde, whose hospitality, advice, and encouragement I gratefully acknowledge. My colleague Robert Slusser guided me through the historiography on St. Petersburg. Douglas Marshall helped me discover several precious Early American documents in the University of Michigan's Clements Library.

Many archivists and curators rendered invaluable assistance by guiding me to archival materials and by freely sharing their expertise in many fields. In France, they are MM. Adhemars (Cabinet des Estampes, Bibliothèque nationale), Audouy, Busson (Service historique de la Marine), Buffet (Ile et Vilaine), Charpy (Finistère), Fardet (Marine at Rochefort), Fouché (Ville de Brest), Gigot (l'Hérault), Heurat (Marine at Brest), and Taillemite (Archives nationales), and Mlles. Beauschesne (Marine at Lorient), Giteau (Charente-Maritime), Lacrocq (Génie), and Mosser (Morbihan). I also thank their staffs and the staffs of the Bibliothèque nationale map and manuscript collections, the Musée de la Marine, the Archives des affaires étrangères, and the city archives of Rochefort and Sète. I also gratefully acknowledge the cooperation of the staff of the Plantin Museum in Antwerp, the Universitatsbiblioteek in Amsterdam, the City Library in Rotterdam, and the Rijksarchief Noordholland in Haarlem. In Denmark and Sweden alike I was extended courtesies that went far beyond what a visiting foreign scholar could have expected. John Erichsen, curator of the Københavns Bymuseum, guided me through his institution, arranged for me to consult with Waage Petersen, architect at the Forsvarets Bygningstienst, and steered me to the collections of the Kongelige Bibliotek, the Stadsarkiv, the Rigsarkivet, and the Statens Museum for Kunst. Erik Lönnroth of Gothenburg and Göran Lindahl of Stockholm responded with interest to my research needs. Curators of the Kunglinga Krigsarkiv, the National Museum, the Kunglinga Bibliotek, and the Lantmäteristylrelsens Arkiv in Stockholm, of the Universitets Bibliotek in Uppsala, and of the Stadsarkiv in Gothenburg, made the task of identifying, understanding, and reproducing literally hundreds of maps and drawings almost easy. The staffs of the Library of Congress Map Division, the Hermon Dunlap Smith Center for the History of Cartography at The Newberry Library, and the Stokes Collection and the Art Collection of the New York Public Library all facilitated my research when I had little time at my disposal.

The Danforth Foundation and the Franco-American Commission for Educational Exchange (Fulbright-Hays Program) assisted me financially when I engaged in research on Louis XIV's new port cities, and the College of Arts and Letters of Michigan State University supported my research on American, Dutch, Danish, Swedish, and Russian port cities.

This list ends with the two intellectuals whose own scholarship first turned me to the study of cities and culture nearly twenty years ago; Lewis Mumford and my father, Milton Konvitz.

I

The Origins and Practice of Port City Planning

I

The Sixteenth-Century Background

The Originality of Port City Planning

Europe in 1600 was an unlikely setting for initiating a century of new port city creation. Most of Europe's port cities had been founded during the Greek and Roman periods of colonization or during the Middle Ages, and Europeans had not created many new settlements since. Existing port cities had ably served efforts to widen Europe's maritime horizons during the fifteenth and sixteenth centuries. By 1600 they were swollen with privilege and tradition, if not also with profit: their very existence made Europe's maritime economy seem an inhospitably crowded environment for the growth of new port cities. Europe's maritime urban civilization might have been left the way it was. Cartographers were certainly prepared to add the names of new places outside Europe as they were discovered; they must have been surprised to find themselves editing maps as new cities were created across Europe throughout the seventeenth century.

The transition to an era of port city development occurred early in the seventeenth century. The successful extension of Europe's political, economic, and cultural power from port cities had only reinforced the impression that such cities were indispensible to sea power. Inspired by this impression, leaders in northern and western Europe began to imagine that new port cities would encourage an even more effective and expansive use of sea power. Such imaginings, repeated and sustained during three generations, marked an unprecedented phase in the history of European city planning. Those who were anxious to increase sea power by developing new port cities and by reconstructing some older ones had much at stake; they were understandably reluctant to abandon such enterprises to chance. The planning process alone, they believed, would make possible a bold and artful reconstruction of the European world.

In the ancient Greek empire, in medieval France and England (and in nineteenth-century America, as well), planners simplified their task by producing a limited number of models for new towns, with the result that new towns founded at the same time look alike. What made planning in the seventeenth century different from other periods when new towns were established in large numbers was the variety of models planners used. Success was no less important to seventeenth-century planners than it has been at other times. Yet, familiar as they were with time-proven methods of city planning from legend, legal precedent, and literature, planners engaged in a prolonged period of experimentation. Why was there such variety in the style and quality of planning from country to country, and within each country? And, given this variety, how can the contribution of city planning to the conquest of the sea and to the creation of a new urban age be assessed?

Only an international European perspective can explain both the variety of seventeenth-century port city planning and development and the success or failure of planning in any one place. Planners and their sponsors and critics assumed that the spatial character of a planned port city and the commercial and military activities based in the city could affect one another, but they often disagreed about the kind of plan a given city needed. Because these disagreements reflected political, social, economic, and cultural conditions for port city growth that differed widely from country to country and from region to region, planners designed a wide variety of urban shapes and forms. A study of the plans for port cities—for those that grew as well as for those that did not—shows how different sets of Europeans assimilated what they knew about sea power into assumptions about how to increase it and establishes links between city space and social, political, and aesthetic preoccupations; it locates the planning process at the center of seventeenth-century Europe's urban and maritime civilization.

The successful French experience with new port cities during the reign of Louis XIV illuminates the entire European practice. Between 1660 and 1715, Louis XIV's government created and developed Brest, Lorient, Rochefort, and Sète to complete a strategic network of commercial and military port cities. Louis and his officers planned each port city (and rebuilt Toulon and Marseille, as well) to play a specific role in the government's politico-military strategy for sea power. The four new French cities were not the most imaginatively designed ones of the century, but their apparent simplicity represented a sophisticated exercise of critical judgment that eliminated irrelevancies and operated in reference to social, political, and aesthetic concepts. These cities were different from other French cities in characteristically similar ways because French spatial design and planned institutional frameworks produced new social, political, and cultural patterns in urban living. The French experience, therefore, illustrates some of the factors involved in successful new port city planning. And, because the sources are available for the study of the actual development of these cities, their story helps us learn what the moral, demographic, social, economic, political, and aesthetic limits to new port city planning were in the seventeenth century.

Three developments of the sixteenth century made it possible for port city planning in the seventeenth century to develop in so many countries and in such variety. Firstly, the ideal city tradition gave European artists and engineers the habit of representing political and social ideas and concepts in graphic terms. It encouraged planners to imagine the ideal port city as a complete unit of which the harbor, river, or canal was an integral part, conceptually and figuratively. Secondly, a practical planning tradition emerged when architects and engineers planned for the growth of existing port cities without copying the forms of the ideal planning tradition. They preserved the characteristic, historic form of port cities, in which harbor, river, or canal was related to the rest of the city as if by accident. Seventeenth-century planners had to choose between two models: they could follow the way actual port cities had grown, or they could retain the assumption of ideal planning that actual, real cities were ill suited to be models for planning. This choice was conditioned by a third development of the sixteenth century. Throughout the sixteenth century, ideal and practical port city planning were most common within the Mediterranean basin, but toward its end, northern Europeans, especially those such as the Scandinavians and the French who had not done much with sea power, began to understand that the sea was a proper setting for their commercial, military, and political activities. Appropriately, city planning was an accessible medium for them to express this new sense of the sea and sea power; the Mediterranean experience was selectively transferred to Europe's Atlantic rim. The choice between the two sixteenth-century traditions was for them an open one. Planners and their patrons could not know in advance, but had to learn empirically, what influences port city planning would have on urban growth in their countries.

Before engaging in an analysis of these sixteenth-century developments, it is well to define those terms and concepts that have been introduced so far, and that reappear in other chapters. The *port cities* referred to in this work were built on the seacoast, on estuaries, and on rivers. Planners treated these geographic differences as incidental; for this reason, the differences they imply are of little importance in this study. In fact, neither topography nor any particular legal prerogative or social quality distinguishes port cities as a generic type. Rather, what distinguishes them, in the past and in the present, is their potential for enormous growth and for contact with distant cultures, societies, and economies. Although the typology and classification of cities remains today a nearly futile attempt to reduce the variety of urban communities to terms acceptable to various schools of historians and geographers, it must be recognized that, historically, the spatial, political, social, cultural, and economic characteristics that have differentiated cities from other kinds of human settlements have been more pronounced and varied at an earlier time in port cities than in cities limited to an exclusively local agricultural base.

Maritime culture refers to how those on land who command, depend upon, or benefit from the exercise of commercial and military sea power understand the technology of seafaring and the advantages gained from its uses. Ordinary seamen and the communities on land to which they belong adapt to seafaring as a way of life; their habits, expectations, and attitudes form subconsciously accepted patterns that are maintained by tradition and experience, and that are a category of occupational folklore.[1] Maritime culture, on the other hand, develops when the need for the conscious manipulation of maritime affairs is felt, most often in literate, economically and politically powerful leadership groups; it is composed of political, cultural, and economic concepts that define and prescribe control over aspects of sea power.

Port city planning historically has involved elites and governments in efforts to endow existing or new port cities with a framework appropriate to their functions in the maritime economy. When these efforts involved adapting administrative, legal, and social institutions to specific local conditions, the planning process for port cities was often no different in practice from that for other types of urban communities. What gives port city planning its distinction are its *spatial, topographic* aspects. The geography of port cities and the scale of economic activities carried on in them presented planners with a unique set of problems. *Spatial organization* refers to the arrangement of buildings, streets, and topographic features into patterns that are derived from and recondition economic, social, and political activities and values. The planned spatial organization of a new port city or of an extension to an existing one would reflect decisions about the location of the waterfront. Planners who worked on that problem confronted not only the engineering difficulties implied by the construction of a waterfront district, but the economic, social, political, and aesthetic implications and possibilities contained in a variety of solutions. Spatial, topographic planning, the outstanding feature of port city planning since the Renaissance, receives primary attention in this book.

Important aspects of port city spatial organization were handled directly in the *ideal and practical traditions*. The ideal tradition had as its goal the description of the perfect community. Its advocates sought to give the ideal city an identity as the locus of the good society, and they attributed to spatial plans the inherent power to encourage social harmony and morally justified action. In the ideal port city, the waterfront became a fixed element in a complex, usually geometric, overall design; as a result, neither it nor the rest of the city was capable of much growth or change. Existing patterns of economic and social life were not supposed to determine what the place of the waterfront in the ideal port city should be. Indeed, one of the challenges facing planners of such places was to design the waterfront such that the activities taking place there and the changes generated by contacts with a wider world would be contained by the rest of the city. Practical city planners paid closer attention to how actual port cities grew. They relied upon spatial design to sustain and promote the growth of the city and its maritime trade. This usually involved designing a plan that would enable each of the various parts of the city to grow without getting in the others' way. Thus both traditions programmed a population's access to the waterfront, but with very different purposes in mind. The ideal tradition encouraged planners to build the city around the waterfront, so that the latter would become a part of a larger architectonic design, whereas practical planning emphasized what was most relevant to the exploitation of the sea. The open sky and harbor, the

movements of ships, and the activity of the dock all had a place in the European city before the sixteenth century, but then, for the first time, planning
ransomed that place from chance and precedent, and made its determination
an important aspect of maritime culture.

Ideal City Planning

Ideal city planning began in Renaissance Italy during the fifteenth century
with a vision of a city built according to reason and the human measure. This
was the idea behind utopia, a place where reason would coordinate and integrate human nature with those universal laws that conditioned human activities. Humanists in the Renaissance placed the perfect society in an urban
setting, not only because the ancient Greeks and Romans (with whose books
they were familiar) had shown them how to do this, but also because ancient
Athens and Rome appeared to them to have been part of a golden age. To
these acquired notions the Renaissance greats added something of their own.
Utopia took on the shape of the city because Leon Battista Alberti (1404–
1472) and those who followed him believed that architecture could serve man
more completely than other arts in the effort to create a rational and beautiful
vision of society and its ideals. It unified all the arts with philosophical
thought, producing a totality in which the multiple aspects of society could be
harmonized into a community.[2] They believed, as well, that the actual world
of appearance was morally corrupt and aesthetically inadequate, and hence
could not provide the outlines or forms for a vision of the world as it ought to
be. So the architect became a demiurge, calling new forms into creation and
using these forms as a demonstration of his inventiveness, all to prove that
through art a new world could be created.[3] A better society became an urban
product. As inventors of architectural forms, the ideal city planners were only
following the lead of those painters, especially Ghirlandaio, Pinturrichio, and
Botticelli, who had included buildings of a style we now identify as Renaissance in their paintings, when in fact no buildings had yet been built that
could have served them as models.[4] Having rejected the world of physical
appearance as an accumulation of dross and debris, the artist-planner tried to
make the truth behind appearances visible in his forms by making those forms
into symbols of that transcending reality.[5] That reality was within reach, but
the planner of ideal cities believed that only he could make it imminent and
tangible.

  During the fifteenth century, ideal city planners thought the ideal city
could take shape as new architectural forms were added to existing cities.
Their planning still had a practical quality to it. Alberti, for example, was
careful to preserve a balance between beauty ("voluptas") and usefulness
("commoditas"): for him, there was no difference "between the circulation of
merchandise and the circulation of ideas, between foodstuffs, drugs, precious
stones, and news and knowledge of things and all [that] is useful to a style of
life."[6] Alberti knew how to dissemble the obvious and render it picturesque;
he knew how to make the grand manner livable and domestic.[7] In his genera-

tion Venice, Milan, and Florence were being rebuilt in such a way that the Italian city-state could indeed give the artist-planner hope that his work was useful.[8] And if more proof was needed that the work of the imagination could be superimposed on an actual place, the transformation of a city during a festival could have provided it. The planner of ideal cities, therefore, had reason to believe that he was neither a fool nor a dreamer. Because actual cities were being transformed, the effort and ambition necessary to conceiving an ideal city seemed to be worthwhile.

In the early sixteenth century the rise of genuine religious anguish and the destruction of the Italian city-state cut short the ambitions of the ideal city planner. The forms for buildings and for city plans that had been blueprints in the fifteenth century became illusory and impractical in the sixteenth. We cannot satisfactorily explain why artist-planners continued the ideal city planning tradition after the practical basis for that planning ceased. The fact is that, during the entire sixteenth century, the theory and manner of visual representation of ideas in ideal city forms remained identical with the practice of the preceding period. Ideal city designers demonstrated their allegiance to a tradition that neglected the observable world as a basis for art, but they failed to elaborate any designs more varied, complex, or original than those that had already been produced. Michelangelo succeeded Bramante, but no mid-sixteenth-century ideal city planner surpassed the works of his predecessors. Ironically, a cultural movement founded on the primacy of the imagination failed to produce forms according to the truthfulness of imagined artistic space that would rival in potency and complexity the ideas with which the first ideal city planners worked.[9]

Because the artist-planner's concern was with the social and political elaboration of the utopian society or culture in space, the isolation and autonomy essential to the ideal city could most easily be imagined through the spatial setting of a port. Port cities could thrive far from one another and yet be able to trade and communicate. At a time when new islands and continents were being discovered, an ideal port city could well be a place that existed but was still unknown. The image of the ideal port city seemed well suited to convey the appropriate impression of a believable fiction, even though artists who designed ideal cities were equally able to present an image of a landlocked community. The explicitly literary utopias (for example, those by More and Bacon) most often required a maritime setting. In the image of the ideal port city, the elements characteristic of port cities—walls, towers, harbor basins, quays, warehouses—and the practical aspects of trade that they served were subordinated to the image of the whole city and the ideal society that it would contain. The artist-planner who designed an ideal port city was not trying to present a model of a perfectly functioning port city for the merchant patricians of Messina or Antwerp, but was instead using the spatial setting of a port city—transcending its normal operative limitations—to show philosophers, prelates, and princes what Utopia-by-the-Sea would look like.

The forms given the ideal port cities were not abstractions or rationalizations of actual port cities so much as they were a figurative, visual presentation of ideas and observations that had little or nothing to do with the way port

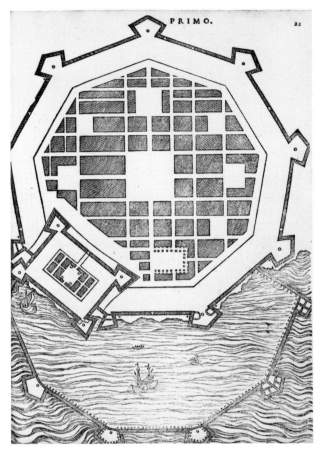

FIGURE 1.1. *Ideal port city by Pietro Cataneo, in* I primi quattro libri di architettura *(Venice: Aldine, 1554 and 1567), p. 22. Courtesy of the Newberry Library, Chicago.*

cities functioned. By examining a variety of plans for ideal port cities, it becomes possible to see that the maritime quality of such port cities was made to serve the image of the city as the realization of a perfectly functioning society. In the drawings of Francesco di Giorgio Martini, harbors and waterways were used to convey an impression of interdependency with independence; symmetry and proportion, aesthetic balance and civic pride were to be found as much in the harbor as in the city itself. Francesco di Giorgio and Pietro Cataneo after him made of the harbor a watery piazza (figure 1.1). One can admire how they tried to compose an architectonic unity out of the harbor, the city, the walls, and the urban space within. Francesco de Marchi drew images that placed the water inside the city, so that the streets and public spaces could be arranged to follow (figure 1.2) or to focus on the course of a river (figure 1.3): in both cases he used a waterway as an urban concourse, an element to integrate into a network of places and streets. These images all have in common outer walls or fortifications that embrace both city and har-

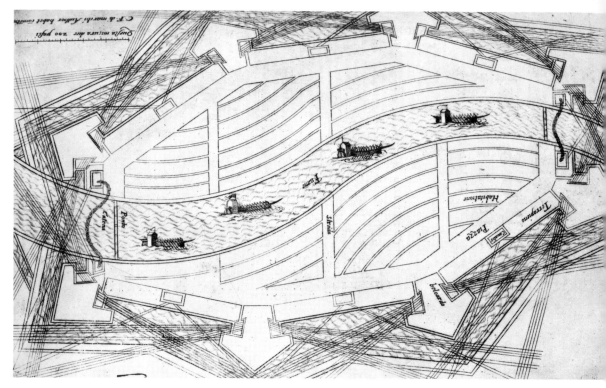

FIGURE **1.2.** *Ideal port city by Francesco de Marchi, in* Della Architettura Militare *(Brescia, 1599), f. 95, recto. Courtesy of the Special Collections Division, U.S. Military Academy Library.*

bor, creating of both parts a whole in which each part is related to the other. But the ingenuity and cleverness—and hence the variations that distinguish one design from another—are found entirely in the land part of the city: in walls, towers, streets, public places. Less variety is found in the conceptualization and elaboration of harbors and harborsides. It seems that designers were most intent on demonstrating their ability to integrate water areas into a cityscape that would be worthy of a self-consciously mature society. These designs were not meant to be blueprints (the cost of building such harbors would have been prohibitive), but inspirations, symbols of man's creative ambitions to recast his world in the image of perfection. As such, these designs use water to admirable effect.

The sixteenth-century designs reproduced here, and dozens of others similar to them, represented the whole as something greater than the sum of the parts, and they graphically demonstrated ideas and concepts that were political and social in nature.[10] Harbor and city were most often composite parts of a whole, and were conceived so as to make it unlikely that either part could grow or change independently of the other without damaging the impressions of unity and balance the ideal city should convey.[11] In particular, the port area was conceived of as less a true working space than as a civic space: it was the city's principal formal element, from which all the other spatial features were derived. This motif of the city as a complete and contained place, finding its raison d'être in itself, encouraged planners to treat water as an urban space that, like a piazza, offered a visual prospect of other parts of the city beyond itself. Water, they learned, belonged not just to ships, longshoremen, and traders, but to the city's sense of itself.

Such was the ideal port city. Ideal city planners had produced a body of designs unrelated to the changing demands maritime commerce placed on an actual port city. Their principal positive achievements had been in the theory of planning itself and in its graphic expression.[12] That they worked primarily from their imagination, and had rejected existing port cities as models, can be seen by comparing their drawings with what several sixteenth-century port cities looked like.

Growth and Change in Sixteenth-Century Port Cities

The great sixteenth-century trading cities are good examples of what Sybil Moholy-Nagy called "orthogonal merchant-linear" urban form.[13] This was

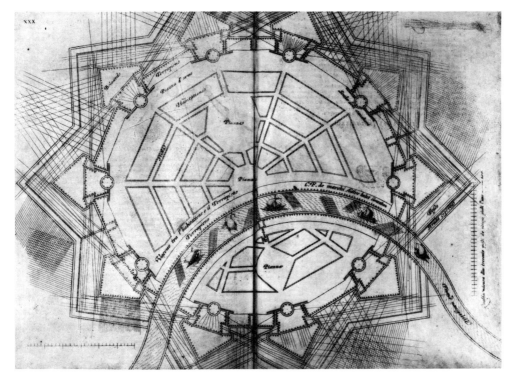

FIGURE **1.3.** *Ideal port city by Francesco de Marchi, in* Della Architettura Militare *(Brescia, 1599), verso of f. 278 and recto of f. 279. Courtesy of the Special Collections Division, U.S. Military Academy Library.*

not the only form possible for such cities, as the pure orthogonal grids of many ancient and modern port cities demonstrate, but it was a form that was highly sophisticated and that made life in a city a rich visual experience. Moholy-Nagy's term connotes cities distinguished by the coexistence of two types of street networks. Small neighborhood streets, usually short and narrow, divided the space of the city into quarters or districts and emphasized communication—that is, the movement of persons, messengers, and goods in small quantities. Longer, broader streets opened the city's districts to traffic, the movement of goods and people in great volume. These streets were conduits, and were not really part of the neighborhoods they traversed. In the port city with both types of street networks, the sights and sounds of all the different activities of a port—movement of goods, ideas, and information, the traffic in bulky commodities such as wood and grain and in dense ones such as metals and spices—animated different spaces that were in close proximity to each other but that did not melt into each other. In both the northern European and the Mediterranean sixteenth-century great port city, the heavy work and colorful activity of trade had its milieu, while the words and numbers corresponding to that activity were written and spoken elsewhere, in the city's corporate organizations, exchanges, and merchant houses.

A complete survey of sixteenth-century port cities would be impossible, but it is possible to examine some of the largest European port cities. These cities were more varied in form than the ideal ones created by artist-planners. In spatial terms, ideal city planners tried to relate the parts of a city to each other, whereas in actual sixteenth-century cities, the processes of growth and change were unequal between the traffic and commercial networks, which shared the same city but did not grow in relation to each other. When change took the form of expanding the facilities available for trade, it necessitated extensions of canals, traffic streets, and quays—but not necessarily of the rest of the city. On the other hand, the city's merchants could also emphasize the construction of greater merchant houses and of larger, more handsome exchanges, bringing change within the network of communication alone. Why one type of growth in one city, another elsewhere? Factors such as geography in Seville and Venice, investment in stone palaces in Italy, and the high cost of constructing quays, which made the expansion of port facilities expensive everywhere,[14] should not imply that patterns of growth, because they usually were determined by purely local circumstances, cannot be understood at a more general level. Because no scholar has yet tried to explain why and how early modern European merchants in each generation related commercial exchange outside their city to patterns of supply and demand within,[15] I can only suggest but cannot prove that the specific differences between growing sixteenth-century port cities resulted not just from the particular physical and social environment of each, but also from the effort made in all of them to preserve both profitability of commerce and control of city growth. This may be the significance of the observation that, in all the cities surveyed here, the processes of growth and change largely preserved each city's already-established pattern of development: in the sixteenth century, practical city planners, relying on the orthogonal, merchant-linear form developed earlier,

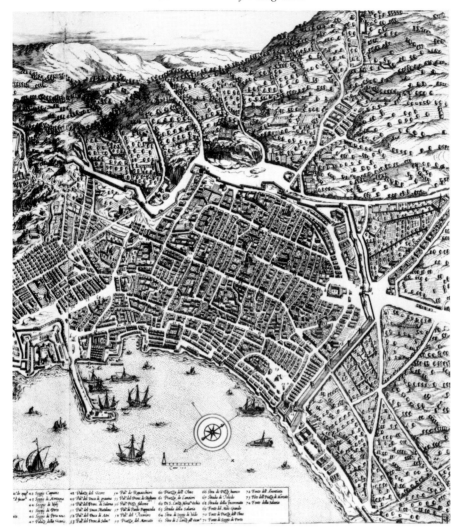

FIGURE 1.4. *Naples, 1566. Novacco Collection 4F232. Courtesy of the Newberry Library, Chicago.*

did not need to innovate in order to sustain commercial expansion and urban growth.

The most common traffic and communications patterns in growing sixteenth-century Mediterranean port cities[16] are worthy of examination. These cities offered a different context for urbanism than did princely Florence or papal Rome. Even though the Renaissance sort of public square was built into port cities and inland capitals alike,[17] port cities shared other features with each other that they did not share with other kinds of cities, features that marked them as a breed apart. Logically enough, the harborfront areas of port cities made them distinctive in characteristically similar ways. Collectively and individually, these city views of Naples in 1566 (figure 1.4),

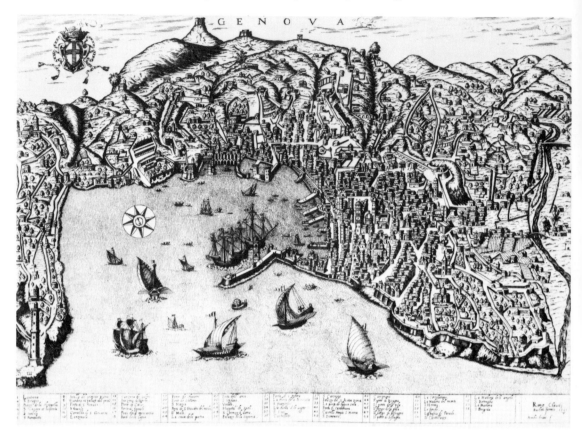

FIGURE **1.5.** *Genoa, 1581. Novacco Collection 4F223. Courtesy of the Newberry Library, Chicago.*

Genoa in 1581 (figure 1.5), and the French port of Marseille in 1602 (figure 1.6) show that a lighthouse as the city tower, breakfronts for harbors, and encircling, embastioned walls were standard features. In nearly each city, the amount of open land adjacent to the harbor was limited, so its principal use was as a quay. The focal points of commercial activities might not be far away, although in Genoa they were. Only pedestrians, not voyagers on board ships, could admire the architectural handsomeness of the merchants' houses. The public buildings, fountains, and statues associated with the Renaissance square were absent from the harborside; although the waterfront was a port city's principal open space and was fit for a promenade as well as for work, planners, architects, and their patrons neglected to embellish it with the spatial vocabulary of the Renaissance.

This reveals a contrast between the vision of ideal city planners, who would have designed a port city as if it had nothing to do with maritime affairs, and the plans of practical city builders, who allowed maritime affairs to determine areas of the city far removed from the waterfront. The pattern of Palermo was typical. There, much of the construction was of palaces for the

FIGURE 1.6. *Marseille, 1602. Novacco Collection 4F137. Courtesy of the Newberry Library, Chicago.*

aristocracy and housing for the workers. The two principal streets added to the traffic network were built by the viceroys whose names they carry, the Via Toledo (1560s), which led from the palace to the sea, and the Via Maqueda (1590s), which connected the two outer walls. A baroque intersection, the Quattro Canti, was built where the two streets crossed.[18] The communications network dictated construction in the rest of the city. In Palermo and elsewhere, the traffic network took the promenade and cargo handling of the quay inland (these streets also made possible a conversion from sedan chairs to carriages), while the communications network of small districts and streets kept business affairs and public life within neighborhoods.[19]

Sixteenth-century construction omitted the harbor area from the contractor's schemes;[20] it remained peripheral to city building practice. The traffic network was enlarged so that the demands of transport on urban space could be kept small; in the rest of the city, changes made within the communications network (besides churches and other structures of public use) were limited to the rebuilding of old and the construction of new exchanges, mansions, and merchant houses in stone.[21] An economy of spatial means kept the functions of the harborfront and the growth of commerce from causing undue stress to the existing urban fabric.[22] This was achieved by allowing the separate parts of the city to grow independently of each other, a pattern the ideal city planner would have rendered impossible. Growth was limited, not by philosophical or aesthetic criteria, but by the financial and political calculations of the city's leaders—no wonder practical city planning survived into the next century relatively intact.

Venice was different from these other Mediterranean port cities because, in Venice, the separation of communications and traffic networks was expressed comprehensively in the political as well as in the social and physical areas of activity.[23] Because of the relationship of the greater and lesser islands to the central city, each area of the city came to have its own economic activities, social organizations, public buildings, political representation, and collective identity.[24] The commercial center was near the Rialto; Wall Street and the City of London share with it the same intensely avaricious use of space. The civic leaders who preserved the Rialto this way also enhanced the Piazza of San Marco and the Piazetta connecting it with the open water with architectural projects throughout the sixteenth century, the century of Sansovino and Palladio, by creating a plastic monument of spatial and architectural patterns that change as one travels between the great harbor and the heart of Venetian civic life.[25] The canals and waterways were conduits of goods and of people, while streets and bridges created a web of lines penetrating neighborhoods and linking them with each other by paths different from those traced by the canals.[26] The canals also allowed Venetians to place warehouses, dockyards, and even cemeteries in separate districts without assuming difficulties in transport. Venice was not the product of a single overarching design; its uniqueness defied imitation.[27] But two fifteenth-century structures created by Venetians in service of the state were widely known and may have been models for other cities: the arsenal, perhaps Europe's first great industrial compound, and the lazaretto, a quarantine fort built on an island to house crews and voyagers as a first line of defense against the plague. Indeed, the city's canals and numerous important public and private structures fascinated those Europeans already disposed to admire the constitution of the Venetian Republic, the intellectual vigor of its university at Padua, its economic power, and its tolerance of religious dissenters. Familiarity with Venice through illustrations may have conditioned the ideas of sixteenth- and seventeenth-century city builders.

In Seville, geography alone determined the separation of harbor activities from the place where the decisions directing those activities were made; the distances involved were so great that it is astonishing that control and coordination could have been exercised. Seville is a supreme example of the center's mastery over the periphery. When Seville was chosen in 1503 to be the metropolitan capital of Spain's Indies Empire, the small fleets of the Atlantic could find shelter on its river and ample supplies and distribution facilities for the import-export trade in the city itself.[28] The small size of Seville's harbor was no defect at all in 1503, but as the volume of trade grew, the size and number of the ships moored there increased. The Casa de la Contratactiòn

FIGURE 1.7. *Havana, date unknown. Cartes Marine no. 76. Courtesy of the Edward E. Ayer Collection, the Newberry Library, Chicago.*

and Seville's merchants became brokers on a global scale, distributing American imports across Europe and collecting Europe's goods for distribution across the ocean. Although Seville's harbor on the Guadalquivir River was inadequate for such a traffic, the vested monopolistic concentration of interests there made relocating the Indies metropolitan base impossible. Gradually the entire river from Seville to the sea was occupied by the Indies trade, creating the first Europort. Ships were repaired between Seville and the sea, first at San Juan de Aznalfarache, a few miles below Seville, and then at two bases farther south, Los Horcades and Borrego. Most ships loaded and unloaded by means of lighters; ships too big even to enter the river were handled at Cadiz. Hundreds of auxiliary river and coastal craft served this traffic. In this way, Seville preserved its commercial dominance while remaining, largely, the city it had been before: the traffic of the river could not be traced out onto a land network of streets and districts. Any other city would have had to expand rapidly in order to accommodate such traffic growth, and such expansion might not have been orderly. Instead, Seville distributed chaos in patterns to which the people involved in the complex European-Indies trade adjusted. The random, ad hoc nature of Seville's solution, logical and useful as it was, would have been abhorrent to anyone who could conceive of an ideal city.

Even the sixteenth-century port cities established and sustained by royal initiative highlight the differences between actual port cities and the ideal forms of artist-planners.[29] Le Havre grew hardly at all during this period; traders from Rouen had not yet exploited it. Its plan, the work of an Italian in the service of François I, had no more detail or vision than was appropriate to a fortified outpost at the mouth of the Seine. Leghorn's trade was significant because nearby Pisa was no longer able to fulfill the commercial ambitions of Florence and Tuscany. Medieval Leghorn had been a town lacking order in its appearance, and during the sixteenth century its growing lower-class population overstretched its limited physical resources. Not until the end of the century was a plan for an extension ordered by the Medici. That plan called for a larger harbor and traced out a grid city with a central square. The new and old parts would be enclosed by fortifications, but the plan did not provide for easy communication between these parts. Instead, it directed all traffic from the port straight across the new city and onto the road to Pisa. Thus, Leghorn was conceived to be nothing more than a transshipment point, the traffic network extension of Pisa and Florence.

As for the new cities in Spain's American Empire, they were built on a grid layout like inland agricultural centers, the seacoast forming one side of the city as if by accident. Cartagena's importance as a port city was not reflected in its spatial design because the monarchy's legalistic, programmatic approach to city planning avoided particular distinctions among cities and identified the functional aspects of planning with its administrative control, and, so, with uniformity. But whence, therefore, the remarkable, undated project for Havana, so obviously inspired by the radial formula of an ideal city planner (figure 1.7)? This was exactly the sort of plan the monarchy would never consider. The material and spiritual benefits the ideal society would

confer were worth hoping for, but there seemed little possibility of introducing them into port cities as they actually were. Utopia had to remain an
indeterminate place in both the New and Old Worlds.

Ideal and Practical Planning Compared

This survey of change in sixteenth-century port cities has shown how different they were from the graphically stunning images of ideal port cities
produced by artist-planners, and has revealed actual port cities to be highly
complex social and physical instruments for the exploitation of the sea. Traffic and communication networks represented a crude spatial division of labor
that worked its way into housing, recreation, and work space as the rhythms of
maritime commerce traced themselves into urban forms. After all, the
greatest ports were not necessarily those with the most complete infrastructure and the largest amount of land for expansion: Genoa, Marseille, and
Naples grew against hillsides, Seville along the Guadalquivir. Land-use control was not needed in the ideal city except to show that everyone and everything had its place; in the actual port city, however, control lacked such an
expression of moral and political virtue and expressed, instead, the ways in
which the wealthy invested their fortunes and provided for the well-being of
everyone else. Change to these cities came only after opportunities to expand
wealth had been seized and turned into profit and power, and then change
was supposed to preserve the port city as a useful container of wealth and
manpower and as a useful instrument for acquiring more. All this suggests
that the orthogonal, merchant-linear form was not innately superior as a form
for a port city, but rather that, by experience, people determined that this
form was a suitable and workable way to provide a certain type of setting for
certain activities. No fundamental transformation of that form was possible as
long as it still worked productively.

These contrasts between ideal and actual sixteenth-century port cities
underscore the remoteness of ideal planning from urban change at that time.
Actual cities and ideal city planning evolved along separate lines of development that were insulated from each other, a phenomenon that influenced
both traditions. Some sixteenth-century designers, especially Cataneo and de
Marchi, like Alberti before them, had cared to treat the space within the city as
if it were as important as the walls around it;[30] their techniques were conceptual and holistic, and made sense because ideal planners still hoped to
influence patterns of urban development. Once it became apparent that city
growth had not yielded to the styles of the ideal planning tradition, ideal
planners specialized in certain types of urban design, and lost interest in
comprehensive urban form. As the designs for military fortifications became
more important and more specialized during the sixteenth century, designers
showed diminished concern for the city within the walls and imposed an
uncompromising logic on it, subordinating streets and public places to the
defense systems.[31] In many designs streets were traced to the bastions, and not
to the gates. Forms most easy to fortify, circles, were most frequently

suggested. At the same time, those designers and engineers who were chiefly engaged in civic, nonmilitary construction chose designs for aesthetic reasons alone, neglecting "commoditas" for "voluptas."[32] The symbolism of street and piazza left no room for defense, trade, and transport. In both cases, the image of the whole was fractured by an inability to relate the parts to each other, but artist-planners, preoccupied with symmetry and symbolism and with graphic perfection, did not seem to notice. Practicality took on the rigid outlines of the military camp, and aesthetics returned to its origins in fifteenth-century paintings and stage scenery. The very devices that had given ideal cities their image of unity and wholeness—fortifications integrated into a network of streets and spaces—were handled with least success in the second half of the sixteenth century. Ideal city planning offered little that corresponded to its purpose: that of being the literal and figurative expression of great ideas.

Neither the practical nor the ideal city planning traditions, as they were sustained in the Mediterranean basin during the sixteenth century, had much influence at that time on port city development in northern Europe. Few cities there were growing significantly, and northern Europeans still acted as if their maritime routes were tributaries of the greater Atlantic and Mediterranean ones that generated the harbor traffic of Spain and Italy. It is important, therefore, to see that, in Antwerp, the one northern port city to experience significant growth before the initiative in commercial and military sea power passed from the Mediterranean to the Atlantic peoples, planners and engineers translated the sort of growth the city experienced into a unified plan, the hallmark of the ideal tradition. This proved to be the link between Mediterranean traditions and North Atlantic developments in the seventeenth century.

The Case of Antwerp

The progressive expansion of commercial and military sea power during the sixteenth century had reinforced the idea that the port city was the instrument best suited for exploiting the sea, but a greater contact with and mastery over the sea had not themselves provoked any new ideas about port cities. Most of the great sixteenth-century port cities grew along lines proved adequate by time and experience. Meanwhile the ideal city planning of that age enshrined a model of conceptual, abstract design that did not need to take account of the problems of established port cities. Only when the opportunistic spirit of Italy's cities had been carried north, like a letter of credit, and had been reinvested, first in Antwerp, and then in the Netherlands, did the interest begin to accrue in the form of new ideas about port cities and their growth.

The growth of Antwerp provoked a consciously new approach to urban change. In the Mediterranean port cities, existing traffic and communication networks provided the skeleton for growth, so that even though new buildings and new streets were constructed, anyone who returned to Genoa or Palermo after an absence of twenty years would have been able to find his way and identify what was new according to the network to which it belonged.[33] Everything was still in its place; the two networks continued to function as separate but interconnected units within the same territory. In Antwerp something different happened. The city as it had existed was left unchanged, but a new district for the traffic network was developed immediately adjacent to the historic core, and that area was in turn made a part of a larger Antwerp by new fortifications that enclosed both the new and the old. By the 1580s Antwerp was no longer recognizably the same city it had been a generation earlier. In Antwerp and in Seville, the traffic and communication networks lost their links and the historic urban core remained intact. Seville achieved an extension of its traffic network only by colonizing the length of the Guadal-quivir. In Antwerp this extension was realized in a neat, well-defined addition to the city along the Scheldt River. This was made possible by successfully combining fourteenth-century Dutch city extension practice with the respect for fortifications common in recent Italian planning. A port city could indeed represent a new cosmopolitanism.

Originally the city fathers of Antwerp had intended to do something less sophisticated and more traditional.[34] From 1543 to 1545 they worked on plans to build a new defensive wall around the old city. The buildings that had been erected outside the city's walls—and that would be most easily threatened by an attacking army—had to come down first, of course, so an order was issued calling for their demolition. This led to a feverish search for available land and shelter within the city. In such a situation tremendous profits could be made at the expense of those who had to relocate. This was the sort of opportunity city fathers of the early modern city often sought to create, but this particular effort to move the suburbs inside the city failed. People who lived just beyond the walls had no doubt been able to economize by doing so; for them, a move would have represented a loss in real wages. Similarly, many small industries, such as those involved in clothmaking and in the production of items distributed by ship chandlers, found it more economical to spread out beyond the walls—and no doubt it was healthier for all that the dangers of fire and toxic wastes be placed as far as possible from the denser parts of the city. Also, an increase in real-estate values within the city would come at the expense of large numbers of lower-class artisans and workers.

Economic handicaps and social tensions threatened to transform real-estate profits into political liabilities for the city. Clearly, the original idea of the city fathers was not appropriate for a city experiencing unprecedented growth and prosperity. Since the rebuilding of the walls proceeded at a slow pace, the passive resistance to relocation among those beyond the walls only hardened. In 1548 the city fathers asked Gilbert Van Schoonbeke to take charge.

Van Schoonbeke had a plan. Taking the pattern of fourteenth-century Netherlands' town extension practice as a model, he conceived of the land beyond the walls to the north of the city along the Scheldt as a new district. A network of canals (old Antwerp had but a few) would extend the harbor—and hence, the waterfront—inland; streets and bridges would connect the new district with the rest of the city. The scale and expense of the project meant

FIGURE **1.8.** *Antwerp, 1550s(?). Sack no. Y5. Bibliothèque nationale, cartes et plans reserve GeDD 655(134). Photo Bibliothèque nationale, Paris.*

that the new district would be laid out at one time, to be occupied as population pressure and traffic growth demanded; the initial costs could be recovered through the lease and sale of property in the new district. This forward-looking project suited those who wanted to speculate on real-estate values (Van Schoonbeke was among them), and was adapted to the needs of a still-growing city. The formula emphasized political and financial control of the old city over its own growth, control it had lacked when growth had taken place beyond the walls. In topographic terms, the form of the extension represented a conscious and deliberate plan that invited growth but limited it to a predetermined area. A remarkable view of Antwerp, drawn in 1556 (figure 1.8), shows the "nieu stadt" (the new city) under construction. This project stands out in urban history as one of the earliest uses of Dutch fourteenth-century town extension practice after that time. For the next century and a half, cities in the Netherlands and in areas in America and Europe open to Dutch influence would be planned according to this formula.

The plan called for fortifications, too—the need for better defenses had been the "primo mobile" of the city government's first actions. Von Schoonbeke intended to connect the old and new parts of Antwerp by enclosing the entire agglomeration with a single fortified wall (figure 1.9). The political situation of the 1560s was dominated by civil war and social disorders; it made completion of the walls imperative. In Italy, bastions had been built in the shape of high, round towers, but this shape limited the ability of defenders to protect their flanks and the walls of the fort. Flat, blunt, and open bastions of a triangular shape were better suited to the use of cannon as offensive and defensive weapons.[35] Lucca was refortified according to this, the latest theory, at mid-sixteenth century. Within a few years Philippeville was completed along these same lines as a new fort in the Spanish Netherlands. Military engineers in service of the Spanish Empire could not afford a cultural lag in their line of work; traffic along the Flanders Road included ideas about warfare as well as means to prosecute it.[36] Antwerp's new fortifications of the 1560s, therefore, represented the latest ideas on siege tactics. The fortifications that enclosed both the old city and its new extension represented an Italian package for a Flemish product.

Antwerp's growth during the sixteenth century took place over a relatively long stretch of time and involved several different phases. Just as it was

FIGURE **1.9.** *Antwerp, 1580s(?). Courtesy of the Newberry Library, Chicago.*

nearly impossible for military engineers to adapt the strict symmetry of their original designs to the outlines and street networks of an existing city, so, too, was it difficult for the idealism and hopefulness of the utopian city plan to be carried out in the adaptation of Antwerp for growth. Civic responsibility was defined by a patriciate, mostly in terms of money, defense, and political control, and even then, it was defined hesitantly and with little direction. The elaboration of traffic and commercial networks in Antwerp changed as a result of the city's extension, but this creative solution was an unintentional, if fortuitous and practical, outcome of circumstance. Even so, it demonstrated what could be done once a certain degree of planning was attempted.

Antwerp's use of planning might not have become an example for other cities to imitate, for it seemed to be the result of an historical accident. Antwerp could have been known, like Venice, as some sort of urban freak; indeed, it might have been forgotten altogether once its economy began its precipitous, end-of-the-century decline during the revolt of the Netherlands against Spain. Someone had to translate Antwerp's practical use of planning into principles of general validity. Dutchman Simon Stevin (1548–1620) did just that. He found real port cities and the way they grew worth studying. Just at the time when artist-planners were treating the ideal city in a manner most allegorical, fantastic, and unworkable, Stevin redeemed the abstract, conceptual moral value of ideal city planning, applied it to the practical techniques of port city extension demonstrated in Antwerp, and produced the first fusion of these two traditions.

Simon Stevin and the Fusion of
Ideal and Practical Planning

Like the ideal city planners, Stevin was most concerned about the organization and moral strength of society. Writing in *Het Burgerlijk Leven (The Civic Life)* (1590), Stevin appeared thoroughly conventional in his statement that order and authority were expressive of the community's existence and essential to its stability and welfare. Were he known only for his repetition of a formula having the validity of common sense, his fame would not have been great. But Stevin was quartermaster general to Prince Maurice of Nassau, he supervised the new fortifications erected in the United Provinces, and he perfected the sluice as a tactical defensive device, allowing the Dutch to flood parts of their own country. He was a very able mathematician, as well: Descartes was not the first mathematician to correlate city planning with clarity, order, and moral authority. So, when Stevin lectured at the University of Leiden in 1594, his ideas were probably taken seriously. At that time the university was one of the most advanced in Europe, and its student body was both large and cosmopolitan.[37] We do not know Stevin's lectures on fortification, but only his treatise *De Stercktenbouwing (The Art of Fortification)*, published in 1594; Stevin wrote in Dutch because he wanted to demonstrate the language's modern aesthetic and practical possibilities.[38]

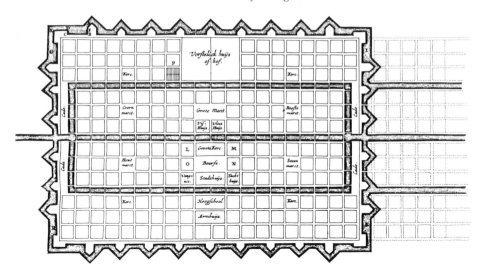

FIGURE **1.10.** *Ideal port city by Simon Stevin, in* Burgherlicke Stoffen, *printed in* Materiae Politicae *(Leyden, 1650?), plate between pages 26 and 27. Courtesy of the Newberry Library, Chicago.*

In the earlier work, *Het Burgerlijk Leven,* Stevin approached the rights of the individual to free expression of conscience with the same scepticism about what people say and believe that can be found in Montaigne. Stevin accepted "the fear of God" (religion) as useful and necessary, but then avoided choosing which religion or sect was true. Instead, he praised the civic responsibility of the individual who shared the religion of his community, and urged someone not so fortunate as to fall into that category to either observe publicly what law and custom required while keeping his real beliefs private or move to a community where his religion was openly and freely practiced. Stevin did not expect people to be happy with their lot; his answer to dissidents was scarcely more subtle than a slogan of the late 1960s: "America—love it or leave it." His approach to the world of public affairs lacked the optimism about man and the vision of truth found in early ideal city planning. Like Montaigne, Stevin was at once a participant in and an observer of prolonged civil war, and he realized that there was little time or energy left to spend on constructing an Abbey of Thélème. His political philosophy accepted the world as it was. It did not lead him to search for the truth in the public arena of civic life; perhaps he, like Kepler, Galileo, and Descartes, suspected that mathematics provided a better grounding for the study of truth. His was a practical approach to the rebuilding of a society that needed cohesion and allegiance to the common good to survive.

Stevin found a way to delineate the separation of private and public affairs in the techniques of practical city planning. In doing so, he elevated those techniques from the particular to the general. Although his planning reflected the moral and social preoccupations of those who worked within the ideal city tradition, Stevin's use of spatial forms represented an understanding of urban change quite foreign to that tradition. Stevin's ideal city was adapted to the military and commercial exploitation of the sea and to the prospects for growth that the successful use of sea power offered. Using the same planning methods that Antwerp had applied to its extension, Stevin demonstrated that a city could be planned to grow.

How did Stevin accomplish his original synthesis of port city activity and growth with the ideal of a politically and morally mature culture? Stevin combined housing, public space, canals, and the grid plan in such a way that the same elements that provided for urban growth also protected the public interest and guaranteed a measure of personal freedom (figure 1.10). He selected the grid plan because it allowed for uniform blocks to be built up on all four sides. And he knew what kind of house to erect on each block: it was recessed from the street by an arcade, rose to a height of four stories, had windows placed side by side to form a continuous line, and was covered by a roof that could not be seen from below. In other words, the buildings of Stevin's planned city would be barren of the architectural elements, such as doorways, facades, window frames, and rooftops, that were most easily embellished. I believe Stevin used this severe anonymity to protect the privacy of those who would live in the buildings. The grid plan contributed a rigidly regular pattern well suited to this kind of construction.[39]

The grid plan also provided for a separation of public from private affairs in a manner not unlike the elaboration of two networks in an Italian port city, except that, in Stevin's design, the points of contact between shipping and the city would be multiple and extensive, since the linear traffic pattern of canals interlaced and bounded the entire city. The principal public areas—the prince's residence, the great church, asylums, schools, the exchange, a place for foreign merchants—were placed in such a way that none became more important, or more prominent, than the others. Rather, they were located as equals in a path of blocks that extended from one side of the city to the other, the only distinction being that the buildings and areas most frequently used were placed in the two center sections. Smaller churches and neighborhood markets were placed at a remove from the center, where they were more accessible to their clientele. The grid plan, therefore, allowed Stevin to separate the public from the private without sacrificing the supremacy of the former over the latter.

Canals also symbolized Stevin's philosophy of community; his insight into their potential uses transformed them into the key element in the city's structured growth. Like the grid pattern, canals separated residential and public areas from each other yet kept them adjacent and the passage between them easy. Extended beyond the city walls, canals provided a matrix within which the city could replicate the grid pattern on land it would annex and, at the same time, they related any new suburb to the city's center. Canals supported the city's prosperity by maximizing accessibility to the waterfront and by minimizing the costs of waterfront land; they sustained the social order by preserving a balance between public and private life; and they provided a way for the city to grow without jeopardizing the basis of its prosperity or of its social order. Stevin's city's growth would represent the conscious decision of the community and its control over its resources, as well as its successful commercial enterprise. It was Stevin's idea that such a city, in its physical, spatial dimension, could no more represent the ambitions of an individual or of a special-interest group than could the community serve the interests of a minority against the wishes of the majority and the best interests of the common good.

In this way Stevin brought an understanding of how cities change to the holistic, conceptual vision of the ideal city planning tradition with its emphasis on introducing social changes through urban form. Stevin's effort to do this may not have inspired many seventeenth-century planners, however, because the publication of his writings was erratic and slow. In any case, we do not know what he discussed in his university lectures, with colleagues, or with the many civic leaders with whom he came in contact: the diffusion of his ideas may not have needed printers at all. His ideas, or something rather close to them, can be found in the many seventeenth-century Dutch projects that built community control over growth into the very structure of the city itself. From the beginning of the seventeenth century and for over a hundred years, Europeans building new port cities were persuaded that contemporary Dutch practice was as good as, and maybe better than, Italian city planning theory.

The Cultural Setting of Late-Sixteenth-Century Maritime Expansion

At the time when Stevin achieved a fusion of practical and ideal city planning, an unorthodox view of the sea and of seafaring as an activity fit for man, a view that Stevin supported, coincidentally began to emerge in Western culture. The interplay between city planning and the cultural setting of late-sixteenth-century maritime expansion is the subject of this section; it is a suggestive, not an exhaustive, approach to the possible impact of one cultural phenomenon upon another.

Seafaring at that time was associated with terror: prayers were appropriate before a voyage. Even today superstitious taboos surround the lives of fishermen in parts of Europe.[40] The fear of the sea in the early modern era, however, had a theological foundation that it has largely lost today. To early modern Western Christian man, the sea was a part of the original matter of the world, and its storms could still be the judging work of God, just as in the days of Noah or Jonah. His instinctive fear of the high seas was physical and spiritual, and very real; most sailors, even those engaged in long-distance traffic, stayed close to the shoreline whenever possible. The theological, aesthetic, and philosophical meanings the Christian man of this time derived from the sea have not yet been explicated in the way Marjorie Nicolson has treated the meanings of mountains.[41] Nicolson described the traditional early modern view of mountains as a sign of man's fall from grace, and then accounted for the new understanding of mountains in the search for the sublime and the natural during the late seventeenth, eighteenth, and early

nineteenth centuries. In the absence of a similar study on the meaning of the
seas, it is possible only to suggest that perhaps port city planning spread across
seventeenth-century Europe as an expression of a new, affirmative sense of
the sea. Simon Stevin, for example, placed himself against what he saw to be a
traditional view that man should not exploit the sea for his own ends when he
wrote: "Some people, seeing the extraordinary power of the sea and large
rivers, take this on the whole to be God's work, about which men trouble
themselves in vain. To which we say that it is evident that all is God's work, but
it is useless to believe too simply that men trouble about this in vain, for they
sometimes divert the large course of rivers."[42] This devout Calvinist knew
what man could do with nature for his own purposes, and he must be included with all those who tried to integrate man's powers over nature into a
morally justified frame of values.[43]

The traditional typology of the sea produced few cultural artifacts that
have survived. Lighthouses of the period, for example, were archaic devices,
symbolic of the fact that man had not yet achieved an understanding of
nature. They were marginally effective as markers to men at sea because, until
Argand's smokeless oil lamp of 1778 provided a light of five candlepower
magnified and focused 400 times by mirrors, lighthouses were in fact nothing
more than fires atop turrets. Because they were so ineffective, few lighthouses
were even built before or during the seventeenth century, perhaps not more
than forty. Seamen located the shoreline by various devices of reckoning,
including visual identification. The height of the early modern lighthouse
alone was probably as functional as the light of the fire built at the top of it.[44]
But lighthouses were built to be tall for reasons other than that of compensating for an unadvanced technology. In form, they were simply urban towers
that had been transplanted beyond the city walls, either to a point adjacent to
the harbor (as at Genoa) or to an isolated spot along a dangerous stretch of
coast (as at Cordouan, in Gascony).[45] Although their practicality was marginal,
lighthouses such as the sixteenth-century masterpieces at Genoa and Cordouan were treated with all the respect the people of the time believed they
owed to the contemporary descendants of the great Pharos of Alexandria.
Lighthouses were decorated and embellished in high style, and this expense
was borne precisely because the symbolic value of the lighthouse was as important as its practical role.[46] The replication of a structure perfected in antiquity
was believed to be a worthy ambition. More than that, however, lighthouses
were as much a marker of the seacoast for those on land as they were a
signpost of the land for those at sea. They represented the values of material
civilization as it developed on land and emphasized the safety, well-being, and
foresight that made urban life attractive. Thus, lighthouses identified the
point beyond which people on land should hesitate to go; they were reminders
to them of the perils of the sea. Similarly, like the towers of a rural lord and
like the turrets of the city, they marked the channel or highway by which it was
safe to pass.[47]

That greater reliance upon and control over sea power might become
critical to the commercial, political, and cultural development of northern
Europe was a new idea, one that the Spanish-Dutch wars of the late sixteenth
century validated. The Spanish had created a seaborne empire earlier in the

century, and they carried fortunes across the Atlantic every year on schedule. The transshipment of the Atlantic trade within the Mediterranean and as far as the North Sea had confirmed a preponderance of Spanish power in those regions, a hegemony the Spanish tried to translate into religious unity and political initiative. Spain's victory at Lepanto in 1571 marked the division of the Mediterranean between Christians and Ottomans and made Spain appear invincible as a European power. Seventeen years later the Armada sailed. The Armada itself was worthy of the predictions that great and terrible events would take place in 1588; numbering 130 ships and carrying 30,000 men and 2,400 pieces of artillery, the Armada was the most awesome fleet northern Europeans had ever seen. Moreover, northern Europeans knew that only the most thorough planning of logistics, supplies, and tactics had made the Armada possible. The defeat of the Armada did not diminish for anyone the lessons about resources, preparation, seamanship, and infrastructure that its sailing had taught. Events in the year 1588, therefore, made sea power seem more important than ever before. At the same time, Dutch commerce grew in response to Spanish military sea power. From 1586 to 1590 a shortage of grain in the Mediterranean was relieved mainly by the Dutch, who organized grain exports from the Baltic toward that region.[48] Behind this opportunism was a sense of urgency: sea power was manifestly no longer incidental to the survival of the United Provinces as a new political and social unit.

Clearly the events of the 1580s went against established beliefs about the sea. Northern Europeans had known that the sea was available to man to use with God's grace and for His ends. At the end of the Middle Ages the Dutch were sending trading fleets into the Baltic and across the Bay of Biscay, but they stuck to these narrow corridors and did not increase the range or complexity of their trade. The competitive setting of the late sixteenth century made them change the way they used the sea. The only fleets with a permanent standing every year in the sixteenth century had been the Spanish fleets that traded across the Atlantic and Pacific, and the Venetian fleets. Even the Armada and the English fleet that met it were created and assembled to do battle once and once only. They were not intended, either of them, to have a permanent presence, and in this respect they were no different from any of the numerous trading or exploration fleets of the day. But by the end of the sixteenth century, efforts were made for the first time in France, Scandinavia, England, and the Netherlands to build up permanent commercial and military fleets, and these efforts were renewed and sustained throughout the seventeenth century. Of course, efforts varied in style, approach, and success from country to country. Nevertheless, these efforts were all based on the idea that the sea need not be left to those who traditionally traded and fished for a living, but could be used even by those who previously had had nothing to do with it. The establishment of stock exchanges, trading companies, and exchange banks in the early years of the seventeenth century were signs of new attitudes toward maritime enterprise in England and in the Netherlands.[49]

Perhaps because of what happened in the 1580s, people, especially those in northern Europe, began to change their views about the sea, seafaring, and seafarers. Little is known about such attitudes and how changes in them were brought about. Late-sixteenth-century Europeans did not find it easy to communicate their knowledge and awareness of the sea. Those who wrote about the sea, for example, either did not know how to or did not care to express the challenge, risk, ambition, and pleasure of making seafaring profitable and a sign of mastery.[50] Despite research into tides and navigation, scientific knowledge of the sea made little progress at that time (advances in oceanography did not come until the twentieth century).[51] Secular history could not yet redeem for the present the virtues of the past, and philosophy was still unable to transform nature from a sign of sin into transcending beauty. In the meantime, writing about the sea remained bound to the imagery of Greek and Roman fact and legend. Hakluyt's works, which first appeared in the 1580s and followed quickly upon Italian examples, showed that seafaring could be an exciting and important subject, but a century later their example had not yet been widely imitated.[52] It took a long time for the world of the real port city to find its way into literary expression.[53]

In painting, the conquest of the sea did not really begin until the early seventeenth century. Dutch marinescapes certainly became common in the Netherlands, but were thought by people elsewhere to be a peculiar genre. In France, Claude Gelée became famous for his mid-seventeenth-century paintings of the coastline. Some of his paintings included fanciful settings of port cities, others did not; his real subject was neither the seacoast nor the sea, but the light upon the waves. In fact, his may have been one of the early attempts to create the feeling that man's relationship to the sea contained elements of the sublime. In the mid-eighteenth century, Joseph Vernet, following the tradition of Salvator Rosa, painted several port cities, and in the 1770s and 1780s, Turner learned to feel and to dream at London's quayside (his seascapes were color-coded pictures of what man could experience with the sea). Thus, in painting as in literature, an awareness of the sea entered into the vocabulary of the arts only after Europeans had initiated a new age of sea power.

This is the reason I am suggesting that, at the end of the sixteenth century, port city planning may have served as an expression of a new, affirmative reliance upon sea power. Sixteenth-century port cities were points of contact between man and the sea, cultural instruments that conditioned maritime affairs. Cities contained a great variety of elements—canals, quays, fortifications, towers—that could be orchestrated to multiply or to limit, to predetermine or to leave unspecified, how and where the inhabitants of the city would take notice of the sea and of the activities by which men exploited it. By the end of the sixteenth century, city planning, in both its ideal and practical traditions, represented a more sophisticated way to stimulate maritime culture than either literature or painting provided. When the theory of city planning had been elaborated, port cities around the Mediterranean were already largely formed. But in the north, urban bases available for sea power had never before been used to create a seaborne empire and to sustain large-scale maritime exploitation. City planning could help northern Europeans prepare to use sea power, and it could also provide a context for them to express the meaning of an expansion of sea power and how they thought it could be sustained. Planning for new port cities in the seventeenth century, therefore, was itself a sign that sea power had become an important part of a new Atlantic civilization.

II

Seaworthy Cities: Planning in the Expanding European World of the Seventeenth Century

Planning and Growth

The development of the ideal and practical city planning traditions and a greater reliance upon maritime affairs were sixteenth-century preconditions for the new urban age that matured during the seventeenth century. Because the Renaissance expansion of Europe's maritime economy had not produced anything more novel in city planning than the realization that cities contributed something to sea power, sixteenth-century Europeans largely took the number and appearance of port cities for granted. Only toward the end of that century, when initiative in commercial and military affairs passed into the hands of northern Europeans, was the connection made between patterns of maritime exploitation and the urban landscape of maritime Europe. This perception seems to have encouraged those who wanted to increase sea power to find new uses for the ideal and practical city planning traditions. In the seventeenth century, statesmen, admirals, and merchants would not take for granted either the number or the physical, spatial structure of port cities.

The age of new port cities began optimistically enough early in the seventeenth century, when Paris, Amsterdam, and Copenhagen were modified and enlarged to make them more suitable as bases for expanding sea power. The approach taken for each city was cautious and reasonable, requiring an initial project that could be executed in a short period of time, and then additional ones that were to be completed as the city grew. This procedure was successful only in Amsterdam. The early development of Paris failed to serve as a model for that city's later growth. And, in Copenhagen, there was so little growth following the initial project early in the century that the relevance of planning to port city growth might have been questioned altogether. But before the lack of growth became apparent in Copenhagen, Amsterdam's success only encouraged planners in Scandinavia to persist in their activities, which they soon extended to the creation of new port cities, in the hope that one of them would develop into an Amsterdam of the North. City planning did not remain a means to an end; it became an end in itself when urban change took precedence over and was seen as a prerequisite for other ways of increasing sea power. The result was the establishment of many Scandinavian cities, of which few were able to grow or to contribute to sea power. City planning promised more than it could deliver, and it nearly consumed itself by its own abuses. Hubris was the sin of the age.

Paris

At the time when the Place Dauphine was built, in 1607,[1] and for more than two centuries thereafter, Paris was a river city whose population was dependent for food and trade on the traffic of the Seine. The sailing ship properly formed the central element in the city's shield; only since the age of the railroad does that symbol need an explanation. The busiest part of the city's riverfront was at the "grève" or bank, where today there is the Place du Châtelet—that is, the area on the right bank directly opposite the central Ile de la Cité. The Place Dauphine was constructed on the western tip of that island, just beyond the law courts. It was as close as it could be to the center of the city's life—even the palace of the Louvre was nearby—and the Pont Neuf connected it with both sides of the river. A more advantageous address for merchants and city leaders was scarcely imaginable, but that was only one of the attractions of the Place Dauphine. The Place itself offered an oasis from the bustle of traffic; open space was the special feature of this addition to Paris' commercial life.

The Place Dauphine, the first residential unit of uniform style in Northern Europe, failed to serve as a model for Paris' growth,[2] for reasons that illuminate both the characteristics of port city planning and the relationship between planning and politics. Henri IV had built the Place Dauphine as a magnificent gesture to a proud city, but also because he wanted to place his initiative and money behind investment in and control over commerce. But the very advantages in location that made the Place Dauphine attractive denied it influence over the city's spatial development.[3] It was inserted into the city's center, whereas the vacant land available for growth was far removed from it, either at a distance from the center along the Seine or inland, beyond the walls. Missing in Paris in the seventeenth century's first decade was a cohesive plan linking the city's commercial center to areas of possible future growth and investment. Perhaps Henri IV became aware that this was so. In 1609 he planned the Place de France to be built along a canal at the city's eastern edge. It was to have had uniform facades along the quay and a semicircular place immediately inland for markets and residences. The Place de France was not constructed; the initial works were abandoned after Henri

IV's death in 1610. Had it been built, the Place de France would have given prominence to an area where future development was possible. By itself, the Place de France would not have been the equivalent of a true master plan, but it could have had a greater influence over the city's shape than could the Place Dauphine.

During Henri IV's reign, no correlation was made between the growth of centralized state power and the baroque capital city. Henri IV's Place Royale (Place des Vosges today) was aristocratic, but the Place Dauphine and the Place de France would have kept the upper class as close to the marketplace as to the palace. The spirit behind Henri IV's projects survived him in the suggestions, which were made during Louis XIII's reign, to dig canals from the Seine inland toward the vacant land along the city's eastern walls. That, too, would have made Paris grow along waterways, as Antwerp and Amsterdam had. Such projects require investments the city's principal residents would not undertake by themselves, and the monies and energies of the monarchy were diverted to the problems of war abroad and unrest at home, problems that eventually culminated in the mid-century Fronde.

Louis XIV's memory of his flight as a child from Paris during the Fronde may well have been an important factor in his decision to live elsewhere than in the Louvre; like a businessman handling his affairs in the city from his country estate, Louis concerned himself with Paris from his châteaux. The city's leaders were unwilling to invest in public construction projects, and accepted the king's suggestions for squares, streets, churches, and public buildings as sufficient opportunities for investment. Since Louis XIV's projects did not call for canals, none was dug. The growth of the city followed the great promenades that lay beyond, not adjacent to, the commercially active quays of the river. Even those projects adjacent to the river, the Ile St. Louis, the College des Quatre-Nations, and the facade of the Louvre, were deliberately designed to be above and beyond the busy harbor. And so the Place Dauphine remained encircled by a city that took on the atmosphere of the countryside as it grew outward toward the fields and hills beyond its walls: the Champs-Elysées started near the Seine but ended at Versailles. Like Rome, whose mantle of imperial glory it thought it had inherited, Paris had become a courtly capital that appeared to be a great port city only by accident.

Given the prodigious construction in and substantial growth of Paris after Henri IV's death in 1610—the large number of hotels, streets, public structures, and residential squares completed during the rest of the seventeenth century—the Place Dauphine and the projected Place de France may seem relatively unimportant. Nevertheless, such a conclusion would fail to account for the differences between planning under Henri IV and growth under his successors. Had Henri IV lived longer, his projects might have endowed Paris with a spatial framework along the city's edge better suited to the city's needs than continued development of the historic core proved to be. A substantial number of the post-1610 projects were placed into the existing urban fabric with little or no concern for how they might be related to the rest of the city as it was then or as it might become. One serious problem, for example, was transportation: neither the carriage of goods nor the movement of individuals was easy, efficient, or pleasant in seventeenth-century Paris because of the city's unusually high population density and concentration of activities. (Only along peripheral boulevards and forest paths could the carriages of the wealthy pass.) Louis XIV had a clear sense that urban construction without a master plan was costing Paris some of the beauty and utility that should have accrued from so much construction and growth, but he and his collaborators found elaboration and implementation of spatial planning difficult for two reasons. Firstly, it involved rebuilding so much of the rest of the city, a costly enterprise subject to legal delays initiated by uncooperative landowners and, secondly, the government did not want to encourage the further growth of a city it considered to be already too large. Louis XIV's demolition of the city's northern wall allowed the city to expand in that direction but did nothing to render growth orderly. Building on vacant land bordered by canals or along the riverfront, away from the historic center, as Henri IV's Place de France would have required, would have facilitated further planning efforts; concentrating construction within historic Paris, as Henri IV began to do with the Place Dauphine and as Parisians continued to do after his death, rendered the task of planners more difficult. Because Paris was a port city, its economy could sustain continued demographic increase, but the absence of spatial planning placed the burdens of growth on the existing city. The Dutch understood such matters and used the progressive extension of the city along the waterfront and canals to add land to a city as its population and commerce expanded. Analysis of Henri IV's Paris leads to the study of Amsterdam as a port city with the sort of master plan for growth that seventeenth-century Paris lacked. Comparisons underscore how subtle was the interplay between the imagination and talent that went into planning and the political, social, and economic circumstances that placed the planner in the hands of fortune.

Amsterdam

The municipality of Amsterdam initiated and sustained a master plan for urban growth as public policy. The city government's sixteenth-century building ordinances had established municipal authority over land-use planning and over construction methods while preserving the initiative of private builders within this framework. These precedents, and the city's independence from the monarchy, made Amsterdam more receptive to planning than Paris. When the land in Amsterdam up to the Singel Canal, which marked the city's limits, was occupied, the city fathers decided to extend their authority over additional lands around Amsterdam. They selected a plan that largely preserved the city's historic core, permitted new land to be added and occupied as the city's needs dictated, and projected a pattern of development on the city's extension.

This plan was the famous "plan of three rings" of 1607 (figure 2.1). The Singel, the canal that then formed the city's edge, was to serve as a model for three additional encircling canals: the city's edge was to be repeated three times across the vacant land beyond the Singel, and each new canal would in

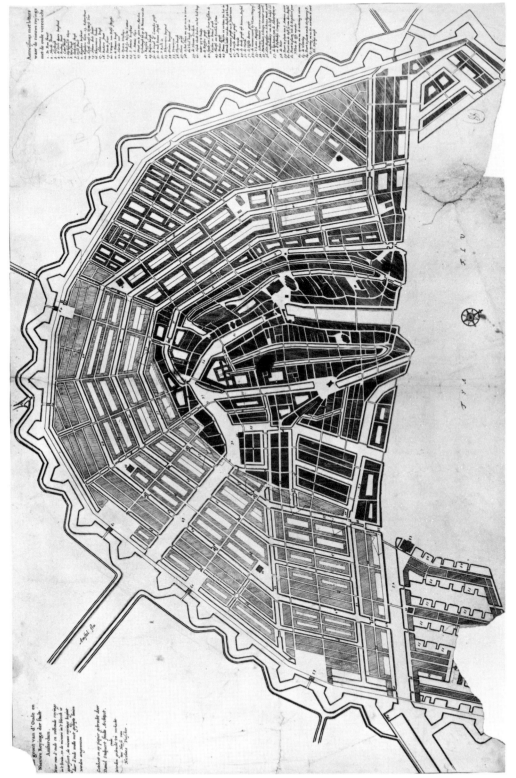

FIGURE **2.1**. *Amsterdam, c. 1650, plan by Daniel Stolpaert, printed by N. Visscher. Bibliothèque nationale, cartes et plans GeC 9092. Photo Bibliothèque nationale, Paris.*

turn become the city's new limit. Boldly, the city planners conceived of the entire area for growth as a complete unit, yet designed a plan that called for construction in stages, to be completed as the city grew. This gradual approach was a major advance in planning, and it must have been attractive to people who knew that economic and political fortunes were unpredictable. And so, just as the rings of a tree tell the history of climate, the canals added to Amsterdam tell a story of good and of bad years, of irregular demographic rhythms, of bad investments, and of risks turned to profit. This does not mean that each new area of the city was distinctly different because a different generation built it. Daniel Stolpaert saw the plan through from inception to completion, from 1615 to 1676. He specified the activities and land uses appropriate to each area of the city's extension at the start, so the variety of activities and residences of the entire city formed a pattern of predictable complexity and overall harmony.

Amsterdam, like Venice, that other artificial city on reclaimed land, made water the primary element in its form. Venice seemed so brilliant and powerful, but those who admired what it had achieved could not imitate its architecture and spatial layout, because the city's physical forms corresponded to a setting duplicated nowhere else. Amsterdam was a man-made environment capable of being replicated; the designed regularity of Amsterdam's canals made this so. Indeed, the canals represented one of the greatest achievements of practical city planning. They offered Amsterdam the facilities to handle traffic efficiently throughout periods of growth, for the plan of 1607 meant that the city would never hinder the harbor.

The Dutch had not devised the plan for Amsterdam because it represented their ideal of what a city should be, but because they thought it would work. Its success lay precisely in the way in which such improvements came with an understanding of the practical needs of those who would use the city as a base for trade. This success needs to be underscored. In Amsterdam the diverse activities of the port city were not contained in isolated individual forms, as in several of the great sixteenth-century Italian port cities, but were enclosed within a single form, including both the activities and their connections. The ideal port city often posited a single topographic form, but did it in such a way as to restrain the city from growth; to that end, ideal city planners traced abstract geometric designs onto the land, suggesting that growth would destroy the desired symmetry and perfection. Amsterdam's canals, however, provided for the integration of the parts of the city into a whole, and for the progressive extension of the whole through the parts at the same time; a working space, and not an idealized, conceptual shape, suggested the city's appearance and pattern of growth. The result, moreover, extended beyond the significant practical gains in economic efficiency and spatial distribution of activities and social groups that such planning yielded. Amsterdam's extended waterfront offered the city's residents multiple opportunities to witness maritime activities as a part of everyday life. Even if such activities were only incidental to their own occupations, they could have no illusions about the basis for the city's growth and the reasons for its appearance. This access to and familiarity with waterways encouraged Amsterdammers, like Dutchmen

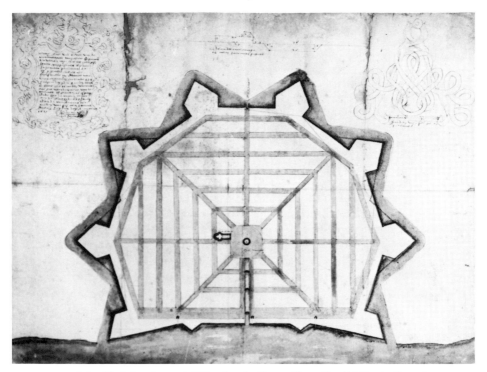

FIGURE **2.2.** *Christianshavn, 1617, plan by Semp. Kongelige Bibliotek, Copenhagen.*

in other cities and like Venetians as well, to develop a sense of play about their fabricated natural environment. At a time when no one visited the seashore for pleasure, they made the city's waterways into a principal public arena for social life and for the aesthetic enhancement of the city's architecture. In Amsterdam the waterfront developed as a civilized and domesticated space, while at the same time fulfilling the primary economic and political goals that had justified constructing a city as waterscape in the first place. With good reason, Europeans recognized that because of its size, shape, prosperity, and beauty, Amsterdam represented something new in urban culture.

Those who wanted to establish a commercial empire as dynamic as the Dutch one imitated Dutch techniques of enterprise, including city planning. Just as a Third World country today might import technology from an advanced country in the hope that it will become able to alter its own economy and, eventually, its relations with others, so several European nations hoped to create opportunities for expansion by applying proven Dutch techniques.[4] But the Dutch record was often translated abroad—incorrectly—to mean that planned port cities were essential to sea power. People interested in making port cities grow transformed Dutch procedures into an ideal type, the best possible way to build port cities. Inevitably, Dutch models were inappropriate as ideal types, but not until later in the seventeenth century did anyone try to study why and how the Dutch used planning with such care and success.

Copenhagen

The first city affected by the diffusion of Dutch city planning was Copenhagen. Those who imitated the Dutch often came to use water as a port city's first resource, and no better example of this can be found than in the way Christian IV (1577–1648) replanned Copenhagen. Copenhagen had grown in a medieval shell, and without much apparent order. Arsenal and shipyards, merchants' area and exchange, and the castle were all concentrated near each other along the harborfront. By 1600 there was little room left for growth. The activities within the shipyards were poorly organized, and new, enlarged fortifications were needed to protect Copenhagen from attack. The new district of Christianshavn was built to correct these defects; it was supposed to be the first unit of a completely new and large port city, very different in form and shape from what it had been previously.

The first plan submitted in 1617 (figure 2.2) would have been as unsuitable as old Copenhagen itself. The planner, a Dutchman named Semp, suggested a layout reminiscent of the ideal planning military camp with its radial-concentric grid. Modified only by a canal leading from the harbor to the central square, the plan would have been difficult to extend if growth made an enlargement necessary. The king rejected Semp's first plan, but chose his second, made three months later. That one (figure 2.3) called for canals that went through and around a grid network. In this plan, Semp revealed a surer understanding of water as part of urban form. Perhaps in his first plan he had hoped to satisfy a ruler's presumed preference for symbols of centralized military power; in the second plan Semp presented Christian IV with what he really wanted, a district usefully integrated into a growing port city.

As the creation of a mercantilist king who wanted to concentrate and secure his power, Christianshavn represented the winds of change that blew across the old city of Copenhagen early in the seventeenth century.[5] In social composition, Christianshavn remained different from the rest of the city as if it was a colony, a district marked out for exploitation. From the 1620s on, many from the royal administrative and mercantile establishment chose to live there. Those who were attracted to it responded to commercial and political opportunities; they found it useful. But Christianshavn did not grow larger. Not until 1735 would the physical, commercial growth of the city provoke Andreas Bjørn, the leading shipping magnate of the day, to make use of additional reclaimed land to the southeast of Christianshavn. All Copenhagen's growth after the foundation of Christianshavn and until Bjørn's development (and largely thereafter as well) was concentrated on the other side of the harbor. There were reasons for this: Copenhagen's growth during the seventeenth century was slow; lower development costs made it easier to contemplate projects for the area adjacent to the old city than for land that would have to be reclaimed next to Christianshavn; and no unifying scheme for Copenhagen existed to relate Christianshavn with new developments that took shape next to the old city.

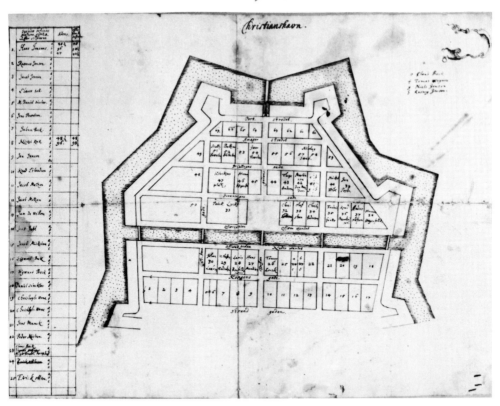

FIGURE **2.3.** *Christianshavn, c. 1640. Kongelige Bibliotek, Copenhagen.*

Given Copenhagen's halting gains in commerce and population, it is most remarkable that the lack of visible growth did not stop planners. Planning had given Christianshavn its place in the city, and planning, it was believed, could make other projects successful, too. Neither the king nor his planners wanted to wait for population and traffic pressures to accumulate before providing a more adequate urban setting. Instead, they saw the vast harbor area and vacant land that had been brought together and circumscribed by fortifications as a domain that they could fill in, at least on paper, as they wished. Their projects show us not only the real Copenhagen of the seventeenth century, but also images of what they thought that city might become. As if to suggest that a city could call itself into existence, planners submitted sketches that depicted what Copenhagen might look like if those projects were built. Projects were made not only for the area adjacent to the old city, where some growth actually took place, but for an expansion of Christianshavn, which did not grow. This marked the beginning of a new pattern in port city development. Heretofore the planning of actual cities had occurred during or following periods of a city's growth. This was true for Leghorn, Antwerp, even Amsterdam. Changes were proposed for Copenhagen before that city grew, almost as if the changes themselves would cause the city's population and

FIGURE 2.4. *Copenhagen, 1648, plan by Heyder. Forsvarets Bygningstienste 1/1/1, Copenhagen.*

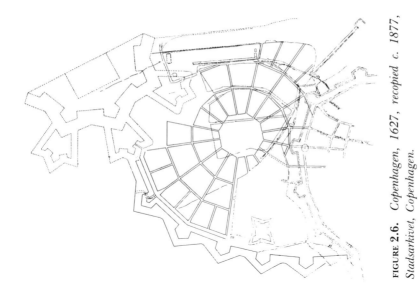

FIGURE **2.6.** *Copenhagen, 1627, recopied c. 1877, Stadsarkivet, Copenhagen.*

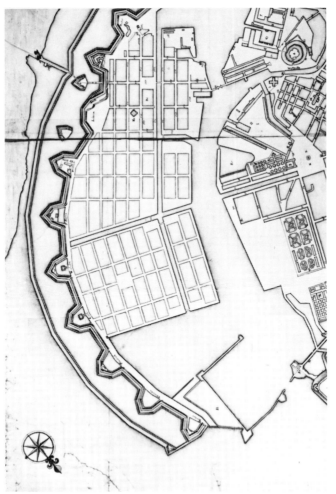

FIGURE **2.5.** *Copenhagen, date unknown. Kongelige Bibliotek, Copenhagen.*

41

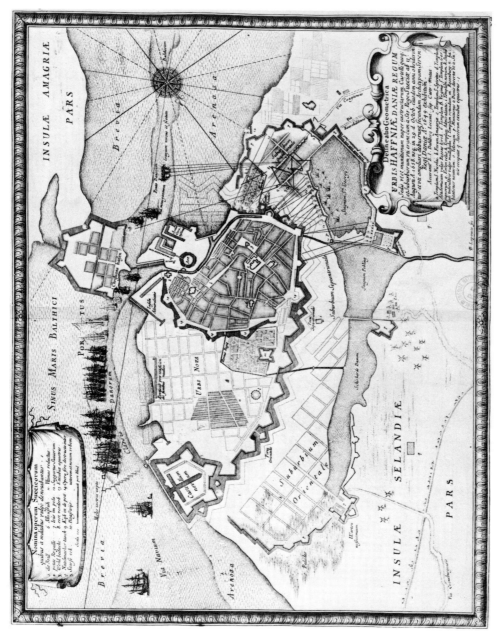

FIGURE **2.7.** *Copenhagen, 1649, print by Dahlberg. Bibliothèque nationale, cartes et plans GeDD 3621. Photo Bibliothèque nationale, Paris.*

economy to keep pace with the builders. Projects for Copenhagen symbolized that city's lack of commercial and demographic growth as much as Amsterdam's three rings of canals symbolized that city's success. With the belief that the forced appearance of a great port city could preface and prepare for the growth of commercial and military sea power, the age of new port cities had begun.[6]

The proposals for Copenhagen called for parts of the city to be developed according to Dutch practice; this is not surprising. What is striking is the absence of any overall coherent, conceptual framework to which these parts could belong. Such a framework had been the great achievement of the Dutch. A descriptive analysis of the projects for Copenhagen—those that were executed as well as those that were not—shows that planners started with the future line of fortifications as a given boundary, and then proceeded to develop the space contained within the walls. The city was not allowed to set its own limits; rather, the fortifications determined those limits and new developments filled in the empty space between the old walls and the new. The various units of the city were not logically related to each other, but belonged to the same city only because the walls locked them into the same space.

The plans to extend Christianshavn are typical of the ways Danish planners misunderstood Dutch techniques. Christianshavn itself was built on reclaimed land, and some suggested that if the line of fortifications was extended around it out onto the harbor and to a point opposite a new castle (figure 2.4),[7] then the area enclosed by the defense works could also be reclaimed. Several different proposals were submitted for this expensive undertaking, and they varied only according to the future form and function of Christianshavn's extension. Figure 2.5 is typical of seventeenth-century extrapolations of Christianshavn. It shows the old city's characteristic juxtaposition of spatial forms, the new district of Christianshavn directly opposite, and the artist's conception of what that district would look like if its shape was replicated on yet-to-be reclaimed land adjacent to it within the defense perimeter. Planners simply used their imaginations to conceive of yet another variation on the theme of Christianshavn, while omitting from their drawings any formal distinction between what was already built and what was as yet mere fancy. This particular drawing is also of interest because it shows that, on the old city side of the harbor, other new developments were also projected, and that the new projects on opposite sides of the harbor were visually and functionally unrelated to each other.

By far the largest number of projects dealt with the future uses of the land between old Copenhagen and its fortifications. Christian IV had wanted to double the city by adding land to the northeast, and he began to surround this land by extending the fortifications toward a site at the harbor's mouth, where a new fort would be built. The first and most dazzling project for this area was made in 1627 (figure 2.6). It clearly showed the edge of the old city (bottom of illustration), the new defense works, and the new fort. The plan called for a pure radial-concentric design around a central open square, surely the influence of Italian ideal city precedent. Obviously, this pattern could not be directly related to the old city or to the waterfront: it was simply inserted, intact, into an existing, vacant space as neatly as possible. Several drawings from the middle of the seventeenth century reveal more of what Christian IV and his son Frederick III probably had in mind. The print by Dahlberg (figure 2.7) depicted rather accurately the old city and Christianshavn. Dahlberg added to the existing city the extensions labeled suburban occidentale, septentrionale and orientale, and the urbs nova. Christian IV intended to drain the lakes near the city and build a plain grid suburb on the reclaimed land. Presumably new fortifications would eventually enclose that district, too. But the most important development was reserved for the space between the old city and the fort, the walls and the harbor. It included a grid pattern, one or two canals penetrating the grid from the harbor, and an oddly shaped, obliquely angled district for lower-class workers, which was the only part of the 1627 radial-concentric plan (figure 2.6) to be executed. Significantly, that district was left alone—no effort was made to redo it according to a new plan (it still exists in the city, distinctively marked by its two-story barrack-like apartments altogether reminiscent of early modern military architecture). Not one of these parts was to be integrated with the others, nor did the street patterns have anything to do with either the fortifications or the royal gardens. Urban squares were noticeably absent. Even in the mideighteenth century, when the unit known as Frederikstad was developed to provide a formal, aristocratic setting for Copenhagen's harborside, no effort was made to coordinate that part of the city with other parts, either nearby or across the harbor.[8]

By the end of the seventeenth century only a few of the projects for enlarging Copenhagen had been built as Dahlberg and others, who composed variations of his scheme, had planned. The planners who prepared for the development of an enlarged Copenhagen had made two errors in the use of Dutch planning: firstly, their plans could not be realized gradually, as the city grew, but had to be executed all of a piece if their scale was to have a felicitous impact on the city's residents and on those who came to it to trade; and, secondly, their plans did not relate the various newer and older parts of the city to each other according to any implicit scheme or order. On the basis of these misunderstandings of the Dutch tradition, Danish planners confronted the empty harbor and land spaces of Copenhagen with projects to fill them. The political and economic context for planning in the Netherlands constrained planners to develop projects that could serve a city as it grew; Dutch planning emphasized incremental developments functionally related to one another. Danish planners felt compelled to conceive of projects that had programmatic value; their projects were not linked in time and space to a process of commercial and demographic growth, but anticipated such growth. The Dutch would have added to the vacant land around Copenhagen as the city grew; the Danes saw all that vacant land as a vacuum demanding to be filled. Had they adhered more closely to the Dutch tradition, Danish planners would have attempted projects of smaller, less pretentious, and more economical dimensions, more appropriate to that city's slower growth. Until the relationship between planning and growth as the Dutch understood it could once again be worked out, planning for new port cities would remain both highly creative and acutely impractical.

The Swedish Experience: From Practical to Ideal City Planning

The new awareness of what sea power could contribute to the growth of the state penetrated beyond the Sund Strait, which separated Denmark from Sweden. Control of the Sund itself was the subject of a long dispute between the two countries because the Danes taxed all the shipping that passed through it between the Baltic and the North Seas. Control of the Sund symbolized and was an important factor in supremacy over northern waters. Conflict with Sweden had motivated the Danes to fortify and expand Copenhagen and other cities as well, principally Christiana (Oslo) and Gluckstadt (50 kilometers northwest of Hamburg).[9] The Swedes, for their part, enlarged Stockholm and initiated a more far-reaching effort to increase their sea power by building new port cities where there were none. They did this mostly from necessity, because their urban infrastructure was, in 1600, much less adequate for sea power than was that of either of their rivals, the Danes and the Hansa League. Knowing that an increase in Swedish sea power could only occur as part of a transformation of Sweden's politics, commerce, and economy, the Swedes intended to use new port cities as the leaven in the dough. Sweden's existing demographic and material resources were so limited that few port city projects would ever have been launched in Sweden or in its empire had large amounts of manpower and money been considered necessary to port city growth.[10] Sweden's new cities were not planned to correspond in number and size to the country's resources. Instead, the Swedes assumed that new port cities would make possible an expansion of Sweden's limited resources by providing the proper kind of setting for the country's new urban, proto-industrial, maritime activities. In Sweden more than anywhere else, planning became a Promethean art.

Beginning in the 1620s, Sweden's planners accepted the challenge to build cities for sea power because they shared a deep personal loyalty to the monarchy. They served the Swedish crown as members of the fortifications corps or the surveyors corps or as counselors. There was friction among them on occasion, not from interservice rivalry, but because alternate views of how the destiny of Sweden might be achieved were thought to be at stake. Willingly and knowingly, these architects, artist-planners, engineers, and administrators helped to reinforce absolutism, concentrate state power, increase mercantilist wealth, defend Protestantism, and consolidate a Baltic empire. They were the radicals of their day, part of a vanguard that was breaking Sweden away from its past and fashioning for it the implementation of political, economic, and cultural autonomy. Intellectually and politically conditioned to change, they could take risks with new ideas. In this they were led by their rulers: Gustav II Adolph briefly corresponded with Simon Stevin; later, Christina, who had definite ideas on city planning of her own, engaged

Descartes on his fatal mission to instruct her in philosophy. The planner's task was even physically adventurous and daring, for it involved giving up the security of home for voyages and the army camp. Like Roman conquerors, the Swedes left the signs of their seventeenth-century empire behind them in the cities they rebuilt or founded in Finland, in parts of Russia, Poland, and Germany, and in Sweden itself: the names of Sweden's then-new port cities amount to a gazetteer of the Baltic, seemingly of more interest to a geographer than to a historian.[11]

Of all those places, our attention is drawn to plans that were typical and can be presented as samples of a larger number, and to plans that reflected a more original treatment of city space. In fact, the variety and proliferation of plans can highlight the close connection between politics and planning in a way that the political record alone, more reflective of Sweden's day-to-day concerns, cannot. Of course, politics gave planning its impetus: at the same time the monarchy called for new urban policies, it created a strong, energetic, reliable centralized admiralty. The political circumstances that surrounded the planning of new cities have already been outlined by Eimer, Michael Roberts, and others;[12] the interested reader can turn to those sources of information. The political record alone, however, does not reveal as well as city planning documents can, that planning linked Sweden's drive for sea power to a European-wide, international cultural movement, and thereby endowed that drive with the visible symbols of success.

Gothenburg was the first major Swedish site to be planned, and the important role it was to play held the attention of planners throughout the first half of the seventeenth century.[13] It was located to the west of the Sund Strait so that trade carried on from there with Atlantic European ports would not be taxed by the Danes. Not surprisingly, the Swedes first turned to Dutch precedents in planning. They were trying to telescope the development of sea power into the shortest span of time, and Dutch techniques appeared to them to promise the best results. (The Dutch, incidentally, were to be associated not only with planning for the city of Gothenburg, but also with its commercial exploitation.) The oldest surviving plan was produced in 1609 (figure 2.8). It called for a grid city embraced by fortifications and enclosing an axially positioned harbor. This plan was not executed, however, because in 1613, the king, Gustav II Adolph (Gustavus Adolphus), relocated the site of the future city to the opposite side of the estuary. By 1620 other plans emerged for consideration. These plans (figure 2.9 is typical) were designed much more in the spirit of Stevin's teachings and in the manner of then current Dutch practice. The city was to be divided in half by a main canal from which two smaller canals would extend. A grid pattern of streets was established in relation to the canals. This layout was varied slightly by one artist-planner after another, and was sustained in its basic outlines throughout the century.

What matters is that most interesting planning variations assumed that the city would grow quickly and would need to be enlarged. Even in its original form, Gothenburg was to be a principal commercial base; clearly its size reflected the hopes of both the Dutch and the Swedish sponsors. In fact, though, it grew slowly—but it grew enough so that the central core of the present city of Gothenburg (that part outlined in the plans of the 1620s) was completely occupied by the mid-eighteenth century. In each of the different plans projecting growth in the seventeenth century (figure 2.10 is representative), the available low-lying land was to be developed as a suburban unit that could be directly linked to the central core.[14] Although artist-planners commonly used a grid network of streets to organize these projected developments, they determined the primary structure by canals. Again in the spirit of Stevin's teachings, canals predetermined the size and placement of these developments; the grid network was simply the best way to divide the land that the canals and fortifications enclosed. Significantly, these projects preserved the city center in any greater Gothenburg. That they did so no doubt reflected the traditional social geography of Swedish cities: the wealthier families would settle close to and in the center, the poorer ones farther away from it. None of those who imagined how Gothenburg might grow tried to change that social pattern of property holding.[15] Swedish artist-planners clearly understood organic, modular planning. What marked the difference between Dutch practice and Swedish design was that these projected developments were out of pace with the actual growth of Gothenburg.

In the center of the country, at the southern point of a vast inland lake, the city of Jönköping was to be enlarged at the same time that Gothenburg was established. Jönköping would serve a function similar to Gothenburg's: it was supposed to control the hinterland and generate its potential exports, to help outflank the Danes. Planning for Jönköping, like planning for Gothenburg, was in the Dutch style; the surviving plans show how well-understood Dutch techniques were in early seventeenth-century Sweden. Before planning, Jönköping had been nothing more than a village extended along the lake. Various plans were made in the Dutch manner between 1615 and 1625 (figure 2.11), all with a canal in the shape of a circle or square around which the city's street pattern was laid out. The variety of differences between these plans was small, but they show, nevertheless, a relative freedom from stereotype.[16]

Designs for Gothenburg and Jönköping displayed a technical mastery of conception and detail; they demonstrate how close to the Dutch tradition early Swedish planning was. Neither city grew as fast as expected,[17] but planners, unable to accept such slow growth, made the mistake of assuming that the rate of growth was higher than it really was. That error cost Gothenburg nothing, because in the absence of rapid growth it could remain bound to its compact form, but it became costly elsewhere, in places that did not have as modest a form as Gothenburg. Having failed to perceive the true relation between planning and growth, planners in Sweden attempted even grander, costlier, and more impossible designs.

Almost all of these plans, produced for cities established or rebuilt in the 1630s and after, shared similar defects of vision, defects that can be traced back to the never-questioned assumption that new cities built sea power. Many of these projects were dazzling and marvelous on paper, but most called for a large city to be executed immediately, a costly procedure. It was almost as if slow urban growth had eroded confidence in the organic, programmatic,

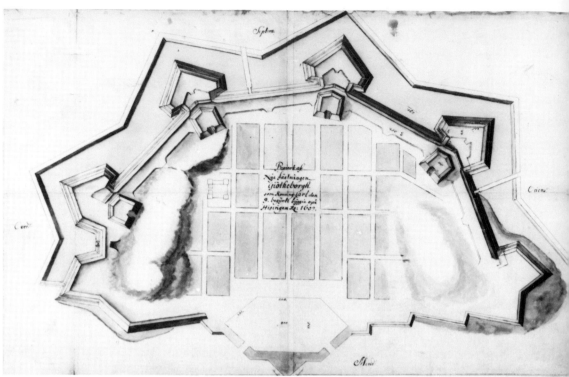

FIGURE **2.8.** *Gothenburg, 1609, no. 74c. Stads-och fästningsplaner, Kunglinga Krigsarkivet, Stockholm.*

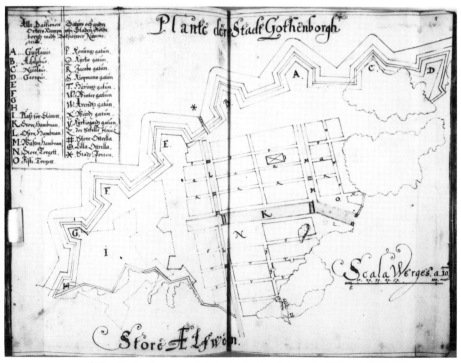

FIGURE **2.9.** *Gothenburg, c. 1620. Uppsala University Library 85(942).*

48

FIGURE **2.10.** *Gothenburg, 1659, plan by J. Warnschiold, no. 81. Stads-och fästningsplaner, Kung-linga Krigsarkivet, Stockholm.*

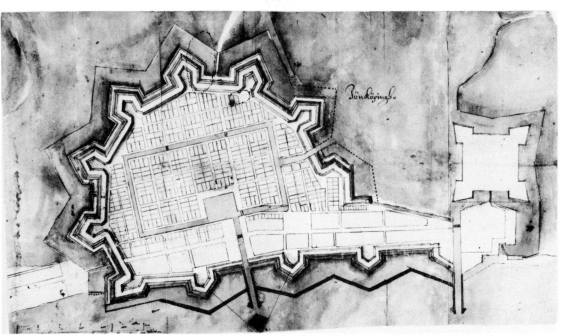

FIGURE **2.11.** *Jönköping, c. 1624, no. 43. Stads-och fästningsplaner, Kunglinga Krigsarkivet, Stockholm.*

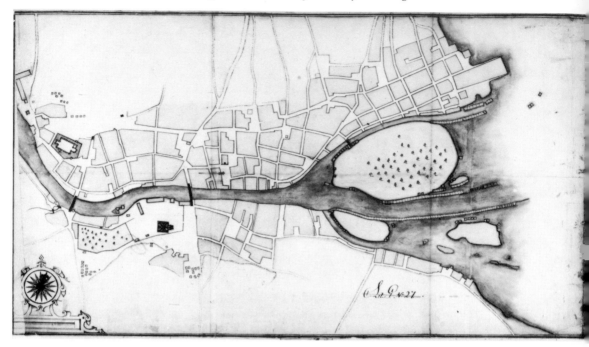

FIGURE **2.12.** *Gävle, 1648, no. 27. Stads-och fästningsplaner, Kunglinga Krigsarkivet, Stockholm.*

incremental planning of the Dutch style, so well suited to Swedish realities. Of course, Sweden might have abandoned the effort to build planned new port cities altogether. Instead, Swedish planners searched for new models for planning with the astonishing belief that their work would make possible an enlargement of Swedish maritime power.

Until the decade beginning in 1650, planners broke with the modular, compact incremental Dutch style by calling for the unwarranted extension of gridiron patterns over areas that were much larger than a city could reasonably occupy. After 1660, mere size and the rigid outlines of a grid pattern that erased topography were no longer enough to create an impression of activity and growth, so Italianate styles were transformed into geometric designs of great subtlety, complexity, and scale. In neither period did artist-planners take into account the monarchy's limited and heavily mortgaged resources. Were these planners, who were close to the court and spent much time in the provinces and in the army camp, so ignorant of the social, fiscal, political, military, and demographic components of Swedish power? It seems unlikely that they were unaware of the contingent nature of Swedish power; it seems more plausible that their plans were an attempt to negate and transcend those contingencies by building cities that were not limited by them in design. As if gradual growth and an uncompleted plan might have been seen as signs of Sweden's failure to build a maritime empire, planners appeared unconcerned to take into account gradual growth or what might happen if only part of a plan were executed. Surely, they may have thought, only a

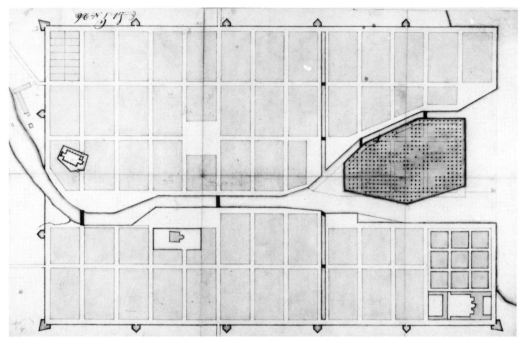

FIGURE **2.13.** *Gävle, 1648, no. 27. Stads-och fästningsplaner, Kunglinga Krigsarkivet, Stockholm.*

finished, planned city could represent Sweden's commitment to its own imperial future, regardless of conditions in the present. From the 1630s on, boldness and impracticality were the characteristics of Swedish planning. As the
following survey of the routine and extraordinary in planning demonstrates,
the slow or even nonexistent growth of Sweden's new port cities never inhibited the energy and imagination, the arrogance and ambition, of Sweden's
new city planners.

Every new city was important to the Swedish crown. Gothenburg's mission as an international trading center was obviously more visible than the
tax-gathering function of dozens of small communities, but even those new
municipalities of the Swedish hinterland and of the Baltic littoral were
planned. Planning for the smaller cities was more clearly an exercise in
abstraction, a simple topographic reordering that provided for blocks and
streets. Oddly enough, this simplistic planning often called for civil engineering works on a scale and of an expense out of proportion to the local economy
or to the state's stake in it: creating straight streets, regular blocks, and linear
quays (as called for in the transformation of Gävle, figures 2.12 and 2.13)
could never be a simple exercise in city building where fiscal and demographic
resources were thin. These plans posed more problems than their simple
outlines suggest. Their rigid outlines made demands not only on Sweden's
fiscal resources, but also on the townspeople themselves: all too often, plans
neglected to provide for a sense of community. Colonial cities such as these
were created to secure the new Swedish empire, but they lacked the enforced

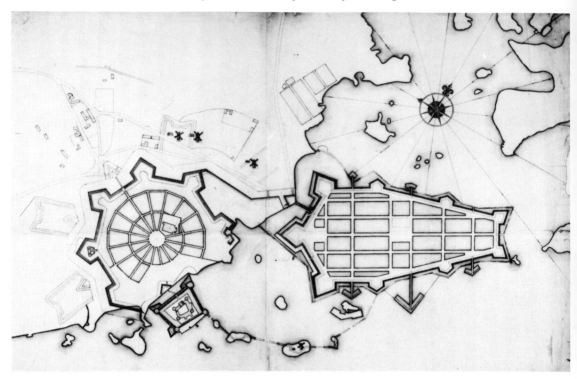

FIGURE **2.14.** *Kalmar, c. 1680, no. 62. Stads-och fästningsplaner, Kunglinga Krigsarkivet, Stock-holm.*

intimacy of the New England town or even of the twelfth- and thirteenth-century bastides of Gascony, which were also colonial towns. Planners may not have felt challenged into creativity by these smaller Swedish communities precisely because their economic and social activities were confined to the closed exchange of an agricultural district; they simply may have reserved a display of style for cities where economic and social growth would set off their achievements. Whatever the reason, planning, as it was apparently understood in Sweden, called for projects that traced out a clearly ordered pattern onto the land.

If planners presented designs for a small and isolated tax-gathering town without accounting for the social or financial costs their designs called for, then certainly they felt at liberty to increase those costs for a busy commercial or military port city. When planners suggested what Kalmar, Karlskrona, Landskrona in Sweden, and Carlsburg across the Baltic should look like, they barely considered the Dutch model at all. As Dutch planning methods became less attractive, Italian artistic techniques were promoted in their place. In the 1650s, Erik Dahlberg (1625–1703), artist-planner, administrator, and courtier, traveled in Italy. After that time, his work reflected the greater preoccupation with the decorative and formalistic possibilities in planning that seventeenth-century Italians and Frenchmen were exploring. During Louis

XIV's reign, Nicolas Tessin the Younger (1654–1728), son of an important Swedish architect, traveled in France, where he became familiar with the architects patronized by the king, who loved buildings. Thereafter he had their drawings sent to Sweden on a regular basis.

Gerhard Eimer has already described this succession in planning styles.[18] Eimer has suggested that the Swedes came to prefer the Italian ideal city planning tradition because it offered greater artistic and conceptual possibilities. Perhaps it did: the artist-planners who adopted Italian models had aesthetic sensibilities that only a more dramatic manipulation of space, form, and line could satisfy. Eimer celebrated the triumph of ideal planning as a chapter in the art history of the seventeenth century, one in which the north and the baroque became linked. But in so doing, he overlooked the context for planning in Sweden. Had the first new cities grown at all, the Swedes no doubt would have continued to plan in the Dutch tradition. It was the failure of those cities that they had planned in that tradition to grow that encouraged them to reject that tradition. Since the practical Dutch style had not worked well enough, perhaps the ideal tradition, they reasoned, might be worth trying. The Italian sources for these Swedish designs had once been part of an aesthetic, philosophical movement with roots in the Renaissance. In Sweden, however, Italian styles were not used to represent philosophical ideas in drawings, but were applied to the task of shaping actual cities. Such planning was supposed to reflect the greatness of Sweden's achievements and the will to sustain them.

Plans for Kalmar, Landskrona, Karlskrona, and Carlsburg can be presented together. They did not resemble each other, to be sure. My concern, however, is not to explain the unique qualities of each plan, nor the many interesting ways in which squares, streets, and perspectives were handled, but to demonstrate that the differences among them can be related to a general process of planning. The few plans presented in this book should illustrate that the variety and number of conceptual characteristics contained in Swedish port city planning were historically significant aspects of the same phenomenon. Planners projected iconoclastic, elaborate, geometric designs to reinforce and enhance each city's particular topographical setting and activities. In so doing, they concerned themselves more with the elaboration of a coherent design than with the specific functional needs of each city—the original justification for planning each one differently. Planners substituted the symbolic virtues of coherent design, symmetry, and perspective for the pragmatic realities of housing, commerce, transport. Water, which in the form of canals and a harbor could enhance the functional aspects of a port city, instead was manipulated to enhance the overall design: arsenal, dockyards, port, and canal were placed for maximum visual and symbolic impact. In this strange way of making port cities seaworthy, the unique, specialized qualities of each city were transferred—perhaps the planners would have said elevated—out of the city's life, beyond the reach of temporal change and spatial growth, and into a rigid abstract form. Such plans were as impractical as the assumption that cities built from them would make it possible for Sweden to sustain maritime ascendency in the Baltic.

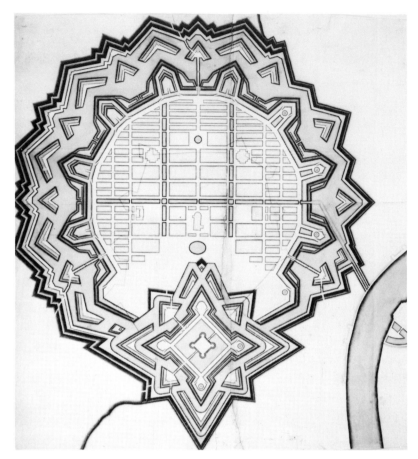

FIGURE **2.15.** *Landskrona, 1680, plan by Dahlberg, no. 113b. Stads-och fästningsplaner, Kunglinga Krigsarkivet, Stockholm.*

Kalmar, on the Baltic, was Sweden's first important naval station. In the original conceptualization, stimulated by Gustav II Adolph, the city (on an islet), the land mass, and an offshore fort were to be placed in relation to each other. When Kalmar burned in 1647, several plans were devised for reconstruction. The grid-plan town to the left in figure 2.14 bears a close resemblance to the king's original idea, whereas the rest of that drawing is a typically ambitious proposal to bring the parts of the district together into a general design.[19]

Landskrona, opposite Denmark on the Sund, passed into Swedish hands in 1659. Karl X Gustav wanted it to become a beautiful and important port city. Tessin the Elder provided two plans, and, ten years later, H. Janssen provided another one, but by 1680, little had been done to transform Landskrona.[20] At that time, the city became the subject of an important controversy: Should Landskrona be developed into a city of 20,000 people, the administrative and commercial metropole of a region? This was what the king

FIGURE 2.16. *Landskrona, 1680, plan by Dahlberg, no. 113d. Stads-och fästningsplaner, Kung-linga Krigsarkivet, Stockholm.*

wanted. But would the nobility bear the expense? And if the project to develop the city failed, would Sweden's imperial policy be placed in jeopardy?[21] Although Dahlberg did not believe in the necessity of elevating Landskrona to the rank of a major city, he nevertheless provided a variety of exceptionally imaginative and monumental designs. A comparison between two of them, figures 2.15 and 2.16, underscores Dahlberg's search for the graphically ideal port city form.

About the same time that Dahlberg was called to Landskrona, the crown decided that a new naval base was needed on the Baltic, near Kalmar. In 1679 the decision was made to create Karlskrona. The city was to take shape on an off-shore island. Dahlberg was called to work on it, and his first plan is shown in figure 2.17. He separated the public and military parts of the city and focused the principal streets on the waterfront. His design was accommodated to a peculiar physical setting, but it also required that the irregular, undulating edge of the sea be rebuilt so that symmetry, regularity, and order would be

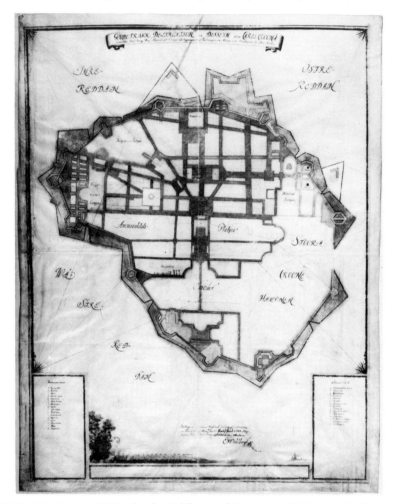

FIGURE 2.17. *Karlskrona, 1683, plan by Dahlberg and Stuart, no. 23. Stads-och fästningsplaner, Kunglinga Krigsarkivet, Stockholm.*

features of the port as well as of the city. Other plans for Karlskrona made similarly unrealistic demands on the financial and technological resources of Sweden.[22]

Carlsburg was among the many cities or settlements in the Swedish maritime empire that the Swedes tried to expand, plan, or rebuild. (Plans for Kronstadt, Nyen, Narva, and Riga are discussed in chapter six, for their influence on St. Petersburg.) Carlsburg was founded in 1674 on a site in Germany near the present-day Bremerhaven.[23] The Swedes intended to concentrate their North German trade there, and anticipated welcoming refugees of differing religious beliefs. There already existed at the site of the future city a fort, which the Danes had built earlier. One of the first projects for the new city was a spiral-radial design, which was rejected for an even more ambitious grid with canal design. Tessin the Elder modified that design (figure 2.18) by emphasizing the intersection of the canals as the setting for prominent public buildings. The entire plan, however, was based on the need for massive civil engineering works, which only the promise of the most startling commercial prosperity in Carlsburg could ever redeem from debt. No wonder, therefore, that somewhat less impractical and less costly designs were also presented (figure 2.19). None of these plans was adapted to the need to build and consolidate a site quickly and efficiently; none of them projected a small city that could grow as its trade and population expanded. Instead, all of these plans—however good any one of them might have appeared on paper—willfully denied the influence of political, financial, and material constraints on the shape or form of the city.

Only after planners had applied more decorative and complex patterns to frontier cities were they asked to apply them to Stockholm, as if that city had been kept apart, the big city after the road show. Actually Stockholm, Sweden's capital and largest city (in 1676 Stockholm had between forty-two and forty-three thousand inhabitants, less than one-tenth the population of Paris) illustrates the transformation of Swedish planning during the seventeenth century well. The settlement of Stockholm had been concentrated on, and pretty much limited to, a small, egg-shaped piece of land, an islet in an archipelago of indented coastline and islands. Indeed, this archipelago, which extended all the way to the Bothnian Sea, provided the city with its principal defense, because no enemy could successfully navigate among the islands for long. For this reason, Stockholm never was fortified with the complex defense works of that era. Without girdling walls to contend with, Stockholm's planners could trace out plans for the city's expansion onto the land north (Norrmalm) and south (Södermalm) of the city center (Gamla Stan), as they wished.

In 1625 the southwest part of Gamla Stan had burned, and, since the island had been completely occupied, the government and Gustav II Adolph, the king, found it easy to decide to make Stockholm a larger, more populous showpiece. Anders Torstensson was among the first to produce plans (around 1640); his plan for the Norrmalm district was distinguished by a grid pattern that took no notice or advantage of the hilly terrain or coastline; streets ended abruptly only where they met water (figure 2.20, although by an unknown artist-planner from the 1670s, illustrates these features of Torstensson's designs clearly). His only concession to effective city communications was to provide a series of squares (for example, the Hötorget) and to guide some of the streets toward a bridge going to Gamla Stan. Canals were deliberately omitted from Stockholm because they called to mind Dutch planning styles and Dutch mercantilism; such associations were undesirable in the royal capital.[24] Whereas water in Dutch planning had determined a city's form by structuring its growth to be gradual and modular, the grid form without harbor and canal deprived water of its functional importance in housing, transportation, commerce, and civic politics. Torstensson and, after him, Jean de la Vallé, executed a variety of grid plans for Södermalm as a separate part of the city, seemingly unrelated to the others. These plans more clearly emphasized

FIGURE **2.18.** *Carlsburg, date unknown, plan by Tessin the Elder, no. 8. Stads-och fästningsplaner, Kunglinga Krigsarkivet, Stockholm.*

Torstensson's concern for the visibility of buildings in a city, his use of urban squares, and his interest in fire prevention and control. These plans were largely followed until the end of the nineteenth century, and were corrected and improved mainly by later seventeenth-century artist-planners, who integrated the grid more pleasingly with the coastline.

Concern for waterscape and monumentality, which was visible in plans for provincial Swedish cities by the mid-seventeenth century, came to Stockholm at the end of Charles XII's reign, when Tessin the Younger made designs for the royal palace and for Gamla Stan in the years 1712 and 1713 (figure 2.21). With sole concern for the symmetrical position of buildings and for how they might be seen from a perspective, Tessin used the water around Gamla Stan as others conventionally used streets and squares. For Tessin, the view of a building with the waterfront formed a complete composition.[25] Water made possible the vast project for Gamla Stan, relating it to Norrmalm and to Södermalm when those parts had never been juxtaposed with each other before. Water, as an instrument for creating a sense of grandeur in Stockholm, allowed the planner to conceive of a design that, even more than the grid plan, depended on the will of the ruler and not the rhythms of commerce or population growth for its realization. So it is perhaps ironic that Tessin's achievement came at the end of a phase in Stockholm's growth and in Sweden's imperial drive: after Charles XII died in 1718, Sweden withdrew from its imperial frontiers, and Stockholm, in turn, withdrew from the Gamla Stan and redirected its growth inland.

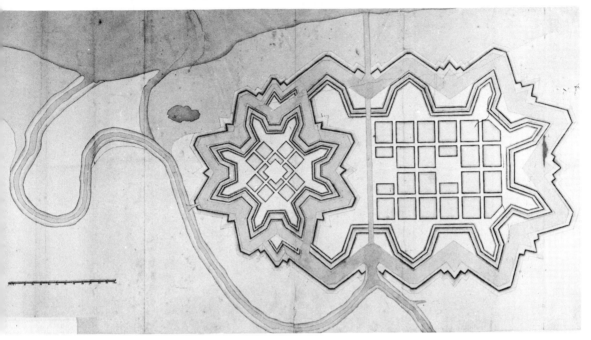

FIGURE **2.19.** *Carlsburg, date unknown, plan by Simpler, no. 21. Stads-och fästningsplaner, Kunglinga Krigsarkivet, Stockholm.*

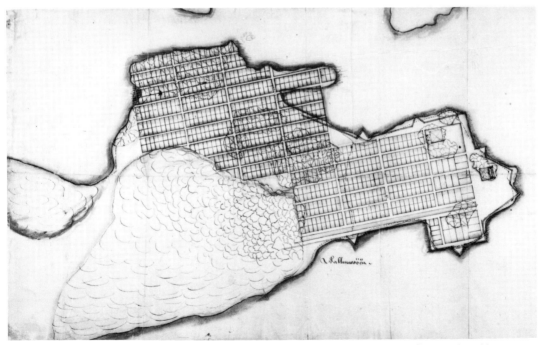

FIGURE **2.20.** *Stockholm, c. 1670, no. 202. Stads-och fästningsplaner, Kunglinga Krigsarkivet, Stockholm.*

FIGURE **2.21.** *Stockholm, 1712–1713, drawing by Tessin the Younger. Cronstedt Collection CC 777, National Museum, Stockholm.*

When Swedish power collapsed in 1720, when the Baltic empire was liquidated, few of the many cities the Swedes had tried to plan had actually been completed. Only the plans themselves—in all their variety—survive to tell us what the Swedes had wanted to do, and why they failed to realize their ambitions.

The Practical City Planning Tradition, 1600–1660

Swedish seventeenth-century new port city planning should be understood in the widest European context. From the beginning, Sweden seemed anxious to channel its drive for power into a cultural, artistic, and technological movement that was already familiar in other European countries. But in so doing, Swedish planners imitated styles without attempting to understand the context in which those styles originated. Thus, they began by adopting methods the Dutch had exploited and, when the lack of growth of new Swedish cities became obvious, they abandoned the Dutch style for baroque forms without questioning the relation between city planning and sea power. While it is true that several planners active in Sweden in the 1630s and thereafter were familiar with the baroque movement Dutch architects had initiated, and that they later looked to French and Italian examples as well, they did not use the new artistic style as Dutch, French, and even Italian artists and planners used it. The baroque had a different impact on new port city planning in Sweden than in other countries. In Sweden, the presence of the new artistic style seemed to make possible a reaffirmation of city planning as the only way to provide a proper setting for sea power. The result was a half-century of unintentionally impractical planning, marked by a neglect of the problem of urban growth. Confronted by slowly growing new cities, the Swedes had had the chance to recover the spirit and methods of the practical planning tradition, but they apparently failed to notice that planning styles were no substitute for demographic and material resources and could not produce city growth in their absence.

In the Netherlands, in England, and in France, decisions about whether or not to plan a given site were handled separately from considerations of artistic style.[26] When the Dutch developed the Zaanstreek near Amsterdam and Nieuw Amsterdam in America, when the English took over that colonial city, and when the French decided to join the race for maritime supremacy, the only important consideration was whether certain activities, and hence prospects for growth, would be compromised if there was no planning. To be sure, the conclusions differed: whereas the Dutch had considered planning essential for Nieuw Amsterdam, the English refused to plan New York. The reasons for these differences are important; they show that the practical planning tradition survived in the close observation of how cities grow. The Swedes lacked the resources to develop as many cities as they planned, while the English, Dutch, and French had the financial and military resources to plan more cities than they developed. And that is precisely the point: the latter understood that the relation between city planning and sea power was complex and circumstantial, and that artistic style was no substitute for the systematic exploitation of the sea.

In this perspective, the most interesting aspect of the Zaanstreek district (called Zaandam today, and known as Saardam in the seventeenth century) in the Netherlands was the absence of any planning whatsoever.[27] Thirty kilometers northwest of Amsterdam, it was seventeenth-century Europe's most famous shipbuilding center. The Zaanstreek was not a town or a city, so general writers about Dutch urban forms have failed to take account of it. But it was large enough to be a sizeable city: twenty-two thousand inhabitants in 1620, and thirty thousand in 1740, even though the shipbuilding industry was shrinking then.[28] The Zaanstreek, in fact, was a collection of narrow villages strung between the Zaan River and some canals: Westzanen and Ostzanen, the most populous, plus the smaller Wormerveer, Jisp, and Krommenie. The Zaanstreek must have confused Dutchmen and foreigners alike. In an age when order was appreciated, in a country where decorum and civic responsibility were important values, in an industry where organization and coordination were critical, the success of the Zaanstreek must have appeared out of place, because the secret of its success was the absence of planning. This was one of Europe's first proto-industrial communities, and, like so many places in the nineteenth century, it grew like Topsy. The largest number of ships was constructed there for the lowest possible cost because the land of the area remained outside any existing urban jurisdiction; land cost less for industry and for housing, so prices, rents, and wages could be lower, too. Competitive, economy-minded capitalism kept these figures lower in spite of the area's fantastic growth during the seventeenth century. No Dutch city could have provided shipbuilders and workers such advantages, and, as long as the Zaanstreek remained a collection of villages, it would provide them. As can be seen in figure 2.22, taken from a remarkable atlas of the district made in 1694, properties extended between river and canal, each property fronting on both. The varying width of the land alone seemed to dictate property size: most of the properties were concentrated where the river-to-canal width was narrowest. Construction of ships was begun in the canals and in the rear of houses, and when ships were ready to be launched, they were hauled across the land to the river. The rhythms of supply and demand alone determined the size and form of the Zaanstreek.

This helps to explain why the area was never planned. Although the Zaanstreek shipbuilding trade competed with established centers in Rotterdam, Dordrecht, and Amsterdam, the leaders of these cities did not interfere with the Zaan producers: after all, a large supply of low-cost ships gave all Dutch merchants a critical advantage in international trade. So, when the Zaanstreek proved its usefulness and productivity early in the seventeenth century, it was allowed to prosper and grow. In the period from 1590 to 1620, an average of one hundred and nine ships per year were built there, and then its production began to climb sharply, to between two and three hundred a year (about half the annual production of the Republic).[29] In 1707 three hundred and six vessels of all sizes were under construction in its sixty yards. Many secondary industries developed there, too—canvas-making, for exam-

FIGURE **2.22.** *Zaanstreek, 1694. Provinciale Atlas, Atl. (492.625) 1, Rijksarchief Haarlem.*

ple, and the processing of imported goods, such as oils. The Zaan district was known for its thousand windmills and was the first area of the Netherlands to be endowed with such a concentration of them for industrial purposes. (The Dutch-style tower windmill had only been developed in the previous century.) Both the large number of small properties and the large number of windmills give a clue to an additional feature of the Zaanstreek: the shipbuilders and processors were not industrialists on a grand scale, nor were they financial magnates, but, rather, they were modest entrepreneurs in business for themselves. The major industrialists, financiers, and shipowners, by providing orders and markets for the Zaanstreek, connected it to the economies of Holland dominated by Amsterdam, of the Republic, and, ultimately, of the growing Atlantic maritime world. The Zaanstreek was dependent upon the economies of larger units, and in this sense, it was a colony that those units patronized. It had started on its own in the sense that the outside interests that benefited from it had not initiated its development.

It is not known what sorts of people went to the Zaanstreek in the years from 1590 to 1620 and demonstrated their productivity. Certainly its social structure in the 1740s (which is known) may have been different from what that structure had been earlier. But it is clear that in 1747 an unusually large percentage of the total district was Baptist (22 percent), and that the Baptists tended to live in the largest shipbuilding areas.[30] Arguments about religion, social structure, and capitalism are still exciting historical issues. Perhaps the Zaanstreek shows a correlation in the Netherlands between small-scale capitalism and a religious minority excluded from participation in the Republic's affairs; perhaps they found security in the Zaanstreek with its distinctive property holdings, absence of municipal government, and productive economy. The creation of a viable, self-sustaining new society out of religious groups separated by irreconcilable differences had been Simon Stevin's concern in the period from 1580 to 1620. The Zaanstreek may have been as effective an answer as any Stevin himself had imagined.

City planning history may not make the Dutch commercial or colonial empires much easier to understand, but it can show that the Dutch applied the practical approach, so useful in commerce and empire, to city planning. Just as the Zaanstreek clarified the relation between city planning and urban form in terms of the Dutch economy, so Nieuw Amsterdam well illustrates that relationship in the Dutch empire. Both communities (and Amsterdam as well) show that the Dutch only used city planning to secure city growth and strength: they never confused the plan with its function by pursuing a plan when it had nothing to contribute. These communities also demonstrate that the Dutch understood the practical uses of water in urban form. Amsterdam's enormous growth during the seventeenth century posed few questions of political and social change,[31] because canals made it possible for the city government to increase the city's size without diminishing its control over new areas. The Zaanstreek's economic role was made possible by the topographic outlines of the district, which were dominated by the navigable Zaan River and an adjacent canal with only a narrow strip of land separating the two. Even without a plan, the settlement of Nieuw Amsterdam included canals in its structure. But if the Dutch understood what they were doing, the English who controlled the settlement after 1664 could not make sense of the Dutch urban form, and they abandoned it.

Nieuw Amsterdam[32] was the most important Dutch settlement in the Hudson River basin. The West Indies Company (founded in 1621) had monopoly control over the New Netherlands territory, and in 1625 it had plans drawn up for a settlement for the tip of Manhattan Island. Only a written description of that plan has survived, but a reconstruction from it includes a five-sided fort enclosing a small town, itself distributed along the walls, a main street, and a square. Farms were outside of but immediately adjacent to the fort. This plan was never executed, for it demanded resources of a scale the early settlers could not provide. Sensibly, the West Indies Company did not compel the settlers to complete a plan when such efforts might have so weakened the colony's resources as to have endangered its survival. The company allowed the settlement to establish itself without a plan, but even so, Nieuw Amsterdam possessed sufficient shape and order to suggest what the pattern of its growth would have been had it remained Dutch. The superb map of 1660 (figure 2.23) illustrates the agricultural nature of the colony as well as a short Broadway leading away from the fort to the territory beyond the colony; it also shows that, in the absence of planning, streets varied greatly in breadth. But it makes clear, too, that even without a plan to follow, the settlers built a canal/harbor and extended it inland. The canal brought the waterfront deep into the settlement.

Since neither Nieuw Amsterdam nor eighteenth-century New York had a plan, it has seemed logical to assume that New York simply absorbed and added to the Dutch settlement. That is only partly true. Had the settlement continued to grow as a Dutch community, the canal might have been extended farther inland, and then back toward the water at a point farther north on the East River. The Dutch would have extended the canal to keep pace with the colony's expansion. But the English, who captured Nieuw Amsterdam in 1664, made no use of the canal, and in 1674 they filled it. Governor Andros called it "pestilential."[33] No doubt it was; no doubt the rest of New York—its streets and its harborfronts—remained so, too. The stench of a canal did not become a valid reason for filling it until the nineteenth century. So the government must have had other reasons for filling in the canal. Perhaps the government simply did not want New York to continue to survive as a Dutch urban form, not for nationalistic reasons, but because it could not accept the consequences. If New York grew—and it was expected to grow— then the canal would have to be enlarged and lengthened or else there would be no sense at all in maintaining it. But to extend the canal would have required the government to interfere with private property by exercising its right of eminent domain. That would cost the government, and might involve it in protracted litigation as well. Such practices were common on the Continent, and Nieuw Amsterdam had had the sort of autocratic government that could do such things. New York's government was more democratic, and it preferred to allow property owners to determine New York's expansion on their own.[34] Perhaps the government simply anticipated New York's growth by abandoning in advance any influence over it. Even though the municipality received jurisdiction over all tidewater lands in the Dongan Charter of 1696, it promptly began to sell the waterfront for revenue. New York's wharves lacked the protection against storm and tide that inland canals provided, and abandoned as they were to the whims of property owners and the elements, they remained remote from the center of city life. By 1750, New York offered shipping the least adequate port facilities of any major colonial city.[35] The Dutch and the English differed in their understanding of new port city planning near the middle of the seventeenth century; the story of Manhattan's canal reveals two fundamentally different views of the way to exploit that island's space within the new Atlantic empire.

This is not an unfair example of what usually passed for port city planning in the seventeenth-century English world. On the whole, the English had no sense that city planning had anything to do with sea power, even though they were undoubtedly familiar with peoples who thought that it did.[36] English traders and agents, diplomats and captains, saw Amsterdam, Copenhagen, and Swedish new port cities, but there is no record that in their observations they transferred foreign examples to English settings for the largest part of the seventeenth century. (Wren's and Evelyn's plans for London are mentioned in chapter six in a different context.)

FIGURE 2.23. *Redraft of the Costello Plan, New Amsterdam in 1660, by John Wolcott Adams, 1916. I.N. Phelps Stokes Collection, Prints Division, the New York Public Library, Astor, Lenox and Tilden Foundations.*

67

France was the only other European country to promote sea power as state policy in the period from 1600 to 1660. At that time, French military power was diverted from the seas by revolts at home and by warfare in Germany, Italy, Spain, and the Spanish Netherlands. Nevertheless, Richelieu has earned a place in French history as the father of the French Navy because he introduced the first enduring naval institutions into the French state.[37] Adequate resources were never available in those years to bring the French Navy to life, but even so Richelieu took advantage of every opportunity he had to organize arsenals (like those at Brest and Toulon) and to perpetuate his ambition for a French naval presence by adopting the imagery of the sea and the insignia of sea power for architectural decoration. His efforts yielded little: How many French sailors who lived abroad returned to France because the Cardinal ordered them to do so? How many foreign ships stayed away from France because Richelieu decreed that French commerce be carried in French hulls? How critical was the French defeat of a Spanish fleet in 1638 when the French fleet, built in haste, lacked a permanent existence? Richelieu's naval policies minimally increased French power, but Richelieu did not include port city planning in his approach. He might have planned for the expansion of existing ports and for the creation of new ones in the hope that such urban bases would yield immediate and enduring commercial and military benefits, much as the Danes and the Swedes had. Richelieu might have used city planning in order to give his projects and ambitions a permanent setting in order to make their realization more likely. Whether Richelieu refrained from commissioning city development projects as a deliberate policy is unknown, but in the perspective of city planning across Europe in that age, France clearly avoided an unproductive flirtation with city planning traditions. Lacking the resources to make full use of permanent bases, and often lacking the loyalty of the principal commercial port cities, the governments of Richelieu and Mazarin kept France closer to the pragmatic spirit of the practical planning tradition by avoiding new port city planning altogether. Later, the government of Louis XIV turned to port city planning out of strength, not weakness; not to substitute for but to complement other efforts at achieving commercial and naval ascendancy. Without French precedents in port city planning to follow, Louis XIV's government was free to approach port city planning by surveying what others had achieved with it until then. The French could redefine the practical tradition in their own terms during the second half of the seventeenth century.

In the years from 1600 to 1660, port city planning outgrew its modest beginnings in Paris, Amsterdam, and Copenhagen to become one of the principal cultural forces in the European maritime world, sustaining ambitions for sea power from America to the Russian shores of the Baltic. Nevertheless, with the exception of a few singular places, most of the cities that were planned were more noteworthy for that fact alone than for their contributions to sea power. Their primary role in the history of European cities is to demonstrate the rapid, widespread diffusion of port city planning in time and space, the often-impossible demands it made on growing nation-states, the underlying unity it brought to European culture, and the variety of urban forms that the persistent search for productive port cities yielded. Some Europeans decided that spatial planning was a precondition for the successful expansion of sea power, some saw it as useful but not essential, and some thought it had no influence on sea power at all, but across Europe, artists and engineers, statesmen and bureaucrats, merchants and mariners had opinions about the potential of spatial urban planning to enhance maritime activities. Surely this ability to conceptualize the relations between urban settings and seafaring can be recognized as one of the distinctive features of seventeenth-century culture. This is why the spatial aspects of city planning have been featured so far: how city space was planned and used is an indication of more general attitudes toward sea power and cities than what can be found in documents based only on the passage of goods, the movement of peoples, and the decisions of state. Port city planning provides the basis for European-wide comparisons that illuminate what might otherwise remain darkened in the shadows of national frontiers.

This comparative approach must be kept in mind as the focus of attention shifts from a survey encompassing centuries to an in-depth analysis of the French scene from 1660 to 1715. In 1660 Louis XIV and his government embraced the hope that port city planning might facilitate a more effective and permanent exploitation of sea power by the French. That decision initiated the creation and development of Brest, Lorient, Rochefort and Sète. How did the French discover for themselves the value and techniques of practical port city planning? What changes to city life in early modern Europe did their planning produce? Did planning alter the relationships between French cities, the state, and patterns of maritime exploitation? Were there limits to what the French government could accomplish through planning? Because these and other questions can be answered for the French new port cities, the next three chapters of analysis highlight aspects of planning that have not received full attention so far. These French cities were important in their own right, and can be studied alone as a chapter in French history—but that is not my intention. Rather, by examining the development of these four cities in detail, I hope to suggest that port city planning in early modern Europe, wherever it occurred, involved the complex interaction between material and demographic resources, cultural values, social patterns, and political ambitions. An understanding of what port city planners wanted to achieve, of their successes and of their failures, can be deepened by a close examination of the French experience under Louis XIV.

II

*The New
Port Cities of France,
1660–1720*

III

The Search for New Port Cities in France

Monarchy and Urbanism

The creation and planned development of four port cities by the government of Louis XIV were important events both in the political history of Louis's reign and in the history of European city planning. Brest, Rochefort, and Lorient, on the Atlantic, and Sète, on the Mediterranean, were established between 1664 and 1666 as arsenal sites where the royal fleet could be built and outfitted, and as land bases for overseas trading companies. Louis and his ministers, agents, and engineers were fully conscious of the specific role each city was to play in the monarchy's overall political-military strategy to achieve mastery of the seas. They planned and manipulated those aspects of city life and form that they believed would influence the ability of the inhabitants to serve the state—legal, fiscal, and trade structures, housing, civil order, and spatial organization. Thus, from the accession of Louis XIV to personal rule in 1661 until his death in 1715, city planning was an instrument of state policy, both spurred and limited by the will of the government to pursue its maritime goals.

In this study of urbanism in political context, the practical *what* in planning cannot be separated from the political *why:* the value of planning was judged by how it would help the people in the new cities live and work as the government intended. We want to see how and why these cities were established and designed as instruments of state policy, the better to understand the changes that port city planning brought to civilization.

The planning of four new port cities may seem today to have been an unremarkable and appropriate activity for Louis XIV and his government; it corresponds so well to the idea that Louis established his power and greatness by concentrating the affairs of France in his own hands. Perhaps this is why the study of these cities has been neglected: Louis's pursuit of absolutism and grandeur deflect interest from the city projects he encouraged to the political sources of his power. The creation and planned growth of these cities have been cited as examples of administrative creativity,[1] but the planning process itself has attracted little attention because it has been understood as just another feature of Louis's bureaucratic, centralized administration. Similarly, the establishment of new port cities has been cited as a beneficial, if fortuitous, by-product of the increase in French military power, but descriptions and analyses of the French seventeenth-century naval arsenal—"One of the first large modern industries the world had ever known"[2]—rarely take into account how life in port cities was affected by or had an impact on naval or national affairs.[3] In urban history, new cities have been identified as an important sign of the vitality and enterprise of a state or civilization, and plans for them are studied with great interest. The names of Brest, Lorient, Rochefort, and Sète have appeared among lists of new cities,[4] and though it is often repeated that their founding says something about new city planning, *what* it says has never been elaborated. To those involved in city planning at that time, Louis's urban projects were a challenge of high order; yet only local historians have paid close attention to these cities.[5]

The establishment and development of Brest, Lorient, Rochefort, and Sète were neither routine nor conventional, and should not be treated peripherally by historians of Louis XIV's France or by historians of European city planning, as if their story would only ratify and not redirect existing interpretations of both subjects. The existence of new port cities in Louis XIV's France should no more be taken for granted than Sweden's Gothenburg or Karlskrona or Holland's Amsterdam. It is therefore appropriate and necessary to begin this analysis with some questions about the relations between the state, cities, and the sea in Louis XIV's France, relations that were reconditioned by the very existence of the new cities. Why did Louis and Colbert (Louis's minister of the navy, with and without the title, until his death in 1683), with little knowledge of the sea, elect French maritime ascendancy as a goal of state policy? Why did they decide that France needed new port cities to support an expansion of French military and commercial sea power? How did Colbert's agents find sites for these urban maritime bases in regions where the local inhabitants themselves had failed to exploit the coastline?

Sea Power as State Policy

Sea power had been a Valois ambition before it became a Bourbon goal. François I and Richelieu, however, had not been able to bring into being arsenals, trading companies, and fleets that would endure (Le Havre, for example, remained an unfinished creation of François I). French military sea power did not exist in 1661, and French commercial maritime enterprise was largely the achievement of trading ports with foreign connections: Saint-Mâlo, Rouen, Nantes, La Rochelle, Bordeaux, Marseille. Jealously defensive of their autonomy and privileges, the merchants of those cities were more eager to share their power and profits with merchant communities in Italy,

Spain, the Netherlands, and England than with the French crown. But Louis's government had a stronger concept of port cities and of the right plans for them than its predecessors had had.

The differences of style and substance between Louis and his predecessors have been a central problem in the historical interpretation of Louis XIV's statecraft.[6] There is little doubt that Louis wanted to dominate French politics and society absolutely, but scholarship today strikes a balance between his legal, administrative, and political reforms (which served his absolutist ambitions) and the obstinate and unsystematic but effective evasion of the influence of Versailles by large and small, literate and illiterate, politically conscious and politically impotent, groups of Frenchmen. Rural revolts, subsistence crises, and the expansion of urban culture by the bourgeoisie and the aristocracy are interpreted as signs of the limits to Louis's power,[7] just as improvements to ports and highways, military organization, and the concentration of political power correspond to the image that the Sun King himself wished to project. It is still difficult to assess that portion of French economic and social change for which Louis's government was responsible and that portion which took place independently of his initiatives.[8] Foreign affairs are no easier to analyze. Louis XIV initiated commercial and military policies to extend his influence as far and wide as possible outside his country. In so doing, did he formulate policies he knew in fact exceeded the capacity of his country to sustain? Or were his policies and programs equal to the opportunities of the day, but failures because of factors outside his control? Politics may be the art of the possible, but few people in Louis XIV's France believed that the state's freedom of action was as limited as historians today find it to have been. Louis's maritime policies, which differed from those of his predecessors because he put the resources of the crown behind them, do not fit easily into a single existing interpretation, but only into a climate of interpretive controversy.

When Louis XIV approved programs Colbert formulated for increasing French maritime strength, he knew little about such matters. He learned little more during the rest of his reign. Louis did not come to seek maritime hegemony on his own; he was too unfamiliar with maritime affairs to have done that. But once his ministers and agents, who mastered the technical knowledge necessary to formulate and execute such policies, made him realize that mastery of the seas was possible, he saw no reason why he should not succeed. Having dominated those powerful local forces—the Protestants, the leading port cities, and the princely nobility—which had used the seacoast and sea power for their own benefit, Louis and his ministers could realize their goals without being diverted by provincial intransigence and domestic political factions. Colbert's patient bookkeeping made it possible to amass the large sums of money a navy absorbed: from a low figure of £112,000 under Mazarin in the 1650s, the navy budget rose to some 8 or 9 million pounds annually in the late 1660s. And a group of Colbert's able friends, colleagues, and relatives served as provincial agents, intendants, engineers, and officers: they guaranteed royal political control of the seacoast and administered the funds used in building and stocking arsenals, constructing and outfitting fleets, and recruiting and training sailors and officers. Louis and Colbert could feel optimistic that time was with them. They knew that they had the first opportunity in over a generation to pursue mastery of the seas, and that they had the means—men, money, and political authority—to try to succeed.

But Louis and Colbert evaluated the urgency and practicality of increasing French sea power differently. Louis did not know how hard it would be to concentrate the energies of the state along the maritime frontier, and he allowed Colbert, his son Seignelay, and their successors in office, the Pontchartrains, to master the charts, tables, memoranda, and letters that alone communicated the problems of administration. Louis was not a frivolous ruler; he mastered many areas of state policy, but maritime affairs was not one of them. Perhaps he thought he learned all he needed to know about the sea from the fanciful image of the maritime world he created at his châteaux out of canals, statues of Neptune, stone fishes in fountains, emblematic anchors and shells, and seascape paintings by Claude Gelée. In fact, Louis's view of himself and his reign made it difficult if not impossible for him to make a purely rational and somewhat cautious assessment of France's potential as a sea power. He understood sea power in his own terms of *gloire* and grandeur, and such terms would intrinsically outweigh any calculation of success or failure. Colbert had presented Louis with the goal of sea power, knowing that the king was ignorant about maritime affairs, but knowing also that he cared that his *gloire*—the fear, awe, and wonderment in which the monarchy was held at home and abroad—was the lesser for the weakness of France's fleets. As Colbert phrased it, "The power of the king is superior on land to that of all others in Europe; on the sea his is inferior; that power must be made uniform everywhere."[9] If Louis could understand sea power in such terms, he had no need to look at the risks involved and could trust his subordinates not to let him down.

Louis simply did not know whether Colbert's estimates of France's potential for sea power were accurate; he thoroughly expected Colbert to deliver France from the status of second-class naval power without delay. France's material resources were not as ample, and the peoples of the seacoast were not as cooperative, as Colbert had assumed when he had encouraged Louis to invest in sea power.[10] Nevertheless, Louis remained blind to the many miscalculations Colbert had made from the start. Instead, when Colbert discovered in the early 1670s that establishing and developing new port cities—a critical step in his strategy for French sea power—proved to be more difficult and time-consuming than he had anticipated, Louis continued to believe that administration could easily overcome the reasons for these setbacks. Had Louis reasonably assessed the odds against France becoming a maritime power, he might never have supported the establishment of the four new port cities. Yet he did support them throughout his reign, and even if years of costly hard work alone made possible their rescue from the miscalculations that had been present at their creation, their existence eventually helped bring France closer to maritime hegemony than anyone in 1661 would have dared hope.

Clearly, the new port cities were the product of theories and attitudes toward state power and sea power that had a self-evident validity to those who acted upon them. From the start, Colbert and his subordinates were inclined to perceive the obstacles to French sea power in terms of solutions the state could develop and impose. Of course this reflects on the nature of French politics: when Louis's administration committed itself to establishing new port cities, Louis knew that such a commitment would cost many thousands of pounds, and he sustained it even when it cost millions, but he had the sovereignty, and his administration the prerogative, to spend that much of France's wealth.[11] It seemed obvious to the French government that they could gain world power only if the state carefully regulated maritime affairs. By altering the character of French trade through tariffs, by fostering the large-scale manufacture of superior goods at competitive prices, and by encouraging an overseas French colonial and commercial presence, France might capture that share of trade and wealth that, in Colbert's opinion, its unadventurous merchant community was not ambitious enough to acquire.

Colbert did not know at first that the existing network of port cities was inadequate to support all of the state's commercial and military policies. After all, there were several great French port cities at that time: Saint-Mâlo, Rouen, Nantes, La Rochelle, Bordeaux, Marseille (Italy alone could boast as large a number). Colbert decided to augment France's urban infrastructure only when he began to see that along a large part of the coastline where no useful commercial or military port yet existed, locations for new port cities might be found. The decision to establish new port cities was not made abstractly, as the best possible thing to do, but pragmatically, as Colbert concluded his evaluation of France's resources for sea power.

Since the very existence of the new port cities was dependent on Colbert's inventory of France's resources, their creation must be studied in terms of how the minister's procedures worked. Colbert instructed officials to survey the condition of the country, to collect all available maps and make new ones if necessary, and to report on everything about the life and institutions of France that could possibly influence the government.[12] The survey was never entirely completed, but the parts that pertained to the navy were presented to Colbert piecemeal throughout the 1660s. Even before the results of his agents' survey were made available to him, Colbert knew that the fleet numbered only one-half the ships Richelieu had commanded, that many sailors and officers had left the kingdom or turned to other trades, and that the few royal arsenals were in disrepair and were barren of essential supplies.[13] However, he did not yet know, but only suspected, that the monarchy lacked a basic network of good ports with adequate facilities. So in 1664 and 1665, he ordered two of his collaborators, Colbert de Terron (1618–1684), a cousin and an intendant in the Charente River basin near La Rochelle, and Nicolas de Clerville (1610–1677), a leading army engineer, to survey the Atlantic and Mediterranean coasts. They examined the great port cities and many lesser ones as well, to see how existing harbors might be expanded to take on a variety of new roles. They concluded that such expansion, while feasible, could not by itself satisfy the government's many new requirements, whereupon they found several unused locations that were fit to serve the navy and royal trading companies, and could also be transformed into port cities that would give permanent support to the great royal naval enterprise. Their recommendations were evaluated, and by 1666 Colbert was ready to commit the apparatus of the state to the creation of Brest and Lorient in Brittany, Rochefort in the Saintonge (the coastal province of the Charente River basin), and Sète on the Mediterranean, in Lower Languedoc near Montpellier.

The final selection of the placement of Brest, Rochefort, Lorient, and Sète was by no means inevitable, for in the correspondence between Colbert and his agents they emerged as the most attractive sites only because they presented the fewest drawbacks. Moreover, there is evidence that some of Colbert's agents, including de Terron and de Clerville, hoped to invest in the enterprise of port city development. They were bound to Colbert as his "creatures" by venal and personal ties, which made royal service an opportunity for profit and speculation. It was expected that they would invest in royal enterprises with which they were familiar, as long as they were able to administer royal affairs dispassionately. Was this the case, then, in the selection of the new port cities? Were these truly the best sites on the French coasts, or, in drawing up their evaluation of their merits—size, defensibility, remoteness from other cities, and strategic value—did Colbert's agents intentionally slant the technical information they forwarded to Paris in order to promote port sites of possibly inferior quality as easy and secure investments?

De Clerville and Sète

How the location of Sète was chosen can be told first and separately because de Clerville alone promoted its selection. By highlighting what participation in the selection procedure represented for his career, it may be possible to establish motives for his conduct and decisions.

De Clerville had begun a career as an army engineer in 1646, and, though never outstanding, he was appointed commissaire général des fortifications in 1662. In 1660 de Clerville was posted to Marseille by Colbert to erect the Fort St. Nicolas and to secure that city's submission to the royal will, which the fort symbolized. Between 1660 and 1666, when not in Marseille, he directed works at Nancy (1661) and inspected Norman and Breton harbors and cities (1663, 1664) and the Atlantic coastline (1665). In 1667 he undertook a major project at Lille, made several major errors (which were corrected by Vauban), and, humiliated, retired to his estate (a gift from Colbert) on the Ile d'Oléron. Colbert, however, continued to trust him after 1667, and sent him to Rochefort and Sète in 1669, 1670, 1671, and 1673. After his death on the Ile d'Oléron in 1677, it was discovered that de Clerville had sold the king's supplies of wheat for his own profit.[14] Had he also acted in his own behalf during the 1660s, when he inspected port sites? He was then near the end of his career, oversaw the disbursement of royal funds for several major projects, and belonged to a generation of engineers that viewed an opportunity to invest in works of their own design as compensation for their efforts.[15] These circumstances may have influenced his judgment.

De Clerville's responsibility, as both he and Colbert understood it, was to develop the infrastructure of harbors and coastal defenses important to naval

power and to an expanding maritime commerce.[16] Marseille, with its secure
and spacious harbor, was a natural and obvious base for the commercial and
military exploitation of the Mediterranean. Toulon, to the east of Marseille,
had been used as a military port under Richelieu, and a new arsenal and
fortifications were planned and built to preserve its defensibility and usefulness. But, west of Marseille, from the Rhône delta to the Pyrenees, there were
no ports for either merchantmen or galleys to call at if attacked by pirates or
by an enemy force, or if threatened by bad weather. This was especially
important, since stormy winter winds forced captains to take their ships to
North Africa along the coastline toward often-hostile Spain instead of across
the open sea. A port between Marseille and Spain had to be found if the
monarchy was ever to realize its ambition of control over the Mediterranean.

But where? The Languedoc-Rousillon coast offered no natural harbor to
a ship in danger. There were no mountains to break the stormy winds that
dominated the currents silting the coastal inlets. In 1662 de Clerville searched
for ports of shelter along the North African coast,[17] and along the French
coast as well. About a colorful harbor near the Spanish border, he wrote ". . .
when one approaches from Collioure or from Cape Créous which is nearby,
the Pyrenees Mountains blow a wind which prevents landings in those
areas."[18] Obviously de Clerville was aware of the problem.

The following year, 1663, he was ordered to survey the entire Languedoc
coast to find the needed port[19] and to inspect the route of Pierre-Paul Riquet's
proposed Toulouse-to-Mediterranean Canal du Midi. Riquet's original proposal of 1662 had revived an old dream to connect the Atlantic with the
Mediterranean via the Garonne River, Toulouse, and a canal to Narbonne
made possible by several ingenious locks. Such a plan corresponded in audac-
ity to Colbert's own hopes for French maritime ascendency and for Languedoc's commercial growth. But de Clerville, on his inspection tour, noticed
how silty and unnavigable the approaches to Narbonne had become.[20]

It was probably on this same trip that de Clerville took serious notice of
the harbor at Sète for the first time. Several months later, in early 1665, he
persuaded the Estates of Languedoc, Colbert, and Louis XIV that a developed port at Sète could serve as a canal terminus and as the Mediterranean
port of refuge.[21]

De Clerville could have found many reasons to believe that an investment
to make Sète the indispensable Languedoc port was sound. The harbor of
Sète lay at the base of the Mount St. Clair, the only elevation along the entire
Languedoc coast. Ships could find shelter from strong coastal winds at its base
and protection from enemies, which an observation fort at its summit could
help provide. The seaport itself could be connected to an inland waterway, an
extension of the Canal du Midi, by cutting a ditch through a narrow strip of
land. It was even thought possible to extend the canal further, from Sète to
the Rhône.[22]

However, de Clerville could have chosen the port of Agde just as easily.
Twenty kilometers to the west of Sète along the same inland canal route and
Mediterranean coast, Agde, once improved, was to carry a tonnage far in
excess of that of Sète and was to become, by 1690, the real Mediterranean

canal terminus. The cost of improving either port for navigation—estimated at £240,000—was the same.[23] Were there differences between Agde and Sète that de Clerville could have noticed? Physically Agde was flat, whereas Sète lay at the base of a mountain, which enhanced its beauty, provided natural defenses, and broke up stormy coastal winds. Socially Agde was the seat of a bishopric and was a well-established local commercial center; Sète was a sparsely populated fishing hamlet, exploited by fishermen who lived in nearby Frontignan. These social or institutional differences were substantial, but the physical ones were not; the qualities that nature had conferred upon Sète notwithstanding, the local Languedoc communities had preferred for centuries to trade at Agde. Clearly Agde was as useable and defensible a port as any along the West Languedoc coast. De Clerville selected Sète because it could be easily preempted, because it belonged to no one and had no interests of its own to defend, and because it could be controlled easily by wealthy Montpellier bankers and merchants, who were anxious to make use of a maritime outlet near their city.[24] De Clerville was influenced by such considerations because he, too, wanted to invest in Sète's future.

The kind of investment opportunity that attracted de Clerville to Sète requires a discussion of its harbor. De Clerville had praised Sète's harbor for its insignificant siltation,[25] a condition that, if true, would have made it unique on the Languedoc coast. The harbor was in fact seriously ensilted at the time, and remained so for decades. It seems implausible for someone as familiar with coastal tides as de Clerville to have believed honestly—if naively—that Sète was exempt from the blight that interfered with access to all other Languedoc ports; he must have known of its real condition. What de Clerville wanted was the contract to construct hydraulic works of his design, which would protect the port in the future.[26] Agde also needed hydraulic works, but de Clerville was attracted to Sète because there he would be free from the interference that Agde, an established community, could generate. De Clerville misrepresented Sète's true condition as part of a calculated maneuver. De Clerville minimized the silt problem in his correspondence with Colbert in order to make the selection of Sète more obvious in the minister's eyes, anticipating that Colbert, once committed to Sète, would undertake necessary improvements as the need for them was made known (presumably by de Clerville), at a later date. (Since de Clerville alone was familiar with Sète's technical characteristics, he could control the information his minister-patron obtained.)

Direct evidence that, as seems likely, de Clerville misinformed Colbert about Sète to further his own interests can be found in a letter written in 1681 by Niquet, one of de Clerville's early collaborators, who later worked under Vauban. Writing to Colbert, Niquet accused de Clerville of having deceived the minister precisely in order to profit from the very hydraulic works projects Sète needed. Niquet implied that de Clerville had always known hydraulic works would be needed there, reminded Colbert that de Clerville and a group of Montpellier bankers received the first contract for those works in 1666, and accused de Clerville of having designed faulty hydraulic works to maximize the king's expense and his own income.[27] (Those works, which indeed were ineffective, cost £10,000 in two years,[28] and in 1668 the contract was passed on to Niquet.) Niquet recalled a conversation with Boussonel, a wealthy Montpellerien who invested in Sète from the start, and explained de Clerville's behavior: "[The reason] was the great profit there was to make." Niquet concluded, ". . . the more one inspects the projects of this man [de Clerville] for this port, the more one notices things contrary to good sense, knowledge and experience."[29]

De Clerville, influenced by personal considerations in his choice of Sète, probably deceived Colbert about its true condition. However, Niquet perhaps exaggerated when he accused de Clerville of deliberately having designed faulty hydraulic works. Such a plot to defraud the king would have jeopardized de Clerville's career and high status. It is more likely that de Clerville, overoptimistic and enthusiastic, was certain that hydraulic works of his design would be effective. Since investment in the king's affairs by royal officers was tolerated, by contracting for these works with the Montpellier bankers, de Clerville tried to make a fair profit. Furthermore, he knew that any Languedoc port would require some dredging and offshore construction, and reasoned that Louis might as well spend the money at Sète, which could be so easily preempted and exploited, as elsewhere. He wanted the port of Sète to be useful: success would have added to his reputation, and he probably hoped to invest in the commerce that would be funneled through it once the port facilities were completed.

The critical factor is the order in which events occurred. There could be no question about de Clerville's selection of Sète had he chosen it on its own merits and then contracted for the needed hydraulic works, but the feature that de Clerville found most attractive in Sète, its isolation, was critical to the advancement of his own schemes, and was not strictly relevant to the monarchy's purposes: Agde could have served as a trading and refuge port just as well as Sète, but de Clerville could not have undertaken engineering projects there as easily. It appears that de Clerville selected Sète precisely because he was confident that his scheme to improve its harbor would make a sound investment, and that he slanted the information he presented to Colbert to promote it.

These personal interests of de Clerville could not have mattered to Louis XIV or to Colbert in 1665. De Clerville had found them the port that secured the future mobility of the galley fleets and the security of Mediterranean trade routes. In the euphoria of relief, they did not inquire how and why de Clerville selected Sète; they insisted only that the port be developed as quickly as possible.

The Atlantic Coast: Rochefort, Brest, and Lorient

Atlantic ports were urgently needed in the early 1660s. Despite the length of France's coastline (it extended from Flanders along the English Channel to the western peninsula of Brittany and then on along the Bay of Biscay to the Pyrenees), there were few ports of national significance, and even those were unattractive to the government for its purposes. Sailors and merchants from Saint-Mâlo, Nantes, La Rochelle, and Bordeaux were active in maritime affairs in areas as distant from France as eastern Canada, the North Sea, and the Iberian peninsula, sometimes on their own initiative, most often following the lead of others abroad. The other Atlantic and Channel ports played a largely secondary role; their influence was more closely associated with the fortunes and resources of their immediate hinterlands. Harbors along the Channel were too close to France's competitors and sometime enemies, and were usually of small physical dimensions—characteristics that hardly recommended them to the government. The great port cities of Brittany and the West were large enough and remote enough from other countries to suit royal designs, but the government did not want to rely on them because they were also far from Paris' centralizing control, and had a long record of municipal autonomy, which had slipped over into secessionist revolt as recently as the early 1650s. Colbert and Louis were going to do what they could to tie these cities closer to the French state, and were understandably reluctant to install new royal enterprises, commercial and military, in them. On the contrary, separate port cities for such enterprises along the Atlantic coast would facilitate government control in those less-trustworthy regions. But the sites for new Atlantic port cities were no more obvious than sites on the Mediterranean had proven to be. Three ports were needed: one for the great Atlantic arsenal where the fleet would be constructed, another for a smaller, supplemental arsenal, and one for an entrepôt for trading companies.

The decision to establish the entrepôt base is discussed first, separately from the military bases, since in fact it was chosen independently. As early as 1664, the Compagnie des Indes orientalles, which was supposed to do for France what the semisovereign English and Dutch trading companies had done for their countries, had begun its own survey of ports. Port-Louis, opposite the future site of Lorient on a south Breton estuary, and Le Havre, on the Channel at the mouth of the Seine, were the principal candidates at that time. Port-Louis had a disadvantage in that it was still controlled by parties that were out of favor at court, and Le Havre was too close to England and the Spanish Netherlands. In order to secure the widest freedom of action for itself, the Compagnie decided the next year, 1665, to gather more information from Colbert's agents, and then decided to expropriate a vacant, broad, and flat area opposite Port-Louis, which became the city of Lorient.[30] Colbert's agents had identified Paimboeuf on the Loire, probably because it was close to Nantes, the commercial port on which the Compagnie relied for wider trading contacts. But Lorient offered the geographic advantage of being closer to the principal Atlantic trading routes, something to consider when long voyages might begin or end during hostilities.

The selection of military ports was, in comparison, a slow, hesitant, even indecisive process, marked by the same dichotomy between private gain and the interest of the crown as the selection of Sète. For this reason, it is also necessary to describe the backgrounds of those royal agents who participated in the selection process, and the man to begin with is the individual who figured most prominently in it, Colbert de Terron.

Placed by his influential relative Colbert in several minor posts before being sent as intendant to Brouage (center of the neglected salt trade) in 1653, de Terron was responsible as well for the Aunis coastal province and for the city of La Rochelle, where he lived. De Terron had ample opportunity to learn of maritime affairs and develop contacts with merchants and ship captains. He invested, for example, in Soubize and Tonnay-Charente, two unfinished bases on the Charente River where the skeletal Atlantic fleet of the early 1660s was outfitted. Thus he developed, over many years, personal and financial ties to the Charente district. Was he loath to leave an area he could control, and did he therefore try to divert Colbert's attention away from new port sites in Britanny and Normandy toward those of the Charente? Largely as a result of de Terron's persistence, Rochefort, located in the Charente region, was chosen for development. He supervised all activity there until 1674, when, weakened by malaria, he left the area to enjoy a semiretirement.

Colbert de Terron's nephew, Pierre de Seuil, was of lesser importance, but was associated with him in all his enterprises. Since de Terron was officially responsible for Brest, he sent de Seuil there in 1661 to take charge as his deputy, but de Seuil was not very capable, and needed to consult with his uncle frequently. He left no record of his opinions about the ports he inspected during the port selection process, and it can be presumed that he deferred silently to the wishes of his influential uncle.

Another secondary figure was Regnier Jansse, an engineer who served on the port site inspection team. Not much is known of him, for he is the author of few letters or memoirs and is only occasionally mentioned in those of his collaborators. A resident of Holland (though possibly of French origin), he was one of the experts Colbert successfully enlisted in 1661 to help build up the navy.[31] He was a "creature" of de Clerville, helping him in return for protection and support, and the two men traveled and worked together in the 1660s. Jansse fit into the port selection procedure much as de Seuil did.

François Blondel and Chatillon were the only other officials who served on the team of port inspectors. Of Chatillon nothing is known. Blondel (1616–1686) had diplomatic experience in addition to a career as an architect-scientist. He visited the Atlantic coast for Colbert just before he was assigned to the Antilles to help fight the English, and upon his return in 1668, became the first director of the Académie royale d'architecture. He was a Parisian on an unusually long assignment to the provinces in the mid-1660s; by contrast, his colleagues were provincials who rarely spent much time in Paris. Their abilities were complementary, but their personal concerns were different. Blondel could not have felt that he had as much at stake as the others in the actual selection of new port city locations.[32]

De Terron was the principal figure of this group. On several occasions between 1661 and 1665, de Terron believed he had found the perfect port site for the navy's Atlantic arsenal, always in the Charente region, where he worked and over which he had control. The first site he fixed upon was Soubize, in 1661: "The project which you propose for me, to establish a work center at Soubize, . . ." he wrote Colbert, "is assuredly very good and strong, because this place has been judged to be suitable and I hope that wood will be found and that once the work center is open, that we will easily have there all sorts of commodities inexpensively."[33] Convinced of its future, de Terron immediately invested in Soubize.

At the same time, he suggested building a port on one of the saline inlets of the Seudre estuary at Chartressac, a place where ships could be cared for and recaulked.[34] But Colbert preferred to build at Soubize, and, early in 1662, de Terron wrote to him that building would start there soon.[35] Only one or two vessels were ever worked on at Soubize, for in 1663 de Terron found other, better, prospective sites for a major arsenal. About Plomb, north of La Rochelle, he wrote that, for £880,000, a port could be built ". . . capable of giving the navy all the advantages desirable for service," and, he added, "we can scarcely do better for cost."[36] That port was never developed. De Terron considered an additional Charente port at this time, too, at Saint-Nazaire, upstream from Soubize, and a map was sent to Colbert showing how a dry dock might look at that site. Even though no decision was made to exploit any of these places, de Terron prodded his cousin Colbert about a Charente basin port and arsenal.[37]

If all this time de Terron was concentrating on finding a port in the region he administered, Colbert had a wider vision, and wanted to know more about Norman and Breton ports, as well. Consequently, he sent, separately, de Clerville and de Terron to study them. As intendant of the Atlantic for the navy, de Terron was responsible for that part of the coast, too, but he openly preferred the Charente region and slanted the facts about harbors elsewhere. His first letter about Brest was the most favorable he ever wrote about that place. In a comparison between Port-Louis and Brest, he stressed how difficult and narrow the entry to Port-Louis was, and how inadequate it would be as a site for a new city, but of Brest's harbor he criticized only some large rocks that were obstacles, and concluded, "Once one has entered the bay, one is safe and in the port there are all the commodities needed for work."[38] Later de Terron distorted these facts. He never denied that Brest was a good, large port (even if prevailing westerly winds were unaccommodating) that would be easy to adapt to the navy's needs. Instead, he stressed the advantages—better weather, more abundant food and naval supplies, and a large labor pool—a Charente port would enjoy over Brest.[39] At the end of 1664, after an inspection tour of northern French ports, de Terron found none fit to be recommended for the navy (Omonville, near Cherbourg, was good but too isolated from supplies,[40] while the winds at Brest were an impediment to efficient naval operations); he promoted Port-Louis, which he had found inadequate a year earlier, as suitable for the newly established Compagnie des Indes orientalles.[41] Thinking that perhaps only one great Atlantic port was to be built, de Terron wanted to be sure that it would be located in territory he controlled.

De Clerville tried to be more objective about the Atlantic ports, for he was concerned only professionally, not personally. He canvassed a greater number of ports in Normandy and Brittany than de Terron, and he eliminated from consideration most of the existing ports on technical or strategic grounds. Dunkerque was too close to the Spanish Netherlands; Boulogne, Calais, and Dieppe were too shallow. He found Le Tréport satisfactory, but remarked that the people there were unwilling to take to maritime occupations. François I's artificial port at Le Havre, he wrote, could be modernized only at considerable expense. He liked Port-Louis, and believed that ten or twelve vessels could spend extended periods of time in the ample bay it guarded. Most of all, and in contrast to de Terron, he approved of Brest, correctly arguing that the winds and rocks offshore that made the approaches treacherous also provided a natural guarantee against attack. Brest was not near France's North Sea enemies, yet it was strategically adjacent to the most critical international sea lanes. Since it would be easy to adapt the town site to the needs of an arsenal, de Clerville recommended that a stone quay be built at once to serve the large number of vessels that could shelter there.[42]

With these reports to go by, Colbert concluded, in early 1665, that it was time to sort through the evidence systematically and reach a decision on new port sites. He ordered Regnier Jansse, de Seuil, and Chatillon to join de Terron and de Clerville in a team effort to survey the Atlantic coastline and make recommendations.

All the ports they examined, without exception, met certain objective criteria—remoteness, defensibility, and size.[43] All were isolated coastal enclaves, places where the monarchy's new arsenal, port, and adjacent city could be constructed and operated at lower cost and without interference from local or regional interests. Detached from existing maritime centers, they were nevertheless accessible by sea to the commodities stocked and traded elsewhere, particularly in Nantes, La Rochelle, and Bordeaux. Colbert and his agents wanted to keep royal maritime enterprise separate from the maritime affairs of Louis's subjects; only in Marseille did the state and merchants share a harbor.

A second criterion was defensibility. All the ports considered were located on rivers or estuaries or in coastal coves. An enemy fleet could not easily penetrate them against winds and tides or around shoals or rocks when pilots were unfamiliar with these conditions; and, once close to one of these places, an enemy fleet could not retreat easily.

Each port had to be large enough to hold a minimum of ten first- and second-class vessels, perhaps as many as sixty of all sizes. Furthermore, enough land had to be available nearby to erect an arsenal and establish a town.

Colbert's agents found no existing port cities on the Atlantic that were large enough, remote enough, and secure enough to support navy arsenals. Therefore, a new city had to be built wherever the navy established itself. In their final recommendations, submitted in May 1665 after weeks of study, they enumerated the merits and defects of several Channel port sites, Brest, Port-Louis, and a half-dozen in the Charente region, and found only one to praise, Saint-Nazaire, on the Charente River. They stressed the value of building one large arsenal (at an estimated cost of £1,600,000) there, rather than two of moderate size,[44] one there and the other in Brittany, arguing that dividing the fleet between two ports would weaken it and make its destruction by an enemy fleet more possible. In addition, they suggested that any other port on the Atlantic should also be built in the Charente region, perhaps along the Seudre, reserving Paimboeuf on the Loire estuary for the Compagnie des Indes and Le Tréport on the Channel for wartime use only.[45] (I have already discussed the fact that Lorient, and not Paimboeuf, was selected for the Compagnie's use.)

It may be coincidental that the memorandum's conclusions about Atlantic military ports corresponded so strikingly with what Colbert de Terron had written in 1663 and 1664, when he had repeatedly and actively tried to discourage Colbert from considering port sites outside the Charente region. Was it the professional judgment of all involved that the navy's ports should be built exclusively in one region, along either the Charente or the Seudre rivers? Or did de Terron manipulate his colleagues and the facts at their command to arrive at this result, so favorable to his own interests? Although it is not possible to know if or how de Terron influenced his colleagues in the spring of 1665, there is evidence that these conclusions did not represent what some of them honestly thought, and that, as a result, de Terron must have taken steps to gain support for the location of one great Atlantic arsenal in the Charente region.

Apparently de Clerville and Jansse disagreed with de Terron about the wisdom of a port at Saint-Nazaire. De Clerville openly preferred a port on the Seudre, which was wider and deeper,[46] and his argument in favor of Saint-Nazaire was so weak—that it would be easy to bring ships to it through the shallow, sandy channel of the Charente—that Colbert grew skeptical.[47] When de Clerville was called to Languedoc in May 1665, Jansse was ordered to bring to Paris maps of the Charente that de Clerville had prepared.[48] Perhaps Jansse spoke freely to Colbert, for, soon after his visit, de Terron learned, first, that while Louis and Colbert were content to establish the great Atlantic base on the Charente, they were not blind to the strategic value of another one at Brest, and, second, that the Compagnie des Indes preferred a site near Port-Louis to the one proposed for it at Paimboeuf.

De Terron's letters of the summer of 1665 betrayed his anxiety over the course events were taking.[49] Every proposal to build a port in the Charente region—at Soubize, Tonnay-Charente, Plomb, and elsewhere—had been dropped on technical grounds. Colbert let him know how impatient he was to find a suitable port.[50] Perhaps Brest, after all, would be chosen. So, in an effort to find a more praiseworthy and less controversial port, de Terron took Blondel and several engineers on another inspection of the Charente and Seudre rivers and first suggested Pilart on the Seudre;[51] Blondel sent plans for it to Colbert in August 1665. De Terron then suggested Rochefort on the Charente, which, he felt, would conclusively remove all doubts about the feasibility of a port in that region.[52] Even though Rochefort was farther from the sea than Saint-Nazaire, de Terron wrote a letter to Colbert in which he stated that Rochefort could accommodate one-third more boats than Brest, which was a true deepwater seaport.[53] As de Clerville had been for Sète, de Terron was willing to misrepresent the facts for Rochefort.

De Terron cited many advantages for Rochefort: it stood near a forest; supplies could be brought to it easily; navigation on the Charente posed no problems; it would be less costly to develop than other sites; and its land could be repossessed by the king from the Protestant and politically-impotent Seigneur de Cheusse.[54] He did not mention how shallow and narrow the Charente River was, nor how unhealthy that seacoast region was known to be (Blondel became ill with malaria in April 1665), nor that he had already invested in land five kilometers away from Rochefort, in Tonnay-Charente. De Clerville had a chance to inspect Rochefort in November 1665, but with the exception of the question of cost, he preferred Pilart on the Seudre.[55] By manipulating the facts, de Terron guided Colbert's judgment so that the government would eventually chose a port in the Charente region. Nonetheless, Colbert saw through the uncertainties that surrounded the choice of a Charente port and perceived his cousin's motive. Colbert accused him of being unwilling to leave the region, and threatened to send him to Brest,[56] at the remote, western end of France. De Terron reassembled his colleagues, advised Colbert to build a port at Brest after all, and humbly offered to go there himself.[57]

In the end, Colbert and Louis did decide to make Rochefort the principal Atlantic naval base, despite their doubts and even after they received advice not to build there, advice that reflected further on the unwillingness of Colbert's agents to give sound judgments. Early in 1666, the Marquis Martel, who had earlier served in the navy on the Atlantic, wrote to Colbert from Toulon:

> I have learned that you want to know the opinion of all the officers of the navy regarding the most appropriate and advantageous location to gather together the King's ships and even to keep them for the winter and recaulk them. . . . The Chevalier de Clerville . . . and several officers of the navy . . . want to prove that the Charente River is a place where a better port can be built than at Brest. I confess to you, Sir, that this completely surprised me. . . . The site of Rochefort could shelter many ships with much work and expense but I do not see that it can be in a state to serve for a long time. . . . Brest will always have the advantages that nature gave it. . . . The harbor of Brest is the most vast and the bay the most advantageous that can be imagined. The countryside can furnish everything but wine. For a moderate expense one can make there in a short while a port capable of holding a hundred [ships] of whatever size you could want. . . . Brest is a port at all tides . . . I do not see what can be spent on Rochefort which would give it that advantage. It is often necessary to wait for high tide to enter it and to leave it.[58]

Why did Colbert reject this advice (the fact that it was offered at all shows that the selection of new port sites was an open process) and instead concur with his agents?[59] The answer can be found in his minute to Martel's letter: first, de Clerville was supported by the principal navy officers in his judgment of Rochefort (a judgment that de Terron had misrepresented to Colbert); second, easy ship movement in the harbor of Brest was impeded by treacherous winds and rocks; and, third, the Bretons had a reputation in the navy as men who were unwilling to serve. Rochefort, thought Colbert, was as close to a sure thing as he might find in 1665, and he felt it could be developed quickly. Yet precisely because caution, prudence, and security were important to him, he felt it would be wise not to neglect Brest altogether. In 1666 he sent de Clerville there to recommend ways to attract Bretons to the navy, and the year after, he sent him back to Brest to plan for an arsenal and for future city growth.[60]

Conclusion

With this, the monarchy's selection of sites for new port cities was fixed: Sète on the Mediterranean, as commercial port of Languedoc and port of shelter for galleys and merchantmen; Lorient, opposite Port-Louis on the same estuary, as seaboard entrepôt of the Compagnie des Indes orientalles (chosen for its large, secure, and remote harbor); and Brest as port of refuge and repair for the great Atlantic fleet, which was to be constructed and sheltered in Rochefort.

Ironically, in betting on the futures of Rochefort and Sète, de Terron and de Clerville miscalculated. The approaches to Rochefort proved to be too shallow for large vessels, and by 1673 Colbert had decided to make of it a secondary port and transfer some of its functions to Brest. After having invested in the region and its future, de Terron, already sick with malaria, moved away and became semiretired from public affairs. Sète's harbor was more difficult to clean and protect from siltation than de Clerville had imagined. By 1668 he had retired financially from the hydraulic operations, and after 1671 he had nothing to do with the plans for those operations, either. By placing their own interests parallel to or ahead of the king's, both men suffered from the poor advice they had given to Colbert. Their actions were worthy of Saint-Simon's observation that "The fate of public affairs is almost always to be governed by private interests."[61] In hindsight, de Clerville and de Terron may have regretted their decisions. And so may have Colbert.[62]

If the process of site selection demonstrates how Louis's pursuit of sea power led to the creation of a network of new port cities, it also shows why France was less likely to achieve maritime ascendancy as easily and as quickly as Colbert probably encouraged Louis to hope it might. The imprecise and indeterminate selection process had distorted the appearance of France's seacoast in the eyes of those Colbert had charged with its study. And when Colbert brought that process to an end by accepting the advice the men he trusted gave him, he probably knew that if France's drive for sea power was to begin at all, there was not enough time to look for other port sites. But the handicaps that de Clerville and de Terron placed on Sète and Rochefort proved to be too great; within a few years, Colbert had to modify the roles each new city was to play in the network of cities for sea power. The time he had tried to gain for France in the 1660s was spent on correcting the mistakes of that decade in the 1670s and 1680s.

Nevertheless, Colbert and Louis had pieced together a network of arsenals, entrepôts, and harbors to sustain the drive for French maritime ascendancy. Men and women would soon congregate in large numbers at seaside places where permanent, thriving maritime communities had not existed before. Significantly, in the search for these locations, Colbert's agents did not pick locations that would make possible a city of a given form or appearance.

On the contrary, they seemed to have assumed that an appropriate sort of city could be planned and adapted to a given harbor. They must have anticipated using port city planning to ready the ports for use as soon as possible and to overcome any handicaps imposed on the port city network.

Colbert's treatment of Paris is evidence that he must have had confidence in his own abilities as a statesman of urbanism. Louis XIV did not like Paris, and the Fronde revolts (1648–1654) had perhaps made him a bit afraid of the city. He loved to hunt and was attracted to Versailles, his father's hunting lodge, early in his reign. If Colbert had not chosen to remain behind in Paris, Louis might have abandoned the city to the whims of its most influential residents. But Louis allowed himself to be convinced by his minister's arguments that Paris was worth his attention. In 1666 a high-level committee studied the city's government and recommended improvements. The outcome was the creation, in March 1667, of a chief police magistrate for the entire city. Other improvements were made subsequently: the old walls to the north were demolished and replaced by boulevards; urban residential squares were developed and new streets were laid out to improve circulation; public welfare institutions, such as asylums for the poor, were erected; new churches were built. In the efforts to improve Paris, Louis XIV, the administration, and the bourgeoisie and the financiers and the governing class of Paris found that, more often than not, they shared common assumptions and interests. But, in the final analysis, the more Paris changed, the more the monarchy could claim responsibility for the city's prosperity and well-being. As Colbert no doubt had intended, the formal compositions that represented Louis's *gloire*— monuments, squares, avenues, parks, public buildings—had been designed to enhance other aspects of city life—defense, housing, circulation, public order, commerce, and trade. Colbert hoped that as Paris became more prosperous and handsome and better administered, the city's reputation would add to Louis's fame. Improving the quality of urban life, therefore, was as important to an urbanism of grandeur as were the formal monuments of the ruler himself. Could Louis and Colbert achieve as much on the French seacoast? Or would their unfamiliarity with the maritime world interfere with the city planning process?

IV

The Government
Proceeds to Plan

Introduction

Louis XIV's government impatiently established cities at the sites of
Rochefort, Lorient, Brest, and Sète to supply an urban setting for expanding
military, political, and commercial activities. In 1665 there were no communities at these locations that could grow into cities: Brest was a village of
between fifty and one hundred families, and the others were barely inhabited
at all. Louis, his ministers, and their agents knew that the transformation of
these places into cities might cost millions of pounds. But the tempo at which
they created legal and fiscal structures, expropriated land, and planned for its
use indicates that they believed new city building to be in the realm of possibility; few doubts were ever raised.

Unquestioningly, the central government assumed that if the cities grew
unplanned, the very influx of workers might create conditions of disorder
that would adversely affect the ports. The government planned each city only
insofar as it felt it needed to, and did not engage in city planning as an
exercise in theory about the ideal shape or structure of port cities. Planning in
anticipation of and in response to problems of growth was often improvisa-
tional, usually empirical and concrete, and, above all, pragmatic, designed to
provide the government with the facilities it needed as soon as possible. This
sort of planning was not always successful. The government's planning efforts
can be divided into two topics: government manipulation of legal charters,
taxation, and trade, which had a negligible impact on the new cities, and
government planning of housing and spatial design, which significantly affected them. These two dimensions of planning are discussed separately in

Sections of this chapter were published as "Grandeur in French City Planning under Louis XIV:
Rochefort and Marseille," by Josef Konvitz, in the *Journal of Urban History* 2, no. 1 (November
1975): 3–42. Reprinted by permission of Sage Publications, Inc.

this chapter in order that the government's failings and accomplishments can emerge more clearly. In both discussions the planning story is told city by city, not only because the circumstances the government confronted in its planning of each city partly determined that city's character and distinctive features, but also and especially because the ways in which the government treated each city separately illustrates aspects of the planning process that only a comparative description and analysis can illuminate.

The story of how each city was planned informs an analysis of planning, but planning did not control all aspects of urban development. The government's planning practice, therefore, deepens but does not satisfy our curiosity about the kind of society that developed in the new port cities. How permanent cities emerged from this planning process is one of the questions that must be answered in the next chapter.

Before describing how royal officers and ministers modeled and scaled each city to the role the government intended for it, the political and strategic reasons for which each was established and used—and for which the government engaged in city planning with such energy—must be made clear. Only then can the separate experiences by which each settlement became a permanent community be seen as part of the process by which Louis's government fashioned a network of port cities for sea power.

Rochefort was to be the king's exclusive Atlantic base, where the great Atlantic fleet would be built and outfitted. From early 1666 on, the previously inconsequential estate of the Seigneur de Cheusse was designed to become a city worthy of its great royal mission. Of the four new port cities, Rochefort was the only one to be built entirely according to a comprehensive plan drawn up at the time it was created.

For this task Colbert called on some of France's best-known architects and engineers.[1] De Clerville, Blondel, and François Le Vau were ordered to draw up plans for the new city: "Work . . . so that [Rochefort] will conform to the grandeur, to the magnificence that I have imagined," wrote Colbert. "It can serve for all our other arsenals."[2] Colbert thought of Rochefort as a large city, occupying as much space as Bordeaux. (The armory, for example, was supposed to hold enough to equip twelve or fifteen thousand men.[3]) And just as Colbert wanted the fleets to be constructed there to rival and surpass those of France's enemies, so, too, did he want Rochefort to rival their great ports.[4] Expressive of this ambition was the following statement: "It will be a great advantage if, using the exemptions which the King has granted the municipality of Rochefort you [de Terron] can make of it a second Sardam [Zaanstreek] of Holland."[5] Rochefort was to be the largest and most handsome arsenal in the world.[6] Rejecting topographic plans by Le Vau and Blondel, Colbert modified one by de Clerville in such a way that the city would have no center of its own, nor any visual or architectural focus of interest. Nothing in the city could be permitted to detract from the importance of the arsenal and its work. It was to be a mute, handsome reflection of Louis's arsenal, obedient to the *gloire* of the king it served.

Colbert wanted the arsenal and part of the city to be ready for use by 1670—four years after the site had been preempted. In 1669 the final plan for the city's space was approved. In that same year, Rochefort was given a charter with a list of special privileges to spur its growth and activity. But difficulties with terrain, endemic malaria, and an uncooperative labor force slowed construction to the point that rumors circulated through the court (perhaps begun by Colbert's enemies) that the king was being cheated at Rochefort. Sensitive to such rumors, Colbert made a strenuous effort to prepare Rochefort; by the start of the Franco-Dutch conflict of 1672–1679, it was operational.

By then, however, Colbert had realized that Rochefort could not be the great Atlantic arsenal. The Charente River was too difficult to enter and leave, too shallow and narrow. In 1670 he ordered that Rochefort and Brest divide the responsibility of arming the fleet, so that it could never be trapped in one harbor or the other.[7] Three years more of naval operations convinced him that Brest had to take the place of Rochefort altogether.[8] But several thousand people lived and worked in Rochefort in 1673, and it could not be "unplanned" so easily. It grew until the end of the seventeenth century, and its arsenal continued to build and supply ships of the fleet (though only second-, third-, or fourth-class vessels, for nearly all the first-class ships for the Atlantic fleet were now built at Brest).

In 1666 Brest had been destined to become a secondary port, complementing Rochefort. At that time it was a simple village on an old medieval site that had been fortified by Richelieu, and it was divided in half by the Penfield River; the right (north) bank was known as Recouvrance, the left (south) as Brest. Initially, Colbert did not know what to do with the site, and in 1667 he asked de Clerville to advise him. De Clerville wrote that few people lived there, that life was spartan and unrewarding. He wondered why sailors and workmen would ever choose voluntarily to remain in Brest.[9] De Clerville understood that a stable working force would be attracted to Brest only if it offered certain comforts and services: he recommended that both Recouvrance and Brest be fortified and built up to attract a population of 3,000 merchants and shopkeepers, whose presence would make life there attractive.

Colbert was not ready to act on this advice as long as Rochefort remained the principal Atlantic base. In the years 1670 and 1671, there was enough housing in Brest for just two-thirds of the labor force of about nine hundred,[10] so, to limit the government's responsibilities, Colbert decided to keep Brest and Recouvrance separated into two distinct communities.[11] In the 1670s some arsenal buildings were erected, and the *maison du roy*, home and garden of the intendant, was laid out, but little else was built. Perhaps Colbert was waiting for the outcome of the war against the Dutch.

The French did not decisively defeat the Dutch in the first year of hostilities, and Colbert may have begun thinking about military engagements in the years to come. On the basis of operations in 1672, Colbert decided (in 1673) that Brest, and not Rochefort, should be the principal Atlantic base. Brest's growth remained undirected at first, but by 1680 many problems had arisen: sanitation conditions were bad, wooden buildings and shacks constituted a fire hazard, public morality was a scandal, a new church was needed, and the city lacked funds. Brest was becoming a great port,[12] and it had to look like a great port city, too. Finally, in 1680, Colbert and his son Seignelay applied to Brest the same forceful comprehensive planning that had been imposed on Rochefort.

What the government did in the next two or three years is the best evidence of its determination to transform Brest as quickly as possible into a redoubtable port city. The new Brest was designed to house and satisfy the needs of thousands of workers. Colbert sent an engineer, Sainte-Colombe, to draw up plans for a new and larger fortified city uniting Brest and Recouvrance, which was to be called "Brest." Vauban studied and approved these plans, which called for the development of spacious and prominent but separate residential and industrial tracts on both sides of the Penfield River. On the advice of Seignelay, Colbert endowed the city with its own local government, taxing authority, and trading privileges, and proposed to create a new parish and erect a new church. By 1683 the government had made great progress toward making Brest the city as important as Brest the arsenal. Thereafter its population increased at twice the 1660 to 1680 rate, reaching over fifteen thousand in 1700. Louis and his government never wavered in their commitment to Brest after 1680, and in peacetime or wartime its future seemed secure.

Lorient had been selected by the Compagnie des Indes orientalles as a coastal entrepôt, and it remained the property of the Compagnie throughout Louis's reign. As a wartime expediency, however, the government preempted Lorient from 1688 to 1716, making it into a military port and arsenal. It was during those years that the city was established and its growth planned.

The land of Lorient, originally known as Faouedic, was given to the Compagnie in 1665 to build "ports, quays, dockyards, warehouses and other edifices necessary to the construction of its ships and the outfitting of its fleets."[13] Since workmen did not come willingly, construction of these facilities was completed by forced labor, under the corvée work tax.[14] The site was never attractive, because the fortunes of the Compagnie did not inspire confidence: between 1668 and 1684 only one ship a year, on the average, was outfitted there. The name "Lorient" embraced no more than a collection of barely used port buildings when the government took over the site for the navy in 1688.

As early as 1679 the idea was circulated that Lorient might be more useful as a naval support facility for the fleet based at Brest. To adapt Lorient to the navy, housing would have to be built, the quays extended, the rope hangar rebuilt, and other essential facilities installed.[15] In 1684 Seignelay reorganized the Compagnie and placed the care of Lorient in the hands of Desclouzeaux, the intendant at Brest. Desclouzeaux took an interest in and exercised control over its small affairs, so that when the War of the League of Augsburg began in 1688, Seignelay was able to requisition Lorient for the navy without difficulty. In just two years, from 1688 to 1690, the site was made ready to help Brest build and outfit the French fleets. Louis and his ministers planned to borrow Lorient from the Compagnie for the duration of the war, which no one thought would last as long as nine years.[16] After the war the Compagnie could use its base once again; in the meantime, it would receive rent. Thinking of his wasted investment at Rochefort, Louis rejected suggestions to make Lorient a permanent naval base.[17]

Louis's interest in the development of the city of Lorient was conditioned by his decision to use the port for an unknown but ultimately limited period, during which, albeit briefly, it would be active and important. After 1688 the government concentrated solely on erecting the port facilities it needed as quickly as possible. Since the War of the League of Augsburg continued until 1697 and was followed by the War of the Spanish Succession (1701–1713), the government slowly involved itself in city planning to improve the working conditions in the arsenal. From 1699 to 1705, for the sake of efficiency and safety, royal agents in Lorient ordered the people who lived in shacks among the arsenal buildings to move outside the arsenal compound, and they planned a new residential quarter for ordered growth. They struggled against the indifference of Versailles and the resistance of local and regional interests to create a new parish for Lorient, to erect a new church, and to endow the nascent city with its own tax structure. The history of Lorient shows the decisiveness with which the government acted when it wanted to exploit a port, the care it took to create the kind of community it wanted, and the influence of royal agents in formulating and executing state policy.

Colbert wanted Sète to be of use both to royal galleys and to merchantmen as soon as possible.[18] Even though the Canal du Midi from Toulouse to Sète would not be finished until years later (1681), in 1667 he urged de Clerville and a group of Montpellier bankers, and then Pierre-Paul Riquet (beginning in 1668) to ready the harbor at Sète.[19] De Clerville, for his part, believed that the population should be increased, if only to swell the small labor force already at work,[20] and Colbert wanted between five hundred and six hundred men working there each day, which would give Sète a population of about two thousand.[21] In 1670, three years before the harbor works were completed, the monarchy, for the purposes of encouraging people to come to Sète, established its municipal institutions and defined its privileges. Clearly, Colbert hoped that a larger working population would make it possible to complete the port facilities quickly and that as soon as it could be used, Languedoc's merchants would organize under royal protection to exploit it.[22] Since the government was content to establish Sète for them to use both in its and in their own interests, it intervened to direct Sète's growth less often than in the other, more military port cities.

The government tried to adapt each site with remarkable speed. Brest was planned in three years, Sète and Rochefort within five. Lorient was transformed into an arsenal in three years (although it took longer to make that place over into a city). Such efficiency reveals the energy of Louis's administration, not just in the 1660s, when the king was young and enjoyed the collaboration of several great ministers, but in the 1680s and 1690s as well. There was a continuity of purpose over the years: what the government began to do in Rochefort or in Sète in the 1660s, it could undertake ten or twenty years later in Brest or in Lorient. The creation of new port cities was an event that by itself adds to the renown of Louis's reign, adds evidence of the renewable vitality of his administration and of the forcefulness and vigor with which his ministers and agents pursued his goals—and demonstrates the importance of speed, flexibility, and determination in the planning process.

Charters for the New Cities: Taxes, Trade, and City Growth

The distance between Versailles and the seaboard frontier can be measured literally, in the fortnight or more it took for a letter to leave the one and arrive at the other, and for the answer to return to the sender; and it can be measured figuratively, in the gap between what the government at Versailles wanted to do and what its agents in the new port cities were able to achieve. City planning was one way the government tried to overcome its distance from the new port cities, and the most direct instrument the government could use to that end was the legal document, a city charter. City charters established the new port cities as legally distinct units. The government also used charters to state its long-term goals for each city and to enumerate the privileges and restrictions for each that would enable royal officers to manipulate that city's growth in the future. No doubt the government at Versailles thought that the planning process, to which the terms of the charters were a preamble, would extend royal power from the palace toward the port city as smoothly as water flows in a canal that has been dug for its course.

City charters had been granted in the Middle Ages as a legal device to encourage the proliferation of towns and their role in trade,[23] but the centralized monarchy of Louis XIV could not grant liberties to new cities in the same spirit as rulers had in the past. The government wanted to influence growth while basic construction work was in progress. Rochefort received its charter in 1669, in the same year its street plan was designed. Sète was established by charter in 1670, and Lorient was set aside by charter as a base for the Compagnie des Indes in 1666. Brest had an old charter dating from 1559, but by 1680 the government's plans for Brest required that the city's legal framework be altered; in 1681 the documents issued to unite Brest with Recouvrance constituted a new charter.[24]

The spirit of public utility infused the entire enterprise of granting charters. These new settlements were established to serve the king, and the terms of their charters referred directly to that purpose. The charters were brief, two- to four-page documents that began with a preamble stating what the government hoped the cities would achieve. The powers, rights, privileges, and constraints enumerated after the preambles were designed to facilitate government operations and to encourage city growth; the specific terms were drawn up with each city's character and role in mind. The legal city-state relations spelled out in the charters reflected measures of city autonomy that were greater (in fiscal and local affairs) and less (in matters of land ownership and use) than those common in France at that time. It suited Louis to be generous in matters of taxation and local government, because he believed such terms would attract people to the new cities and would facilitate the conduct of maritime affairs. For nearly the same reasons, to render the cities more attractive physically to new residents and to designate parts of their territory for specific functions, Louis reserved for himself rights respecting land ownership and use that specifically indicated the physical appearance of each city and compelled the inhabitants to conform to whatever topographic plan the government imposed. In these ways, the city charters announced great new ventures and prepared for their success. But the provisions respecting topographic design and land use proved to have an impact on city life and growth that the provisions on taxes and trade never exercised. What limited the influence of chartered tax structures?

The fiscal and trade terms of the charters, by which settlement and growth were nurtured, were adaptations of ways the monarchy exploited the economy of nearly every French municipality.[25] City authorities had for centuries imposed an octroi tax on local, land-based trade of foodstuffs and other common articles brought into their jurisdictions.[26] Early in Louis's reign the central government increased the percentage of the octroi it received to 50 percent; the other half belonged to the city.[27] In addition, the monarchy sought to rationalize the domestic accounts of cities and eliminate chronic indebtedness by specifying that their expenses not exceed income;[28] and it established a fiscal structure similar to the octroi to augment royal revenues and integrate long-distance mercantile trading into the national economy.[29] The income from these measures figured in the two-thirds of the royal revenue that could be raised by indirect taxation in peacetime.[30]

Because the government had in mind the high-priority maritime affairs of state (and not the Treasury's balance sheet) when it composed the fiscal terms appropriate to each new port city, it deliberately modified these conventional tax structures. Thus Rochefort's taille (general tax collected by the city) was fixed at the ridiculously low figure of £2,000; many towns of smaller size in the Charente region paid larger sums. In addition, wines and spirits imported into Rochefort were to be taxed at half the standard rate for a period of thirty years. Of even greater consequence was the charter provision that the city be gerrymandered out of the Cinq Grosses Fermes, the largest customs unit of France, so that the navy would be relieved of the obligation to pay customs duties on its supplies. Instead, the government affiliated Rochefort with the Charente customs unit and created it as a duty-free port. This privilege embraced local merchants and their trade, too. The king encouraged people to live at Sète and establish it as an entrepôt (for the Languedoc-Mediterranean trade) when he created a duty-free port there, as well. Property-owners, including merchants, would have to pay just the customary local taxes. Brest was not given tax credits, but a variation on the octroi system instead. City officials were granted the authority to tax cider, wine, and spirits at lower rates, and Louis XIV explicitly allocated the city's share of half of the revenue for construction and upkeep of civil works and for a new parish church. Lorient's tax structure was never spelled out as clearly as that of the others. It was the only one of the four to be subject to the taxing power of other communities; its unrefined tax structure reflected Louis's decision to return it to the Compagnie des Indes once the wars ended, and thus showed how deliberately and selfishly the government phrased the tax terms.

By the 1690s the fiscal and trade terms of the charters no longer corresponded to each city's actual role in the government's maritime strategy or to the government's own view of fiscal priorities. Having put its own interests first when it used charters to create an appropriate fiscal structure for each city, the government was willing to alter those structures when the policy ends they were designed to serve were revised, when the wars after 1688 increased the royal budget, and when even the navy itself no longer received adequate funds because tax revenues were insufficient. The tax status of each new city was placed in jeopardy; the concept of *raison d'état* was not. Intendants and ministers had to choose between taxing the cities more and more heavily to ransom the debt of wartime expenses and preserving their privileges in taxation and trade; they most often chose the first course of action.

The strange part of this story is that the actions of the officials had little adverse impact on the new cities. In fact, government ministers and agents had miscalculated from the start how government-sponsored tax and trade structures would influence new city growth, because they defined the urban economy according to the interests of the centralized state. The nature of the privileges granted and the process of revision are of interest for what they show of city-specific planning. Moreover, this investigation of the new cities' economies also suggests that some of the limits to the planning process had nothing to do with how efficiently policies were drafted and executed, but had much to do with whether those involved in planning could measure the influence of their policies on the phenomena of urban growth.

Rochefort

When the government decided to put taxation ahead of growth, Rochefort lost only its unique budgetary privileges. The government since 1669 had made an unusual effort to pay for everything the city needed on an ad hoc, year-by-year basis, but in 1692 Louis made Rochefort conform to the octroi tax and budget procedures of all French cities, forcing it to pay its own way thereafter. The inhabitants apparently did not oppose the change. Perhaps the opportunity to manage a budget tempted prominent city leaders, with their limited view of public affairs, to think of the power to be wielded and the profits to be made. Rochefort's population was still growing in the 1690s—an octroi deposited in the city hands would be sizeable and would free the city from dependency on the royal treasury for yearly subventions.[31] But the same demand for additional revenues that led the government in 1692 to reduce what it spent on Rochefort by granting it a budget limited to half the octroi led it, in 1703, to cancel trade privileges, as well. Until 1702 Rochefort's intendants had successfully defended the city's local privileges against the tax farmers of the Cinq Grosses Fermes, whose revenues were diminished by the city's trade. But, during the War of the Spanish Succession, benefits to Rochefort became less important to the government than an increase in tax revenues, and, in 1703, Rochefort's duty-free privileges were removed.[32] Rochefort, however, had already been ruined as a great port city by the continued silting of the Charente River: a surprising fact is that the government maintained Rochefort's tax and trade privileges for twenty years longer than it maintained its principal Atlantic base there.

Brest

The government had provided Brest with a traditional octroi regime when it moved the Atlantic naval headquarters there from Rochefort in 1680. Louis directed that the city's half of the octroi, levied on cider, spirits, and wine sold at retail, be used for all city improvements,[33] and in fact the city was able to pay its own way until the early 1690s. From this revenue, subventions were paid to house principal government officers, to maintain the hospital, and to finance both civil and military engineering works. By 1686 income totaled nearly £15,000,[34] and since, at this point, income exceeded expenses, the government decided to build a church with the surplus octroi funds that would accumulate over the next several years. Revenues appeared sufficient for such an undertaking: expenses for the church were estimated at £75,000, and between 1686 and 1690, octroi revenues averaged over £20,000 yearly, totaling £101,472.[35]

In the 1690s the government suddenly and unexpectedly found that octroi revenues were inadequate for all the new projects it wanted to complete in Brest. The octroi had to cover such unanticipated expenses as the purchase of city offices from the crown, the salaries of a bourgeois militia, and the cost of major fortifications. Moreover, gross irregularities (especially embezzlement) appeared in the accounts, worsening the effects of the inevitable deficit.[36] The government increased tax revenues as it could, drawing on the surplus octroi of Landerneau, a neighboring town,[37] and imposing taxes on real estate adjacent to the arsenal, on which people had built houses.[38] As far as Louis was concerned, the city still had the responsibility of raising £18,000 yearly. To avoid long-term indebtedness, both city and province suggested that Brest be established as a free-trade port,[39] but before the government acted on this proposal, the War of the Spanish Succession began, resulting in a substantial rise in both expenses and revenues. For instance, in 1700 the octroi had to cover, as an extraordinary expense, outlays of £28,000 for housing for 564 soldiers and 99 officers;[40] yet in 1704, a good year, total octroi taxes yielded only £30,000[41] (a sum double the octroi revenue in 1686, but still short of expenses). To increase revenue as the war continued, Louis imposed on Brest the exceptional wartime taxes, such as the *dixième,* that he imposed on other cities, and resorted to forced labor (corvée). Despite the size and nearly constant growth in the octroi itself, the almost endless capacity of the government to push expenses beyond its income flawed the effort to make Brest self-supporting. The government-sponsored fiscal regime taxed the secondary effects of urban growth instead of the traffic in men and materials, the cause of that growth and of the city's principal financial burdens.

Lorient

Lorient benefited from no established tax or trade privileges because the permanent character of the privileges would have impeded any effort to return Lorient to the Compagnie des Indes. When the navy opened its Lorient arsenal in 1689, local inhabitants were taxed lightly: the tax farmers from nearby Hennebont controlled the sale of wine in Lorient,[42] and inhabitants of another village, Plemeur, collected a taille. All the while, of course, Lorient lacked any revenues of its own. At one point it was discovered that, during fiscal years 1710, 1711, and 1712, Plemeur had overtaxed Lorient to the extent of £8,000. Remarkably, the sum was returned to Lorient and spent partly on the church, partly for houses for people displaced in a recent fire.[43] Yet when residents demanded that the fiscal exploitation of Lorient cease because they wanted the government to recognize Lorient as an established community deserving of a permanent fiscal structure,[44] the answer from Versailles was that Lorient should not be considered similar to Brest and Rochefort.[45]

On occasion the royal agents in Lorient could delay the introduction of a new tax; the *droit du pied fourché* on butchered meat was imposed in 1713, nearly eight years after its levy had been proposed.[46] But as the government's need for revenues increased, extraordinary taxes on trade,[47] income, and real estate[48] were levied on its inhabitants. Louis could stick to his goal of keeping Lorient for the navy on a temporary basis only because people came to work and transformed the site into an important naval base despite the severity of taxation; he did not feel the need to grant autonomous tax and trade privileges to Lorient in order to make it attractive to newcomers. But Louis and his ministers never learned the lesson Lorient taught by example— namely, that tax and trade structures had little influence over the new cities' patterns of growth. Louis's institutionalized treatment of Lorient did not prevent Lorient from gradually taking on the appearance of a permanent community; Lorient emerged at the end of Louis's reign showing every likelihood of enduring. Although there is no sure way of knowing, it seems that, if Lorient could grow under a harsh fiscal regime designed to cripple it, in all likelihood neither Brest nor Rochefort needed any of the advantages in tax and trade matters that the government had granted them.

Sète

The controversy between Sète and Louis over tax and trade privileges is an equally telling demonstration of Lorient's lesson that the state's tax policies did not have the desired effect on new city growth. Sète performed well as a trade port and as a harbor of refuge, but not as well as Colbert must have hoped: Agde captured more than half of the Canal du Midi–Mediterranean trade. To promote Sète the government had freed it from the taille and did not grant it an octroi levy (in 1713 the town finally was awarded an octroi on wine for local consumption, to reduce its accumulated debts).[49] Additionally,

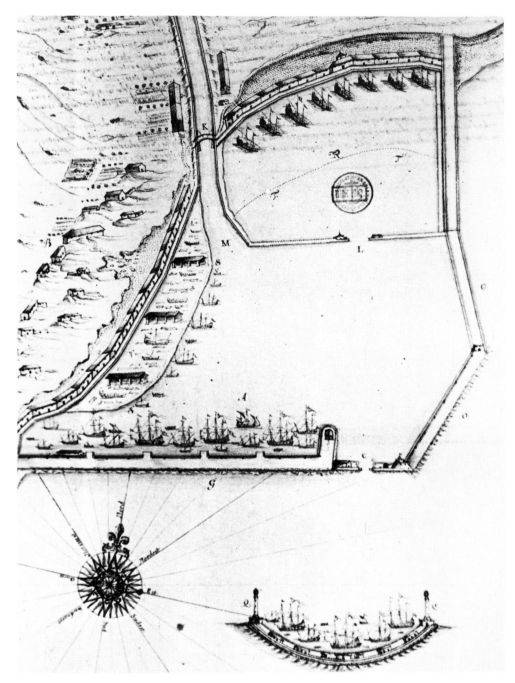

FIGURE **4.1.** *Sète, 1680. Bibliothèque nationale, cartes et plans Hydro D73bis/10/44. Photo Bibliothèque nationale, Paris.*

Sète's charter of 1673 provided that local and maritime commerce be exempt from duties. But these privileges were not enough to divert existing and new maritime traffic away from the more established routes, which terminated in port cities already familiar to French sailors and merchants. Instead, meeting little competition in Sète, foreign traders expanded the already significant share of Languedoc's Mediterranean trade they controlled. There was little Paris could do by way of tax and tariff legislation to transfer the expertise and entrepreneurial initiative of foreigners into the hands of the French.

The leverage Marseille exercised over Sète further illustrates the structure of Sète's trade. In 1669 the monarchy had ordered all ships in foreign trade to stop in quarantine at Marseille, and had granted that city authority to levy 20 percent fines on all foreign and French shipping not stopping there.[50] Marseille stationed agents in Sète to collect the fines.[51] The justification for Marseille's monopoly was that only there could ships and their crews be quarantined to prevent the plague from entering France. The fines had the secondary purpose of encouraging French traders to hire French ships, since French ships were taxed only if they did not call at Marseille, while all foreign ships were taxed, even at Marseille. Foreign traders came to Sète and paid the fine, but Languedoc's merchants did not enter into maritime commerce in large numbers, even though they could take advantage of their nationality.[52] In May 1671, three Genoese craft stopped to load wine. That December, fifty-two craft called for the same purpose; only thirteen were French, the rest Italian or Spanish.[53] Sète's charter was a call to Languedoc's merchants to make Sète a French port, as all they had to do was stop at Marseille for a quarantine inspection, but throughout Louis's reign, they were merely trying to catch up with their foreign competitors, who had to pay 20 percent fines to do business.[54] Serious but unsuccessful attempts were made to organize a French-sponsored commercial traffic tied to Languedoc's merchant and banking interests,[55] but in the end those interests were involved in Sète's trade as suppliers, not as shippers. They sold large quantities of wine to foreigners who came to Sète, and they capitalized the industrial transformation of wine into spirits for export.[56]

Nevertheless, Languedoc's bankers seriously identified Marseille's quarantine as the obstacle to their participation in Sète's trade. Finally, they urged that a quarantine facility be built at Sète.[57] The idea of an offshore quarantine at Sète was old: there are maps showing designs for one in 1665, 1672, and 1680 (figure 4.1). In 1688, 1692, 1698, and 1701, however, Louis rejected proposals to allow direct trade between the Levant and Languedoc.[58] In 1701 Sète's merchants received the privilege of exporting wines and spirits without paying tribute to Marseille, but ships from the east still had to call there to undergo quarantine. When Louis finally allowed Languedoc to begin construction of a quarantine at Sète in 1710[59] (which was not completed until 1723) and lifted all taxes on its trade,[60] he had not so much decided to open Mediterranean trade as he had agreed to grant a favor to the financiers from Languedoc who were supplying the war money he needed.[61] Sète's interests, and even the medical requirements of quarantine, were a secondary concern; Sète's role as a commercial port was less central than the identity of those who controlled and profited from it. Sète's story only confirms the overall pattern: the government was more concerned with its everyday sources of revenue than with understanding the nature of the French urban economy.

Conclusion

The fiscal controversies in which the new cities and Versailles engaged as unequal adversaries are interesting for what they reveal of the planning process. They illustrate that the new cities were not free, as were older and more autonomous cities, to negotiate with the central government; that the government failed to increase its income through financial manipulation and political pressure; and that even though privileges were withdrawn and obligations increased during the fiscal crisis at the end of Louis's reign, neither city growth nor government operations were permanently crippled as a result. All four new port cities continued to grow even when the government exploited their economies at their expense, but Louis and his ministers never reevaluated their assumptions about the impact of tax and trade structures in the light of this phenomenon. A closer look at the French economy is necessary to spell out in greater detail why Louis's attempts to influence new city growth through fiscal policy did not succeed.

Louis's government did not clearly grasp the nature of the nation's economy, and its outlines remain indistinct to us, as well. The limitations of documentary evidence mean that there are many unanswerable questions, and that the information we possess does not cover any single topic adequately; for example, more is known about how Louis spent his money than about the sources of his income, a situation that probably also corresponds to seventeenth-century realities. Louis's government persisted in believing that its policies on taxation and trade could influence new city growth because it lacked the means to assess how the sum total of its fiscal policies affected the disparity between rural and urban life.[62] During Louis's reign (1660–1715) France had some 19 million inhabitants, most of whom worked on the land. Although the value of agricultural production directly consumed by the producers is unknowable, it is likely that gross agricultural production amounted to approximately one billion pounds. The French peasants and their rural landlords accounted for more than three-quarters of France's population. The agricultural sector provided, in turn, nearly three-quarters of the king's income from taxes—and the king preempted about one-fifth of the value of agricultural production in this way. A percentage at least as great as that went into other forms of taxation and rent at the local or provincial level. When, during the wars at the end of Louis's reign, the state's expenses were annually twice what its income was, the state found that it could increase taxation, but that the greater tax burden itself, coming as it did during a deflationary period, raised the specter of rural bankruptcy. Peasants simply could not respond to the state's fiscal demands by increasing productivity or total production value.

Commerce enjoyed relative advantages over agriculture. Municipalities were the exchange points that, when connected together, composed a national market. Commerce gained from cities the greater elasticity in demand of urban populations, the increased productivity of semiskilled and skilled labor, machines, and volume transactions, and instruments of credit; cities gained from commerce the capacity of merchants to increase profits and productivity in response to changing economic, social, and political conditions. Commerce may not have contributed much to France's total wealth or to Louis's income through taxes, but its very nature magnified the differences between city and country life, differences that unpredictable and calamitous meteorological conditions, rising taxes, declining agricultural production, and falling prices brought home to farmers and merchants alike. Even though Louis's taxation of commerce increased during the long wars at the end of his reign and warfare itself increased the risks to merchant trade, commerce—both in the new port cities and in long-established ones—grew substantially more in the period from 1700 to 1715 than it had earlier in Louis's reign, proof that it was insulated against the agrarian fiscal regime of the state.

Because Louis and his ministers did not know that the government's imposition of new and higher taxes and restrictive trade policies still left the cities more attractive than the countryside, they perceived the failure of their tax and trade policies to direct patterns of new city growth as accidents of fate that overcame their best efforts. The increases in the new port cities' population (from a few hundred persons to fifteen thousand in Brest and Roche-fort, five to seven thousand in Lorient and Sète) can be explained in part by the same processes that encouraged so many Frenchmen to move to other cities: Paris, Lyon, Bordeaux, Marseille and many others contained tens of thousands more people at the end of Louis's reign than they had at the beginning, the result of rural-urban migration, not of natural increase. The government's taxation of agriculture probably had a greater impact on the new cities' growth than did the city-specific fiscal policies it had so carefully elaborated. But in that age, when Cartesian and Newtonian styles of scientific explanation were perfecting the study of physical nature, people did not need to be reminded how inadequate by comparison was the study of human affairs.

The government's attempt to use tax and trade policies as instruments of city planning reveals how the government tried to adapt each new port city to play a role in its network of cities for sea power, and focuses attention on factors that, in addition to planning (but outside government control), influenced the pattern of new city growth. French officials responsible for the material and social development of Brest, Lorient, Rochefort, and Sète made more of an impact through their manipulation of each city's spatial aspect, which is the subject of the rest of this chapter.

Housing, Spatial Planning, and the Government's Concept of Order

The sudden arrival of workers and their families in Brest, Lorient, and Rochefort, and the presence of their hastily erected, shabby housing, too close to the port or arsenal, jeopardized the government's intent to secure trouble-free city growth. Living within or near the arsenal compound, residents had ample opportunity to steal from the king's stores. Accidental fires could start easily in their simple wooden shacks and spread to arsenal buildings or even to boats, and the government feared the possibility of destruction by arson, as well. Workers had built their shacks wherever they found land, creating a random yet dense housing pattern that prevented sanitary disposal of sewage and proper land drainage. Government agents reporting these conditions and the ministers who read their reports agreed that deplorable housing threatened to keep community life in a state of disorder and to prevent efficiency in the work of the ports.

In the hope that spatial order would influence and improve public morality and maritime affairs, the government imposed topographic plans and functional land-use policies. Its concern for housing may seem to have been motivated by an appreciation of practical matters alone, but its approach, like that of the Dutch, Danes, and Swedes, was also based on abstract considerations of state. Louis's regime linked urbanism and the interests of the monarchy because it recognized moral imperatives and political principles in the appearance of order. The government wanted to find in each new port city a reflection of its own *gloire* and power; it unconsciously overestimated both the threat the behavior of the masses posed to the arsenals and the potential of spatial planning to remold popular culture and reconstruct work patterns. But the government's exaggerated hopes for spatial planning only made the construction of Brest, Lorient, and Rochefort according to a topographic design more likely: a government involved in schemes for Paris, Marseille, Versailles, and Lille, among others, was not going to retreat from the opportunity to build metropolitan colonies on France's maritime frontier in the royal image. The government may have stumbled when it manipulated the new cities' economies, but its misunderstanding of what spatial planning could achieve did not interfere with its efforts at designing and imposing land-use policies. Therein lies our interest in the attempt at spatial planning: to Louis's administrators, artists, and engineers, making the connections between city space and social, political, and aesthetic values was a creative challenge worthy of their best efforts, and they tried all the harder because they thought they were succeeding. And spatial planning did have an impact on the new cities, for it endowed them with the visible signs of permanence and security with which they survived Louis's reign.

I discuss, first, how Rochefort benefited in matters of housing from having been thoroughly planned at the time it was founded; second, how and why the government forced residents of Brest and Lorient to relocate and rebuild their housing; and, third, how residential social patterns in all four cities were influenced by the presence or absence of planning. Insofar as the planning of housing districts is the subject of this chapter, Sète is not a part of it. Because Sète's waterfront was barely wide enough to contain even the essential port buildings, people built their homes at some distance, and for this reason, housing did not threaten to disrupt port activities. In the third section, for its own sake and as a comparison, Sète is included.

In appearance, these cities today owe only their topographic layout to the seventeenth century. Brest and Lorient were destroyed by Allied aerial bombardment during World War Two; all that could be salvaged from the debris were the original street plans. Had they survived the war intact, however, Brest and Lorient would probably have told us no more about what they looked like in the seventeenth century than Rochefort and Sète do today; all four cities, which have been rebuilt at least once after 1750, document how adaptable changes in building technology are to street plans of another age. The visitor to these cities who is anxious to exercise his historical imagination cannot even depend on topography: he is denied access to the military ports of Brest and Lorient; he finds the Charente River a miserable stream so badly silted that it is barely fit for canoeing; and he must close his eyes to that half of Sète which has been built on land reclaimed since the days of Louis XIV. Only distant views can remind the visitor of what moved those seventeenth-century pioneers: the vast bay of Brest, so promising as a place to fill with fleets; the flat terrain of Lorient, so fit for building ships; the isolation of Rochefort, which kept the king's maritime affairs separate from his subjects'; and the commanding vista of the Mediterranean from Sète.

Rochefort: Renaissance Planning in the Seventeenth Century

Of the three new Atlantic port cities, Rochefort was the only one to be planned before it grew. In the late 1660s, Colbert still anticipated that Rochefort would be the only major new port settlement on the western coast, and he wanted to plan its layout so that no aspect of development would be left to chance. Topographic planning was a deliberate attempt to encourage the inhabitants to work in an orderly and disciplined way for the king. The city was a stage for their work; topographic planning was to correspond to and enhance their activities and, thus, the king's *gloire*. Because Rochefort was the first to be planned in this way, it is useful to begin with a statement about how Louis and his associates approached the problem of translating *gloire* and grandeur into city form and function.

Louis wanted statements about the greatness and power of his monarchy to be clearly and literally rendered in the architecture and city planning of his reign,[63] an ambition which meant that architectural and urban planning styles should be no more ephemeral and transitory than his own power. By the time Louis began his personal rule of France in 1661, the new science of the seventeenth century had reinforced traditional ideas about vision, order, the perception of truth, and the concept of style based on absolutes.[64] Louis XIV was among those who believed that proportion and symmetry expressed grandeur and nobility, and his patronage nurtured theories of urbanism and architecture that authoritatively codified truth and knowledge in the visual arts.

Louis XIV founded an academy of architecture in 1671 to disseminate an orthodox aesthetics of building, and François Blondel, a geometrician and member of the Académie des sciences, became its official theoretician. Blondel's *Cours d'architecture* of 1675 was the equivalent of Boileau's *Art poétique* for poetry;[65] it is an exposition of the idea that order based on reason and science renders a building comprehensible to the mind.[66] His statements on order, proportion, harmony, and the truth of nature perceived through reason are Cartesian in tone and substance.[67] Like Descartes, he found superior those buildings which reflected one architect's comprehensive, ordered vision. Indeed, Descartes presented an excellent model of city building (one of which Blondel and Louis XIV would have approved) in the *Discours de la méthode*. Descartes contrasted those cities which reveal the many stages of their growth in the crowded, disordered layout of their streets with "the regularly constructed towns which an engineer has planned according to his fancy on an open plain." He concluded that because new cities so visibly illustrated "the will of a few men using reason," they were superior to older cities built by "chance." As Descartes expressed it, the more nearly total the exercise of reason, the greater the visible mastery of the thinker over the subject of his thoughts. Harmoniously constructed districts would call to mind the power of the king who built them; just as "the principal apartment must be higher than the others to signify the eminent dignity of the occupant," buildings and districts erected by a king would stand out by the greater degree to which reason and reason alone provided for their design.[68]

Blondel's concept of worthiness, as well as his belief that grandeur and *gloire* could be expressed architectonically, derived from the Italian Renaissance writings and achievements of Leon Battista Alberti, Leonardo da Vinci, and Andrea Palladio, among others. Starting with a revival of the Roman Vitruvius and an archeological search for classical buildings, the Italian masters formulated a new humanistic, metaphoric use of architecture and urban space. For them, architecture was a moral discipline unifying the arts and sciences; it could illustrate the moral quality of institutions and directly influence behavior. For example, churches should be circular because, to quote Palladio, the circle disclosed "the unity, the infinite essence, the uniformity and justice of God." A church's geometry could evoke in the congregation a consciousness of God's omnipresence. The designers believed, like Plato, that one responded instinctively, without rational analysis, to pure architectural forms. To enable the beholder to perceive these qualities, the church was isolated by its decoration and placement from whatever else represented everyday life in the city.[69] Thus, the Italian Renaissance church was erected as a statement about God.

The result was a style in which form and harmony had unquestioned status as the primary aesthetic values. Asserting proportion and geometry to be the most immediate and intuitive expressions of form and content, Palladio wrote authoritatively that "beauty will result from the beautiful form and from the correspondence of the whole to the parts, of the parts amongst themselves, and of these again to the whole."[70] An architectural composition based on mathematical proportion and geometric order could express not only the omnipresence and supremacy of God, but also the power of the ruler over his subjects. Palaces, villas, ecclesiastical properties, town houses, and public buildings were designed with emphasis on symmetry, proportion, and

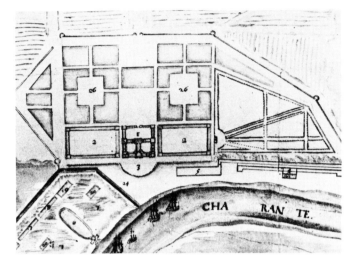

FIGURE **4.2.** *Rochefort, 1666 or 1667, plan by De Clerville. Bibliothèque nationale, cartes et plans Hydro 53/1/3. Photo Bibliothèque nationale, Paris.*

visual perspective as the best way to convey the inherent superior qualities of those who used such buildings. What was valid for individual structures was also true for the layout of cities: urban projects were planned to illustrate the commercial and military power of those who built them.

The Renaissance artist-planner tried to make the truth behind appearances visible in his forms by making those forms into symbols of a transcending reality. The city projects sponsored by Louis XIV were also supposed to refer to a reality beyond themselves, but they were intended to communicate Louis's power rather than religious or secular philosophy. Renaissance principles were simply adapted to new subject matter. In Louis's government, aesthetics in architecture were handled no differently than civil order, the economy, and the law: all were given the same moralizing treatment, and were administered so that the sovereignty of state and ruler might be strengthened.

In moving from the theory of statecraft to the administration of public affairs—whether in law, politics, military or fiscal affairs, or in city planning matters—Louis depended on his ministers and their collaborators. They articulated what Louis understood by his *métier du roi*, his profession of ruling, in the orders, decrees, and inquiries they initiated in his name and, usually, with his knowledge: they transformed the theory of statecraft into the practice of government. This proved to be difficult in city planning. Rules on public order, tavern hours, vagrancy, and the like were relatively easy to compose and distribute to municipal authorities across France, even if such rules were enforced and observed unevenly. But urban projects could not be planned according to a model developed in Paris. Each project had to be planned differently, not only because of obvious factors such as topography, but especially because the activities of a given city required a particular spatial setting.

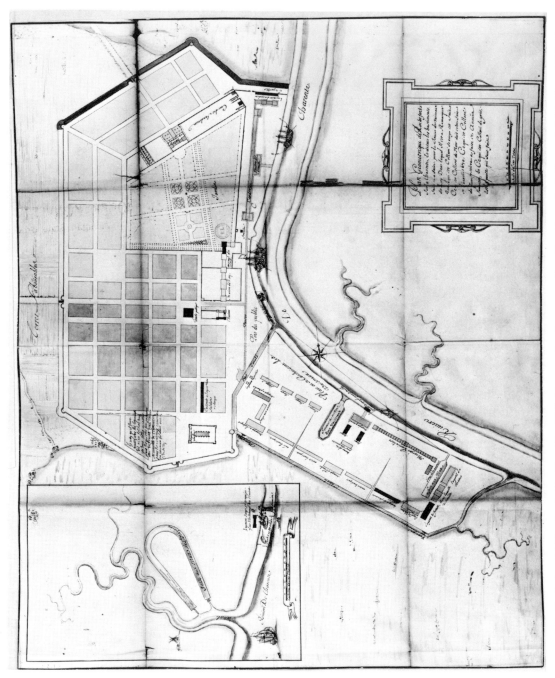

FIGURE 4.3. *Rochefort, 1669, plan by De Clerville. Bibliothèque nationale, manuscripts, Cinq Cents de Colbert, vol. 123. Photo Bibliothèque nationale, Paris.*

The type of planning that would enhance the reputation of the king in one city might appear so out of place in another that the king would look ridiculous.

Theories about city planning were translated into actual plans for Rochefort under Colbert's guidance. He started out with the idea that Rochefort would be built to look like a great port and with the hope that its appearance would enhance its role. An arsenal surrounded by a chaotically growing city was unacceptable to a government afraid of urban disorder. Thus, the government planned Rochefort so that urban growth would not impede arsenal operations. How much and what kind of formal design would be necessary to achieve these goals were questions that Colbert answered in his reactions to sketches for Rochefort submitted between 1667 and 1669.

The first design was submitted by Nicolas de Clerville. He modified his plan for Rochefort three times until, in 1669, it met with the minister's approval. In 1668 Blondel constructed a design (now lost),[71] and in 1671 and 1672 François Le Vau revised de Clerville's final plan.

De Clerville began with an imaginative and complex design fit for a display of royal splendor. He sketched his first plan into the upper-right-hand corner of a map of the Charente basin (figure 4.2). It displayed a rectilinear, enclosed arsenal compound with a city adjoining it but separate in design. In some respects the plan was an adaptation of the town of Richelieu,[72] built by Cardinal Richelieu in the 1630s: it had the same two residential squares on which market and church were located, connected by one street and surrounded by more residential blocks. In Richelieu, however, the château was at one end of this street, placed where the large park would have been in Rochefort. By contrast, de Clerville placed the *maison du roy* (at once command post and residence of the leading royal official) in a dominating, symmetrically arranged position overlooking the arsenal and the river. He framed the building with two compounds for the navy's officers, thus pushing the town firmly inland. Appropriately, the park was reserved for navy personnel, not townspeople: its radial walks started at the government compound.

Colbert de Terron, first cousin to Colbert and the royal officer responsible for Rochefort, liked this plan, preferring it to a design Blondel had prepared on his return from the Antilles.[73] But Colbert did not agree. A record of his objections is not preserved, but it is possible to suggest what they may have been by comparing two other plans by de Clerville with his first one.[74]

The differences in opinion between Colbert and de Clerville demonstrate Colbert's willingness to analyze a design in terms of its function. The minister disapproved of Versailles because it was monumentally wasteful, and conceived of order, careful planning, and efficiency as the values to be stressed in strong government and absolutist organization; he did not want Rochefort to be designed in a courtly and decorative manner. Colbert rejected those parts of de Clerville's plans which sacrificed the city's efficiency as an arsenal to pure form; he wanted a design that would enhance the city's strictly utilitarian role. That plan might be embellished—time and money permitting—to represent Louis's *gloire* more strikingly. But Colbert concentrated his efforts on a plan to make Rochefort an efficient and productive arsenal city. A city solely designed for shipbuilding would sufficiently enhance Louis's *gloire* by its very existence and activity.

In his next plans de Clerville retained something of the two principal squares that he had copied from Richelieu, but he modified the rest of the plan drastically. The park still started in the administrative sector, but that district had been greatly reduced in scope. The officers' quarters were eliminated and the *maison du roy* was less imposing, less like a nobleman's château. Residential blocks were more fully extended throughout the city and around the park. In the first of these two plans, the church was imposingly centered in a large square of rather sophisticated design, but in the second, that square was removed and the church's location was not even identified; presumably it was to be erected on any one of four open squares. These modifications reduced the autonomy and distinctiveness of the city to the monotony and grid pattern of an army camp: formal squares to enhance housing districts were rejected for a pattern of simple, vacant blocks.

Perhaps Colbert wanted Rochefort to be a city without any distinctive topographic features. Although the city was large enough to provide space for the more than ten thousand people who eventually lived there during Louis's reign, people were not to be overawed. Nothing, not even the *maison du roy* itself, was allowed to detract from the importance of the arsenal in de Clerville's final plan (figure 4.3). The grid pattern was taken to its dullest and most economical extreme: all the blocks but one (a cemetery) were designated for housing, and the market was placed close to the port in one of the squares left empty in the third plan. Several blocks (to the far left of the map) were reserved for barracks for twelve hundred soldiers. By contrast, progressively greater attention was paid to the variety of geometric patterns in the *jardin du roy*. De Clerville, in his first plan, had gone too far in the conscious use of proportion, symmetry, and design to set the city apart as a unique creation. In the final plan, Rochefort no longer reflected the imagination that went into Vitry-le-François, Richelieu, or Charleville—the smaller, quiet noble-estate towns of the sixteenth and seventeenth centuries—or the boldness and drama reserved for Marseille and Paris.

When François Le Vau[75] visited Rochefort in 1671 and 1672 to supervise the execution of the final plan, he could not resist the opportunity to enliven its monotonous features. He believed, moreover, that his proposals would add harmony and unity to Colbert's more austere concept. He wrote, ". . . for the order and the beautiful decoration of all the buildings . . . at Rochefort, it would be desirable that [the buildings] be better distributed and connected to each other to form a regular shape among themselves, which would present a magnificent appearance by their grandeur and by their number, . . . such as one should desire of such a superb enterprise."[76] In Le Vau's opinion, a handsome appearance was required for Rochefort, lest it be unworthy of its royal sponsor. He wanted to extend the city toward the port area with a semicircular arrangement of walls and buildings, erect a church in the middle facing the market, and construct three units of housing and offices reaching from the *maison du roy* on one side of the church to an armory on the other (figure 4.4). The four main streets of the city would end along this complex.[77]

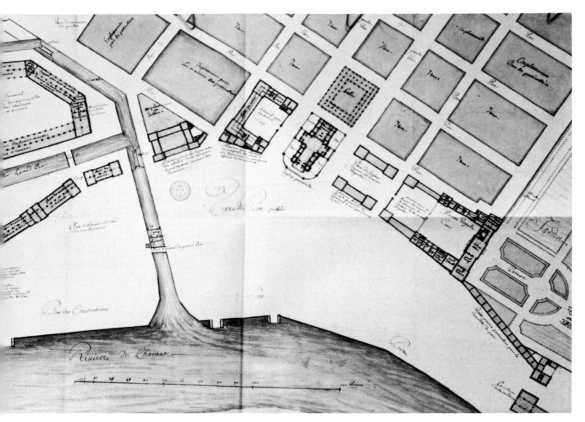

FIGURE **4.4.** *Rochefort, 1671, plan by Le Vau, Maps 144–177. Manuscript Collection, Service historique de la Marine, Paris.*

It was a sophisticated design, worked out with three perspectives in mind: that of the ensemble from the river (as such, this was one of the early French examples of architectonic planning from the point of view of the water looking onto the land), that of the royal compound (housing, offices, parade ground, church, and garden together), and that of the city (market and church, with all city streets open toward the port).[78] There is, unfortunately, no record of Colbert's reactions to this more obvious attempt to express grandeur. Le Vau himself raised the objection of expense and, given Colbert's dissatisfaction with fleet operations at Rochefort in 1670 and 1671, it is understandable why the minister never pursued the project. Le Vau's plan would have enhanced Rochefort's appearance without making the city a more effective, efficient naval base.

When simple grid patterns have been used in city planning, it is often because a more imaginative design has not been conceived. Rochefort's grid plan, however, was the result of a process of elimination, an effort to select the most appropriate design. In fact, the aesthetics of grandeur were worked out on a very reasonable if subtle and unambitious scale in de Clerville's final plan. Colbert was critical of what de Clerville would make of Rochefort, but not because he rejected the theories behind the plans. Grandeur and *gloire* were effective components of state power that Colbert could manipulate more imaginatively than de Clerville or Le Vau. Under Colbert's sponsorship the facade of the Louvre was redesigned to express grandeur in statecraft with obviousness, but there was no reason for Rochefort to make that sort of impression. Grandeur and *gloire* would emerge from Rochefort in the form of fleets and shipbuilding. Colbert wanted Rochefort to be a famous city, not on its own account, but only as the construction site of the king's fleets. Thus the city was designed pragmatically to emphasize and enhance that activity. The functional spatial qualities of the final plan were evident in the separation of the arsenal from the city, in the large proportion of that city reserved for housing, and in the unadorned grid that focused the city and its inhabitants on the navy and on the king's service. It was the intention of the plan to form the inhabitants into an effective and docile work force whose activities would bring fame to the city and *gloire* to the king. Visibly, the city's only reason for existing was to serve the monarchy. Because its spacious, zoned, and ordered street pattern clearly showed itself to be a product of a single, coherent vision, Rochefort managed to represent the order and power inherent in and necessary to Louis's maritime ambitions.

The story of Rochefort demonstrates that the interests of state did not dominate city planning easily; it indicates what Colbert achieved by directing the spatial imagination toward new opportunities in the service of the king. When Colbert thought that visually potent and purely symbolic forms would express *gloire* and grandeur, as in Paris and Marseille, those opportunities involved costly and elaborate designs. But when he ordered the king's ships decorated with costly and artistically rich designs because "ships should give some idea of the grandeur of the king by their beauty,"[79] he limited his artists to designs that corresponded to the seaworthiness of the ships.[80] Colbert was interested in the appropriate form for a given function. The simplicity of Rochefort's final design can be explained in those terms, even though written evidence alone cannot account for the city's form and appearance. When other validating textual evidence is lost, pictorial documents such as maps and plans can suggest the thinking of the city's builders. These maps and drawings are at once the only evidence that an effort was made to plan Rochefort's topography and the only sign of what the social or political preoccupations of the planners may have been.

A study of housing reveals how planning affected Rochefort's development. The comprehensive city plan of 1669 dealt with housing insofar as it provided for the separation of workers' homes from their places of work. This reduced the danger to the arsenal from fire and strengthened the maintenance of security, but the wide streets and airy housing districts were also supposed to lessen the spread of disease, which they did not: planners were surprised when they found that, as Rochefort grew in size, the incidence of malarial fever rose.[81] More importantly, Louis and his agents could cope with the sudden, then continuous, arrival of newcomers because they had designed the city to grow as the arsenal increased its activity. Theirs was no small achievement.

To guarantee the success of the plan, the government not only compelled all residents to build within its regimented pattern; it also assisted them financially in constructing housing. Louis wanted people to settle in Rochefort and he was willing to make a move to Rochefort financially rewarding for the common people. In particular, he was willing to listen to Colbert de Terron, who advised that an offer of free housing might be one way to induce people to settle in the new city.[82] This produced an order to build numerous wooden and stone cabins and houses on royal land, and another permitting all newcomers to pay a minimal property tax. Concerned that a lack of housing might disturb the ordered pattern of military life that he desired,[83] Louis became the city's principal landlord and contractor. Naturally, some people with means took advantage of these offers and speculated by reselling the land or by demanding exorbitant rents as if they, not Louis, were the rightful owners. Eventually, such profiteering was punished.[84]

Because he owned nearly all the land of the city, Louis could control housing to a considerable extent. He owned all the blocks closest to the area of the *maison du roy* and to the entrance to the arsenal. These were considered more desirable than the privately owned blocks, and were the most densely developed until a shortage of land forced people to build on the periphery. But in the 1680s (coincidentally, at the time he transferred Rochefort's prominent role to Brest), Louis decided to sell his property to use the profits to underwrite construction of new arsenal buildings.[85] In this way he yielded some of the government's initiative over housing to private interests he had previously chastised. In 1681 he sold twenty-five lots for £8,030. The properties had increased in value at an average of 3.8 percent per year—not a bad return on the royal investment in housing. This was a limited operation affecting a small number of people and properties, but among the buyers were many of the principal merchants and royal officers of Rochefort.[86] After 1687, when Louis decided to get out of the business of owning and renting housing altogether, the rest of Rochefort's housing was presumably built privately. An important exception was made in 1700, when it was ordered that houses built of wood should be rebuilt in stone to prevent fire, and royal funds were provided to help defray costs.[87]

Even after housing became a totally private affair, it remained as ordered as the government wished it to be. Over the previous two decades, people had separated along streets according to status and occupation, so that the grid pattern became a matrix of social organization. That the housing plan thus became an element of social life no doubt helped perpetuate the original layout. But by the 1690s, because the city's population continued to grow even though most of the available land was in use, people began to settle outside the walls, along the road to La Rochelle. Although the government was reluctant to plan a suburb, it ordered the intendant, Bégon, to direct any future new housing along that road and to discourage housing parallel to the city's fortifications.[88]

The steps the government had taken to zone and regulate housing showed results. During thirty-five years of port activity, tens of thousands had come to Rochefort without provoking disorder. What occurred in 1705, when the navy ceased to pay its employees regularly and people started to leave, might have been common from the beginning had there been no housing plan predating the settlement of Rochefort: government agents could do nothing to prevent poor families from living as squatters within the arsenal compound, these squatters pilfered regularly from the arsenal's supplies,[89] and they tried to set fire to the entire compound.[90] Orders came in 1706 to force the squatters out and destroy their shacks, but not until 1707 were they obeyed.[91]

Planning Brest and Lorient

In contrast to the situation in Rochefort, housing in Brest and Lorient came under the immediate responsibility of the intendants in charge, who faced a shortage of housing in each city when its port first became important. In the years 1670 and 1671 there was enough housing in Brest for only two-thirds of the labor force.[92] At Lorient conditions were worse, for barely half the work force found housing there (the rest stayed in adjacent villages.)[93] This had a pernicious effect on the arsenal's work, because the many workers who lived at a distance began work later than those who lived close to the arsenal. Louis would not have tolerated such conditions in Rochefort in the late 1660s.[94]

At first, and on their own initiative, the intendants encouraged newcomers to live in the arsenal, which solved the problems created when workers had to travel sizeable distances each day. In Brest, de Seuil built up parts of vacant quayside land into warehouses, shops, and housing in 1673 and 1674. He also allowed people to build there after paying rent at one sol per foot of frontage, which was one-tenth of its value.[95] Even so, many workers simply squatted on arsenal grounds or lived in unused arsenal buildings. This had the effect of keeping the population of Brest-Recouvrance within the dense, historic core of the city so that, despite the increase in population, by 1680 Brest and Recouvrance were not much more spread out than they had been ten or fifteen years earlier.

The situation was not much different in Lorient. There, too, workers were permitted to live close to the buildings in which they worked. Céberet, a director of the Compagnie des Indes and an early administrator of the arsenal for the king, allowed this situation to develop when he provided newcomers with old wood with which to build shanties and cabins.[96] He even asked the king to build barracks for four hundred workers, arguing that despite Louis's decision to use Lorient for a short time, the buildings would not be costly and could be used afterward by the Compagnie.[97] The next year, 1692, he was still providing lumber to workmen so that they might build their own housing,[98] and what he did not offer, they pilfered from the arsenal.[99] As in Brest, clusters of shanties within the arsenal were a threat to the navy, and, for both Brest and Lorient, the only solution was to separate housing from the work site so that both could be ordered more effectively.

In 1680, finding these conditions insupportable and wishing to make a great port city of Brest, Colbert and Louis ordered Sainte-Colombe, an engineer, to make a master plan for its growth. That plan provided for the spatial separation of activities and for a vastly enlarged residential district within an outline of a larger, unified city composed of a regimented, unbroken, unembellished grid pattern of blocks. Sainte-Colombe anticipated the need for fortifications embracing an enlarged Brest-Recouvrance (figure 4.5), but he did not make the mistake of composing a design that could only be completed if the entire space enclosed by those defense works were filled in at once.

Vauban had an opportunity in 1681 to suggest improvements, and he inserted into Sainte-Colombe's scheme a unified composition for Brest of church, market, and formal residential square to enhance the city's appearance as a government creation (figure 4.6).[100] He placed the market near the main street and close to the city's gate, and planned to attach it to the courts and town hall. By placing the church between the market and the *maison du roy,* Vauban built the connection between church and state into the topographic fabric of Brest. Most important, both church and market would be surrounded by a formal residential square, "the best placed district in the city."[101] Vauban explicitly stated that he wanted the church, market, and homes to form one district at the access point between the city and the arsenal. He wanted new city growth to focus on buildings that spoke clearly to all inhabitants of Louis's power over their lives and of his influence over their city. Significantly, Recouvrance, whose former autonomy and greater size symbolized a time when government control was incomplete, was so entirely absorbed into the newly enlarged city that it received none of the public buildings around which city life revolved. The new Brest was created on royal initiative to serve Louis's power, and through his placing of public buildings, Vauban imposed an architectonic expression of that initiative onto the city's grid plan as effectively as Colbert had in Rochefort. Both men achieved the same results; the topographic, physical difference between Brest and Rochefort, which their plans respected, was in fact superficial.

In Lorient the government's agents moved toward the same separation of housing from arsenal in 1699, several years after the government had begun to use that site and then only because it was clear that exploitation by squatters would continue. The government's agents intended to plan a new city outside the arsenal walls, one large enough to support a population of eight thousand.[102] Mauclerc, Louis's senior agent at Lorient in 1700, thought that the removal of the workers would pose few problems. He wrote that the best cabin was not worth more than ten écus, and that most were owned without title and had been built at the expense of the king, anyway. Mauclerc thought that the workers could rebuild their shacks on land outside the arsenal, which would be purchased by the monarchy from its present owner (the lieutenant general of the admiralty at Vannes) and be sold to the new tenants at a profit (which could be used on public buildings, such as a church).[103] In that same year of 1700, therefore, all those who had crowded into the arsenal compound were ordered to live outside, on land on which a city would be built.[104] Thus the housing problem at Lorient presented an opportunity for Louis's agents to transform the temporary arsenal and its colony of workers into a more permanent, efficient, and handsome community.

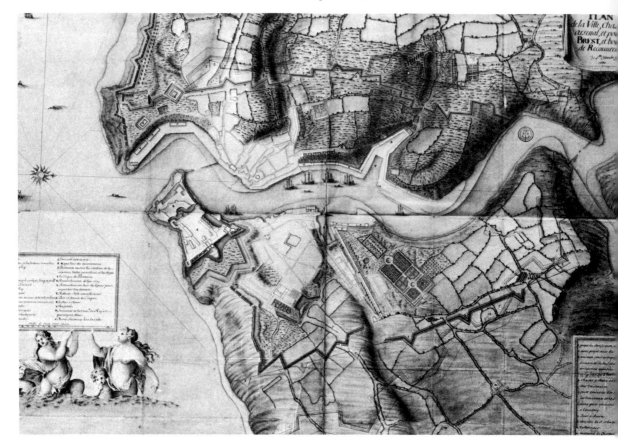

FIGURE 4.5. *Brest, 1680, plan by Sainte-Colombe, Maps 144–186. Manuscript Collection, Service historique de la Marine, Paris.*

Once housing and arsenal activities were officially separated—in Brest after 1681 and in Lorient after 1700—how did each city grow? Was spatial order introduced, and were living and working conditions improved, as the government had intended? The government certainly wanted people in Brest to live in the new districts marked out by Sainte-Colombe. In 1681 Seignelay, Colbert's son and brilliant successor as minister of the navy from 1683 to 1690, visited Brest to supervise the execution of the spatial plan. He ordered the squatters in the arsenal to leave within two weeks, and insisted on the strict separation of arsenal from residential districts to the point of ordering that a principal navy warehouse standing outside the arsenal be moved.[105] Vauban even urged that people be given land, arguing that the construction of new houses would increase the value of the king's investment.[106] But Louis, now giving up his role as landlord in Rochefort, did nothing to help in the construction of new housing in Brest, citing a lack of funds.[107] And since he took no financial interest in the new construction, it was harder for his agents in Brest to compel people to build within the boundaries of the plan. Some

FIGURE **4.6.** *Brest, 1683, plan by Vauban, after Sainte-Colombe, 8/1/1/7. Archives du Génie, Paris.*

inhabitants, especially navy officers, no doubt continued to build on navy land in defiance of Louis's orders.[108] More important to the agents was the fact that even after the plan of 1680 was introduced, some people felt free to build where they wanted outside the arsenal. The government did not use force against resisters,[109] and only in the 1690s did it begin to expropriate their land and impose the outlines of the 1681 plan on those who had built contrary to them. Louis might have done better to have become Brest's principal landlord. Most of the city's land fell into the hands of a few urban seigneurs who rented rooms, houses, and shacks to people of standing and to workers alike.[110] Population pressure and full employment encouraged landlords to charge steep rents. Louis tried to stabilize rents and additionally tax the landlords' excessive profits several times, but without apparent success.[111] When Louis finally expropriated land, the value had risen so much that he tried to avoid giving full value; but the landholders, including the Duchess of Portsmouth, engaged a lawyer to represent them in Paris, and secured a favorable decision in the end.[112]

Nevertheless, most townspeople and landholders cooperated with the government by building and living where the government wanted. Sainte-Colombe's plan apparently absorbed Brest's fourfold increase in population from 1680 to 1705. His plan of 1680 (figure 4.5) had called for fortifications well beyond the existing city perimeter to enclose new city blocks conforming to topography. By 1694 many areas within the fortifications boundaries were built up: on the right (or north) side of the Penfield River (the part formerly called Recouvrance), housing was still limited to the old district near the quays, and the vast area on top of the cliffs was still uninhabited; on the left (or south) side of the Penfield, the old core, close to the arsenal and port, remained, but there was much new housing around the church, the market, and the *maison du roy*, most of it conforming to the plan. The government had decided in 1680 to make a great port city of Brest, and a plan was provided at that time to order its growth. The government was rewarded with a large measure of success because royal agents worked hard to execute the plan, and because the city's rapid and continual growth in population encouraged landholders and newcomers alike to make use of the clearly delineated blocks of land it provided.

The difference a usable plan makes can be measured by comparing Brest and Lorient. The government wanted to maintain Lorient as a temporary naval base, not establish it as a permanent city, and so was reluctant to do more than decree a separation between arsenal and housing. The order expelling those living within the arsenal compound was not followed up immediately with any provision for alternative housing or with a spatial plan orienting the development of a housing district. Thus many people remained where they were within the arsenal compound: officers kept their quarters there and many of the shacks were never razed. In 1701 the Compagnie des Indes found 139 heads of households residing on its property, of whom more than half were artisans employed in the arsenal.[113] Even in 1719, when another census was taken, 114 shacks were occupied.[114]

Those who did move out after 1700 built their homes where they wished. Clairambault, the government's agent, observed that streets had never been traced out:[115] the homes outside the arsenal ran along two or three haphazardly defined streets (figure 4.7). A spatial plan only emerged because, in 1705, when the government decided to enclose the new residential area with fortifications, Clairambault seized the opportunity to make the city permanent through topographic design. He wanted to create for Lorient a future that, as a temporary naval base, it was not supposed to have.[116]

Clairambault was allowed to proceed only because he found a way to make his scheme self-financing.[117] A report from Lille gave him the idea of buying the land with royal funds, duly compensating the owners, laying out new streets and squares, and then reselling it to the former residents at a profit measured by the increased value of the land within the plan. The profits, perhaps £20,000 (or nearly double the investment), would go to the king.[118] (Clairambault may have hoped to speculate on and profit from these land sales, too.) Within a few months, an engineer, Langlade, had contributed a plan for a layout of a new city within walls that made use of the streets the

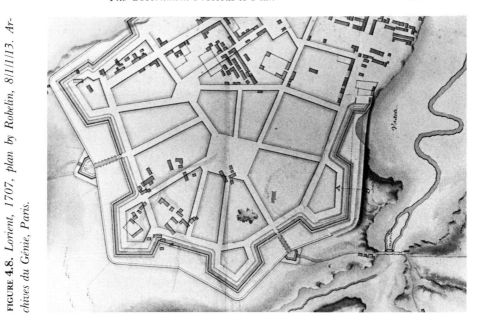

FIGURE 4.7. (left) Lorient, 1703, 8/1/11?. Archives du Génie, Paris.

FIGURE 4.8. Lorient, 1707, plan by Robelin, 8/1/1/13. Archives du Génie, Paris.

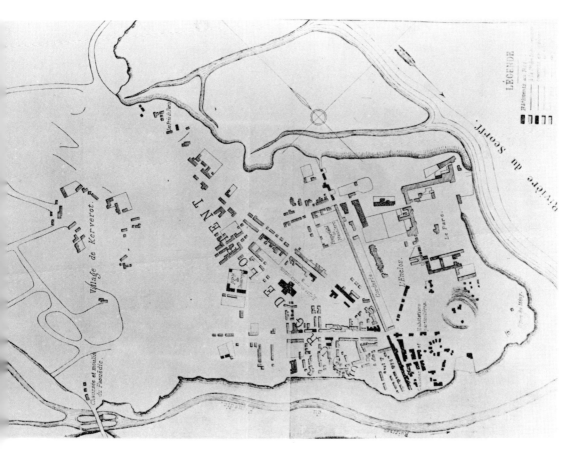

homeowners had created inadvertently.[119] In 1707 Langlade and Robelin, senior engineer at Brest, revised this plan to structure the housing pattern that had developed spontaneously into a network of new streets and public squares (figure 4.8).[120] Once Vauban reviewed the plan, Louis approved the financing.

Work proceeded with forced labor drawn from neighboring towns;[121] but by the end of Louis's reign, the plan had been only partly executed. Many people wanted to build according to the new plan once they understood that it could make Lorient more attractive and could increase the value of their property,[122] but many others, who objected to being told where to live, moved outside the planned boundaries, or else refused to move off their land at all. Finally, Clairambault asked for and received a royal order forbidding residents to build outside the planned layout, on pain of destruction of their homes,[123] but the process of expropriation and compensation that followed was complicated and lengthy. Louis himself gave contradictory orders, for at the same time that he ordered people to build according to the plan, he allowed existing farmlands within the walled perimeter to remain under cultivation (these were years of grain shortages).[124] Thus, despite the government's will to persevere and turn plans into marked streets on Lorient's soil, the people were at liberty to build and live where they wished. Lorient's housing remained a problem for Louis's agents, not only because arsonists tried on two occasions to set fire to the tawdry complex of shacks and sheds which composed that arsenal city, but also because the incomplete plan seemed to symbolize Lorient's uncertain future as a royal naval base.

This comparative study of the planning of housing districts illustrates how the individual character of each new port city was molded by the ways the government used and planned it so as to improve maritime operations. This explains why Brest and Lorient, with fundamentally similar housing problems in 1680 and 1690, respectively, were treated so differently. Although the government was concerned about the social consequences of bad housing in Lorient, it dispensed at first with an effective housing plan because it intended Lorient to remain a temporary base; Lorient was allowed to take on the social and visual features of a permanent city only when there seemed to be no other way to order its existence and growth. The government's hesitation when dealing with Lorient was largely political in nature, as was its eagerness to improve living and working conditions in Brest through spatial planning. The thousands who moved to Brest during its period of most rapid growth (1680–1715) were able to find or build housing along well laid out, regular streets away from the arsenal. The government's response to the housing problems in these two cities is a clear example of how boldly and thoroughly it could adapt each city to its role.

Social Geography

In the newly laid out cities of Brest and Rochefort, once a grid pattern was created, people separated themselves by wealth or occupation and thus established permanent social communities. Perhaps the very opportunity to do so helped make the effort at functional land-use planning succeed. In these cities, shopkeepers, merchants, and officers tended to live in close proximity to each other and apart from laborers. Housing patterns derived from fiscal registers are evidence that residents established themselves in a traditional mold for European urban society. The wealthier residents of Brest, those who paid an average tax that was twice the mean tax for all residents, lived along three streets. Of the 146 servants employed in Brest, 85 were employed in households there. Along these same streets resided 29 of the 38 royal officers, 73 of 104 merchants, 25 of Brest's 28 taxpaying members of liberal professions, and skilled craftsmen and shopkeepers in large numbers. But only 5 of Brest's 53 carpenters lived among them. In contrast, one-third of the day laborers and sailors lived on two other streets.[125] In Rochefort, too, streets traced by a grid pattern assumed the social character of those who lived on them. Nearly half the merchants, as well as many artisans and some members of the liberal professions, lived on the four streets closest to the city's center. Their average tax assessment was greater than that of the city as a whole. No sailors or day laborers, and only a few carpenters, lived with them. The less-well-off residents lived on the periphery of the city and in its nascent suburb, beyond the walls.[126] Louis cooperated with the bourgeoisie of Rochefort to house all the military personnel in barracks on the far side of the city,[127] sparing householders the burden of billeting. Lorient did not follow this pattern, for even the 1705 new city plan did not become a topographic or social reality during Louis XIV's reign. If there was any impulse among Lorient's residents to organize their housing by wealth, position, and occupation, it was frustrated by the lack of a topographic layout along which the social differences between people could be plotted. But enough of the plan and its promise were sufficiently visible to royal agents and to the townspeople so that they came to believe Lorient was about to become a permanent social community like the other cities.

The government abstained from imposing a spatial plan on Sète because geography provided the natural organization for housing separate from the port. Brest, Rochefort, and Lorient began as vacant, undefined territories with no distinctive geographic outlines. Sète began differently. When de Clerville was constructing the first breakwater, the workers lived in shacks on the cliff overlooking the port. As the community grew, the shacks increased in number, forming a row on either side of a long and narrow street on the cliff that extended as far as the church. Most of the people who lived on this street did not own their homes, but they did own and cultivate small vineyards on the terraced sides of Mont St. Clair above.[128] Senior royal officials, merchants, and bourgeois, who owned most of the property in Sète, lived on more spacious tracts on the open, gently sloping ground between the church and the water. How different in quality was their residential district, composed of open space and gardens, from the narrow street along which the laborers lived in small hovels, either against the city walls or on the edge of the cliff. Of the landowners, 5 percent were royal officers who, collectively, possessed 38 percent of the land as assessed by its value. In contrast, 25 percent of the landowners were workers, but they owned just 3 percent of the land as assessed by its value. The church was erected exactly at the point where the level street on the cliff along which the workers lived broke to descend to the quays. One flight of steps brought them down to the church; another stairway brought Sète's wealthier residents up to it. Architectonically, the church with its two flights of steps gave public expression to the division of private property, according to Sète's natural geography, into socially defined districts.

For all the Atlantic cities, and for Sète on the Mediterranean as well, the transformation of space into distinct social patterns made that space and the community that orchestrated itself within it seem permanent and public. Public, because the different parts of the city and the social groups located in each were visible to all, and permanent, because such segregation described not only the existence of social groups, but the conditions of their cohesion and survival as well;[129] social geography translated the organization of space into a self-validating and self-sustaining framework for daily living. To the extent that the overlay of social and topographic features may have impressed the inhabitants with a sense that the city belonged to them, spatial planning, and at a minimum the separation of housing from port, could have worked against the government's aim to fashion each new city in its image. But this did not happen. Even during the fiscal crisis of the 1690 to 1715 period, Brest and Rochefort did not engage Versailles in controversies over taxes and trade, and Lorient and Sète, which did, were unable to influence the government's decisions much. No new port city released itself from the government's network of port cities to which it belonged by adopting a willful pose of municipal autonomy. The new cities had little or no control over how, why, or when they grew, or over the spatial form that growth took. Despite size, social complexity, and spatial permanence, they remained metropolitan colonies of Louis XIV.

Spatial planning reveals how the new cities became established. In the final analysis, it also illustrates where city space belonged in the government's understanding of maritime exploitation. Clearly, the government of Louis XIV believed that city space conditioned port activities and thus indirectly influenced trading opportunities and naval engagements. The French did not substitute spatial planning for the husbandry of material resources and manpower, for the development of commercial and military maritime affairs or for the skillful administration of the navy itself, but they did understand that the treatment of port and city as autonomous yet interrelated places could make those tasks easier. If, in addition, Louis and his associates thought that spatial planning could play a moralizing role in the life of the new communities, at least they also understood that urban forms do not have abstract, absolute, a priori values but only take on values in particular settings. Their feel for spatial planning was marked by a balance between tradition and flexibility that was at once sophisticated and practical.

V

Civic Order
and Patterns of Growth
in the New Cities

Two Societies

City planning cannot by itself explain how large numbers of people living in the new French cities formed permanent settlements. Clearly, spatial planning had more of an impact on city growth and on the usefulness of the new cities to the French state than did deliberately phrased and manipulated legal, institutional, and fiscal structures. But all these efforts at planning encouraged the transformation of settlements into cities only by providing each place with the appearance of permanency. The government could try to attract people to the new cities, but it could not compel them to come or to stay. Indeed, it did not need to. Why did the French move to the new cities, and what process of acculturation bound them into new communities? A global history channeling the arrival of thousands in Brest, Lorient, Rochefort, and Sète into social patterns cannot be written from the few surviving parish registers, tax records, and government memoranda. However, enough can be learned from these documents about demographic patterns, social structures, city-region interaction, and popular life to indicate how the new cities grew and in what ways they were different from other port cities in France.

For the purposes of this study, it is inconsequential that the date for each new settlement becoming a metropolitan colony of Bourbon France cannot be specified more precisely than the early 1670s for Rochefort and Sète, the early 1680s for Brest, and the early 1700s for Lorient. What counts is the fact that the new cities were characteristically different from other French seaports in similar ways. They sheltered two societies that were separated not by material wealth and status so much as by political power and culture. One was composed of the many who came to the new port cities because France's drive for sea power provided opportunities for work; it looked upon life in those cities opportunistically. The other, composed of the few who served the French state as its administrators and agents, had as its mission oversight of the first group. Although the two societies lived in one space, each used that space and perceived the other group in it in different terms. Neither the workers and their families nor the royal officers and agents seem to have learned much about each other from their contacts in the new cities; each group continued to perceive the other with values and prejudices acquired elsewhere. Nevertheless, each group, each society, needed the other; they all understood that the destinies of the new port cities were not theirs to determine. Neither group could transform its energies and hopes into the autonomous exploitation of the sea, neither was free from the dictates of state policy and open to the rhythms of discovery, innovation, and enterprise, as were workers and the upper class (who acted with more unity of effort) in Saint-Mâlo, Rouen, Nantes, Bordeaux, and Marseille.

Secular and Spiritual Authority

In 1669 the navy hired several score Dutch carpenters to go to Rochefort to teach what they knew of shipbuilding. They came in several separate groups to work in an area where for over one hundred years the Dutch had been helping the French build dikes to contain salt evaporation pans. Soon, however, Colbert de Terron advised Colbert, "... as regards the Dutch, I am of the opinion that more should not be brought in a hurry.... unless they be Catholics who come to settle.... It will be better if they come singly rather than altogether; we will Frenchify them better [nous les franciserons mieux]."[1]

Making Frenchmen of the newcomers meant getting them to give up their respective political and cultural identities (the better to serve the Bourbons). The task that de Terron felt was his when the Dutch arrived in a remote and unhealthy Charente enclave also confronted the intendants of Brest and Lorient when they received workers from Brittany, the Basque country, and the Saintonge. Knowing that the newcomers lacked feelings of patriotism and notions of service to the state,[2] royal officers, following the example set by Louis XIV and his court and armies,[3] worked to suppress provincial loyalties and patterns of popular behavior, which in their eyes symbolized insubordination and immorality. The regulation of morals was a common feature of urban life in France at that time because in most communities social groups and institutions existed that claimed responsibility for the welfare of the common people. In the new port cities, however, justification for such regulation and the means to enforce it were markedly different—the state itself, and not a local authority or patriciate, defined the rules of acceptable behavior. Directly involving itself in this task, the government tried hard to create a new urban culture in its own image, to make work in the arsenals and life in the new port cities uniquely French experiences. It used administrative authority and the Church to mold the inhabitants into an obedient and ordered community: edicts, sermons, searches, inquiries, roundups, and lists of names became commonplace. Efforts to reform popular life hint at what can be known of that life and indicate how arrival and residence in the new port cities became a process of acculturation.

With nothing so obvious as a red-light district to frequent, men nevertheless had ample opportunity to find prostitutes in the port cities. The women apparently picked up trade in the streets or taverns; the disease their presence spread was undoubtedly one reason the navy maintained a hospital in each arsenal city.[4] However, health was not the only concern that spurred the government to take steps to remove the prostitutes: it also found their trade morally offensive and corrupting. Prostitutes were either locked up in a country house[5] or simply expelled from the city.[6] Louis preferred that the women be punished publicly—placed in stocks, dunked in water, or beaten and branded.[7] Yet he also encouraged more constructive measures: in Brest, for example, some were housed at state expense (£6,000 yearly) and were put to work making textiles for the navy.[8] As for the men, it was proposed that they might better occupy their time with gymnastics or with games such as lawn bowling.[9] "But they always return,"[10] wrote Arnoul from Rochefort, and any intendant might have said the same. Prostitution remained a problem. Moreover, believed the intendants, it was brought on by the women, who were the corrupters to be punished, and not by the men, who had to be saved from them.

Debauchery was not the only release the government tried to deny the workers. Troops of comedians were expressly forbidden to stay in Brest on two occasions because it was feared they would turn the men from their work and take their money.[11] For the same reasons public dances were outlawed in Brest and its environs; if any took place, dancers and musicians would have to raise £30 between them to pay a fine.[12] To curb drunkenness, drinking hours were regulated in Lorient by restricting the sale and consumption of wine and spirits to a canteen with fixed hours,[13] and in Brest by forbidding tavernkeepers to sell drinks after 9 P.M., " . . . to prevent the disturbances which usually occur."[14]

Certain behavior was morally or socially inappropriate, and unacceptable, in the new cities. Worse, there was the fear that people who were rowdy, drunk, or disorderly after work hours might remain so at work. Knowing that many (if not most) workers were unfamiliar with the work discipline demanded in shipbuilding, the intendants tried to regulate as much of their lives as they could, and promised to carry out orders to keep the men on the job.[15] Those who could not adapt, those who remained subversives, malcontents, troublemakers, did not belong, and insofar as it was possible, were evicted with the prostitutes. To execute the order to expel "all unknown and idle persons," those who might start a fire or provoke a riot,[16] intendants ordered that the residence, place of origin, and occupation of all people not employed at the arsenal be reported to them.[17] In addition, lists (now lost) were made in Lorient of the residence of every inhabitant, the length of residence, and the rent that was paid.[18]

Foreigners were under collective suspicion. Welcomed in the 1660s and 1670s, when they could teach the craft of shipbuilding to the French, they could not stay in the port cities in the 1690s and after, when they were no longer needed. If any number of the thousands of Irish exiles who arrived in Brest in the 1690s were to stay in that city, their presence might radically alter town life and affect arsenal efficiency; they would have to assimilate elsewhere. Those who were not French could not serve the French king: Protestants and Catholics alike from countries allied with France were expelled.[19] In 1695 Louis XIV ordered all foreigners, except those married Irish who were employed in the arsenal and who had children, out of Brest in a fortnight. Nevertheless, no foreigner, not even those few Irish, could be trusted to serve Louis loyally. Warned Pontchartrain, ". . . on the subject of the Irish who remain in Brest, you cannot take enough precautions against these people."[20] (Xenophobic attitudes still pervade French navy regulations, for although foreigners may enter army or air force bases, they are strictly forbidden to enter navy arsenals. French citizens may enter any of these military bases freely.)

Only one instance can be cited in which the government reversed itself and consciously exploited the parochial, regional identity of workers. When an arsenal was established in Lorient, an effort was made to send Bretons to Rochefort and Basques and Gascons to Lorient.[21] The government hoped the men would work more diligently if they were isolated as groups, linguistically and socially, in a new and disorienting environment. They could not make contact with the people who lived around them, but only with each other and their employers. The result was disappointing for the government. Bretons had visited the Charente coast for generations, as sailors engaged in the salt trade; they integrated easily. The Basques left Lorient at Easter to return home, with the excuse that not enough Basque-speaking priests served in Brittany; many did not return north later that spring.

The government's lack of success in this case is rich with a comic irony, because the workers were able to turn the government's strategy to their own advantage. The government acted with more enthusiasm than knowledge or understanding when it tried to manipulate regional or national identity as a police measure, but this should not diminish our respect for Louis's administration, which was engaged in a task without precedent. Louis's maritime ambitions called for more cultural and technological innovations than the proto-industrial economy of the *ancien régime* could absorb, but efforts at direct social control in Brest, Rochefort, and Lorient hint at modernity nevertheless. Political and industrial revolutions a century later cracked traditional ways of working and patterns of allegiance more decisively than did Louis's pursuit of grandeur, and modern governments, more grasping and powerful than Louis's, have exploited disciplined work forces and patriotism with considerable results. Louis's innovations, like Piranesi's prison drawings, preface the transformation of absolutism into totalitarianism.

In the seventeenth-century world, religious life and institutions and secular notions of order were so intertwined that their separation can only be brought about by the historian, for his own purposes. There was nothing surprising about the government's desire to use church and priest as well as administrative sanctions to control the population; after all, Louis thought irreligion might be the cause of civil disorder. As priest-king of France, he wanted the Church to help introduce civil order, first by ministering to the townspeople, and second by forming teams of chaplains to serve the sailors on land or sea. Propagating the Catholic faith was one way Louis had of reinforcing his own temporal power: as his subjects worshipped one God in one faith, they might devotedly serve one king under (his) one law. Thus, when Louis XIV learned that only a few priests were serving the residents of the new cities, and in overcrowded churches at that,[22] he ordered new, larger churches to be built so more priests could have access to the population.[23]

Given the importance of the Church's mission and the power of the king over the affairs of the new cities, it is noteworthy that instead of immediately strengthening social order, these missions became the subject of prolonged controversy. Church construction costs escalated, construction dragged on, new priests did not get along with those already there, and everyone involved argued over what to do. Each party—the government, the Church, and the town—felt its wealth, prestige, and honor at stake. These conflicts prevented the Church from providing an adequate ministry for at least a generation after it had been charged to do so. In each case, the conflicts show that since the concern for civil welfare was primarily the government's, all initiatives for improvement could only be realized with its help.

In Brest conflict over the new church was particularly sharp. Brest proper already had a small parish church, Sept-Saints, in the old section near the port, but since it was too small and its cemetery overcrowded,[24] it was to be replaced by a new church, Saint-Louis, which was established in 1687. Sainte-Colombe had reserved land adjacent to the *maison du roy* for that church,[25] and the Jesuits, who lived next to the intendant anyway, were able to cajole the townspeople to agree that it should be built there.[26] Actually, this was a means by which they could fasten their grip on the curacy of the parish, for they insisted that since the church was to be built next to their chapel, it belonged to them. At this the city refused to follow their spiritual leadership since it was paying for the church building out of its octroi, considered the church its property, and preferred that the priests of another order occupy the curacy.[27] The preference now was for the church to be built in the old town. Meanwhile, Vauban advised Louis that a church near the *maison du roy* would cost less and add more to the city's visual style. Louis adopted this point of view, which was favorable to the Jesuits, and refused to build a second, separate church for either party to the dispute.[28] In fact, Louis supported the Jesuits out of a belief in their power to subdue any rebellious spirit in those who came to Brest in search of work. Pontchartrain agreed to mediate a solution, but there was no common ground for agreement between the Jesuits and the townspeople.[29] Finally, in 1706, the Jesuits were confirmed in their possession of the Church of Saint-Louis,[30] which in any case was not completed until 1708.

When Rochefort was established, the existing parish church, Notre-Dame, stood more than a mile away from where the port would be, and was tended by an alcoholic priest. To assure religious services the government introduced Capuchins in 1669, and erected a chapel for them adjacent to the port.[31] Colbert de Terron spoke optimistically of finishing a new church in the town's center by 1673,[32] but for lack of money it was not completed until 1683, and by then it was too small. This became the Capuchins' church, but they were unwilling to undertake an energetic mission among the townspeople.[33] They were replaced by Lazarists when Louis, concerned for the spiritual safety of Rochefort at a time when the Protestants of the area were forced to abjure, established the church as the parish of Saint-Louis.[34] In addition, the Pères de la Mission were brought in to train chaplains for the navy and to "prevent swearing, blasphemy, drunkenness, quarrels and scandals."[35] They realized that a new church, much larger than the one finished in 1683, had to be built, and in 1687 they suggested that it be erected on a vegetable plot nominally a part of the *jardin du roy*.[36] Money was appropriated the next year, but the sums were never transferred. In desperation, nearly twenty years later, Rochefort's priests established a lottery to raise money,[37] but the townspeople had as little money as the king to spend on a new church. It was not built until the early nineteenth century.

Most residents of Lorient adopted a non-churchgoing routine, perhaps because they lacked any suitable structure in which to pray. When, therefore, the residents of the arsenal compound were ordered to move farther inland in 1700, a site for a new church there—one that gave the new Lorient the central core it needed—was selected.[38] As in Brest and Rochefort (and in Sète, too) the placement of the church building, the largest civil structure of the city, was one way of reinforcing the Church's position of influence and authority in the city's social order. This explains why the erection of Lorient's church was subject to a fight between those parties who felt their positions and prerogatives were also at stake in this matter: Dondel, who was seigneur in the name of the Rohan family over the land outside the arsenal, the Compagnie des Indes, and the rector of Plemeur parish, of which Lorient was a part, all fought to retain control over it. Mauclerc, the government's agent, wanted to solve this quarrel by establishing Lorient as a parish with its own funding, but Louis disallowed it. In 1702 Mauclerc was able to start construction of the new church with royal funds anyway.[39] It was only half-finished in 1705 when construction was halted until Dondel and the Rohan family settled an argument over who should sit where in the new structure.[40] Finally, in 1708, the church, still a part of the parish of Plemeur, was consecrated. Morphy, the Plemeur curate, let another priest take over Lorient the next year "to attract the best subjects there."[41] But since the church lacked an income an independently wealthy priest had to be found, so Father Le Livec, with an income of £1,000 yearly, stayed in Lorient until 1714.[42] For his successor, a rural abbey was attached to Lorient, and the revenues from it supported the parish. Even so, the church stood without a roof until 1720.

The progress made toward erecting new, larger churches, adequately staffed and funded, was always limited by practical and financial problems. The conflicts these problems aroused became important political issues in Brest, Lorient, and Rochefort, and their effect was to prevent churches from becoming useful agents of social and spiritual conformity. The state, and not the church, provided the most visible, pervasive framework within which the new residents adjusted to life. Tens of thousands of people were born, lived, and died in Rochefort, Brest, and Lorient with inadequate spiritual care. Apparently, many of them did not greatly miss such attentions. Nevertheless, had Louis made more money available, adequate financing would have helped religious efforts considerably. The government missed the opportunity to use the pulpit of the Church and the ritual of the altar to bring the people together in a common, patriotic faith. When the penury of the navy after 1704 caused a royal recession in the arsenal cities, the Church lacked the stature to serve as a stabilizing institution in the communities, expressing on a spiritual level the lack of concern for the common people that marked the *crise de conscience et d'autorité* of the end of Louis's reign.

The Crisis of Authority

During the last three decades of Louis's reign a crisis in royal finances developed when a rural depression, deflated prices, and the rareness of specie coincided with and were aggravated by the wartime burden of taxes, disruption of commerce, and concentration of capital in the royal debt. Government expenditures outran income four times over. Funds for the navy were gradually and unceremoniously restricted after the Battle of La Hogue of 1692 until, in 1704, the decision was made to suspend all payments to arsenal employees. In 1709 the government no longer guaranteed credit or grain supplies, and people began to leave the new arsenal cities. The War of the Spanish Succession ended in 1713; the revival of maritime commerce, underway since 1700 and confirmed by the peace, restored some measure of prosperity to the new cities. Marcel Giraud has labeled this period of naval decline the "*crise de conscience et d'autorité,*"[43] and has characterized it by the poverty and threatened disloyalty of the residents of the new ports and by the refusal of many in the navy to defend France and alleviate suffering. Giraud referred to the navy in particular, but his research illuminated conditions that are now seen as having been widespread in France during Louis XIV's last years of rule. This crisis of authority figures in the history of the new port cities because it reveals, more dramatically than a discussion of their early growth can, their fragility and dependence upon the government that created them. The situations and solutions specific to Brest, Lorient, and Rochefort represent the contingent, purely French aspects of this story, but because the impact of the crisis on these cities and the reactions of the government to it describe how they emerged at the end of Louis's reign as enduring urban societies, this story should also be understood as an example of the difficulties that stood between many early modern port city projects and the self-generating growth of mature urban centers. (Sète is not mentioned here because its fate was linked to the monarchy's crisis indirectly, through the financiers of Languedoc and Louis's need for their credit.)

There is the possibility that royal officers vastly exaggerated their accounts of political unrest and poor living conditions when they wrote to Jérôme Pontchartrain, secretary of state for the navy from 1699 to 1715, because many workers and officers continued to serve without pay, even for as long as a year and a half. But the exaggeration seems to have been minor: so many officers, craftsmen, laborers, sailors, and shopkeepers were affected harshly by the cuts in royal spending that riots, violence, and insubordination became major problems.

Rochefort's arsenal nearly closed for lack of funds in 1698, but Pontchartrain was able to keep it operational,[44] appealing for funds from the Treasury by citing the danger of violence and subversion. In 1703 workers abandoned their jobs in Brest when they were not paid,[45] and in 1705 and 1708 workers and their families attacked the homes of royal officers in Brest and Rochefort, demanding back pay and food.[46] Early in 1706 workers in Rochefort started a fire, and later that year workers in Brest mutinied.[47] Attacks on royal officers and strikes and riots demonstrated that workers were restrained by neither respect for the king's service nor fear of his officers in demanding what they had earned. The ideal of patriotism could not send sailors to their boats, soldiers to their posts, and workers to their jobs as effectively as regular pay and food. The government grew afraid that seacoast populations might passively allow the Allies to invade.[48] To the extent that Louis's land war interfered with coastal fishing and commerce and with the economies of the new port cities, Louis and his administrators were prudent to worry.

Pontchartrain and his agents did their best, not only because relief measures might prevent disturbances, but also because such actions, they believed, were morally necessary: these workers, after all, should not have to suffer, precisely because they were servants of the king.[49] Orders went out to royal agents, telling them to provide the workers with food.[50] In 1705 the government extended credit to Brest's bakers so they could give milk, bread, and other provisions to the townspeople.[51] In 1709 grain was distributed in Rochefort and Brest; in Rochefort alone, an estimated three thousand persons were fed daily by the government.[52] Pontchartrain believed that rioters demanding back pay and food should receive what was owed them, and be favored, not punished.[53] Nevertheless, it is interesting to note that most disturbances took place between 1704 and 1709, when the government undertook most of these relief measures. Between 1709 and 1714, when the government's warehouses and coffers no longer sustained the workers and their families, an exodus from the new port cities took place, but it was accompanied by few signs of political unrest: people spoke with their feet, not their fists.

In order to understand how the new port cities emerged from the crisis as permanent communities, it is important to note that even when population size diminished after 1704 and 1708 (years when the royal treasury could pay the workers only at irregular intervals), it never decreased to the point of making shipbuilding and repairing impossible. Population figures indicate that each city remained a sizeable factor as a reservoir of manpower, for no matter how unattractive life in them became, many residents no doubt decided that it was better to trust the king to feed them than to try their luck elsewhere. Had Louis and his subordinates cared to, they could have made an

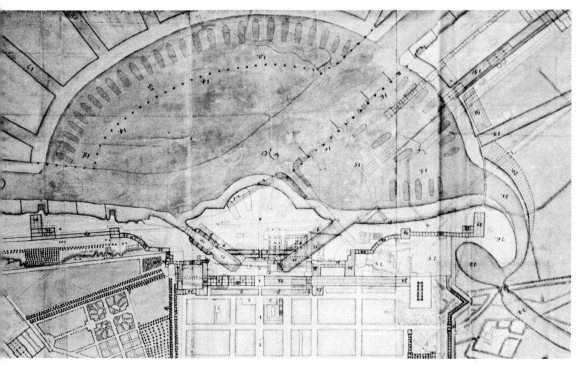

FIGURE **5.1.** *Rochefort, 1684, plan by Arnoul, Maps 144–150. Manuscript Collection, Service historique de la Marine, Paris.*

effort to close the arsenal bases and discourage the growth of the new port cities, even unmake them as human settlements. But they made no such efforts. Instead, Louis's agents tried to keep hopes for French sea power alive by supporting the well-being of those who had come to work, and by adapting the cities themselves to new tasks. The solutions proposed and implemented are evidence, not only of the government's commitment to the continued existence of the new cities, but also of the cities' dependence on the government for a reason for their existence.

The solution for Brest was easy and simple. Its strategic location astride the Atlantic sea lanes and its safe, immense harbor made it attractive during the War of the Spanish Succession to the capitalists of Saint-Mâlo, who, with the king's money and authority, were organizing France's privateering campaigns.[54] The corsairs were outfitted in Brest and returned there with captured prizes. Privateering kept the port active, but it was the result of a temporary circumstance. At least Brest's capacity to build French sea power was preserved intact.

The solutions proposed for Lorient and Rochefort, however, required greater effort. Those responsible for Lorient wanted to remake the city so that it would be fit to play a more important, permanent role as a seaport. In 1700 the small community of Lorient, which had lived in shacks scattered throughout the arsenal, was ordered by edict to move onto open land adjacent to the arsenal. By 1705 the government decided to enclose the new residential district with fortifications, and Clairambault, royal agent in charge, took advantage of this opportunity to plan a complete city with permanent streets. The story of his venture was told in chapter four: work proceeded throughout the depressed years of 1708 to 1713, but by the end of Louis's reign the plan had been only partly executed. What survived were the plan itself and the ambitions that lay behind it. The new Lorient included at least two major civic and residential squares, and the street pattern emphasized their importance. This new city had a character of its own in its new, permanent outline. After so many years of war, Louis finally understood that Lorient was an investment in France's commercial and military future.

By contrast, there was little anyone could do with Rochefort. Its principal handicap was its location on the Charente River, which was very silty. As early as 1683 Pierre Arnoul, then intendant at Rochefort, had proposed a scheme even more ambitious and grandiose than Clairambault's transformation of Lorient. It failed, not because the government rejected it outright, but because its author, unlike Clairambault, could find no source other than the royal treasury for financing.[55] Arnoul's grandiose scheme (figure 5.1) involved widening the Charente and constructing a semicircle of basins across from the city, two symmetrically arranged dry docks on the city side, and a long, complex, and symmetrical group of government buildings between these docks and the city itself. Arnoul maintained that his projects would make Rochefort truly independent of royal finance, since it would be large enough and attractive enough to serve outside shipping and construction business;[56] but his ideas (so reminiscent of many unexecuted Swedish plans of the same period) were judged to be impractical. In 1688 Arnoul was replaced by Michel Bégon, who remained there for the duration of Louis's reign. During Rochefort's depression, which began in 1704, Bégon put the unemployed to work improving the region's roads.[57] Later, in 1708, Bégon took to selling the forests owned by the navy in that district, netting well over £50,000, and he planted industrial and food crops on the reclaimed land.[58] Beyond that, Rochefort's decline was cushioned only because the navy found it a convenient place to stockpile materials and build small ships.

Louis XIV and his agents, it appears, remained convinced that new port cities could continue to contribute to sea power. They assumed that the established nature and permanence of urban bases were important factors in the navy's ability to undertake large-scale operations. Though often unable to amass sufficient financial resources and raw materials during the last two wars of Louis's reign, the government always anticipated being able to make the necessary allocations to the navy at some future date, when the ambition for maritime supremacy might be realized. These ambitions sustained the new port cities when their very existence was in jeopardy—as the same ambitions had justified their creation a generation before. The crisis of authority reveals that, whatever success the newcomers to Brest, Lorient, and Rochefort had in adjusting to conditions of life, they could not separate their futures from the diplomatic, political, military, and financial decisions made in Europe's capital cities.

Acculturation in the New Cities

When ministers learned of conditions in the new port cities of which they disapproved, they expressed shock that irreligion and immorality could persist in cities whose existence was justified by *raison d'état*. They were disturbed by the contrast between popular behavior and the order, precision, and refinement of systems of production and discipline that were essential characteristics of arsenal work.[59] In fact, the government had little to worry about. The disorder that continued to pervade popular life did not penetrate into the arsenals, where, despite abuses and some corruption, work was usually executed efficiently and under strict supervision. Men worked from dawn to dusk, were assembled and dispersed by bells and clocks, and were registered according to a primitive system of punching in. On the whole, French arsenals were a model of organization in their day, and the government's failure to reform popular life was of little consequence to their operation. Large numbers of workers were apparently willing to submit to a disciplined routine in order to work there. The government, however, was unwilling to evaluate life in the new cities narrowly, or to accept cooperation from the workers in the arsenals as enough. Conditions of life could not be separated from royal ideals when the qualities of work, discipline, foresight, and patience were to bring *gloire* to Louis's reign by increasing French power and wealth. As long as popular life was colored by the talk of the taverns, the sight of the prostitutes, and the laughter of fellowship, Louis's agents suspected that the workers were serving the king only so long as they thought it was in their interest to do so. And they were largely right.

Perhaps the most striking feature of the process of acculturation that assimilated newcomers into the king's service was the fact that local, nongovernmental elites played no part in it. In other leading French cities a local oligarchy usually directed the city's economic, social, and political affairs. In the new cities the elites were either Royal Navy officers or merchants dependent on the navy or on big merchant houses located elsewhere. The future of the city in which they lived was not theirs to determine, and it is probable that they realized this. It made a difference for the workers and their families. In most cities the elites tried to reinforce their own position by maintaining the social order, and they used traditional methods, such as control of the grain markets, or new ones, such as the police and the *hôpitaux généraux,* to that end. But in the new cities Louis's agents were the only people who cared about the conditions in which most people lived. And they did so not out of any paternalistic sense of moral responsibility, but according to a new imperative—the interests of the state. It is only possible to guess how the masses reacted to such a remote, abstract, and intangible justification for social control: they were among the first groups in Europe to confront statecraft, not as the king's justice, a royal wedding, or a tax-gathering system, but as a day-by-day bureaucratic routine. The cooperation of the largest number of residents made the new system work, but I want to suggest that they did so without believing in what they were doing. Most workers did not become loyal servants of the king just because they worked hard in the king's arsenals. They and their families intended to stay in the new port cities only for as long as it was in their interest to do so; they did not think of Brest, Lorient, or Rochefort as the only possible place in which to make a home. Most urban communities were held together by a sense of belonging to a particular place: aristocrat, bourgeois, and day laborer alike could agree that they were all, in some sense, *toulousain, parisien, lyonnais,* or *lillois,* just as seigneur, peasant, and farmer could agree that they were all, in some way, *breton, provençal,* or *alsacien.* But it is hard to imagine many of those who lived in Brest, Lorient, or Rochefort thinking of themselves as *brestois, lorientais,* or *rochefortien.* The process of ac-culturation, to the extent that it worked at all, helped transform new set-tlements into permanent societies; but without wars, which gave Louis's fleets opportunities for action, the new cities would have stagnated or declined. Acculturation to the kings' service, therefore, could not produce an autono-mous city, one capable of attracting newcomers and holding onto its resi-dents by its very presence and its ongoing economic activities. Louis's drive for sea power appealed to the different groups living in the new port cities in different ways; it was all they shared, but that was enough to make them willing to live in the same place together.

Population, Class Structure, and Nonregional Influences

Little is known about why people move to cities. Restlessness, adventure, misery, ambition, hope, and despair characterize the emigrant to the city in the works of Marivaux, Balzac, Dickens, and Dreiser. The lucky reader of a novel can know what act of will, what wave of forces, pushes the young hero or heroine toward the city. For the character in the novel, for the novelist, and for the reader, the city is there to go to—only the motive and circumstance need to be explained. But those who migrated to the new French cities do not reveal such secrets to the historian who tries to trace their path. Why did those who chose to move to one of the new cities no longer want to live where they had been living, and then, why did they choose that particular city to go to? If one of the new cities had not attracted them, would they have moved into another city, or would they have stayed where they were? These questions cannot be answered. Moreover, it remains a mystery how news of the new cities spread as far and as fast as it did. The network of communications from the Charente River basin to Champagne, from Brittany to Provence, remains hidden. The common people in France who were literate or had access to literacy read traditional items, largely apolitical and folkloristic in nature,[60] so that their awareness of current events is thought to have been limited to outbreaks of war, signing of peace treaties, and events in the life of the royal family. Even today, information on current affairs is absorbed by only a few of the large number of people who have access to daily sources of news. So it is a wonderment that the existence of the new cities became known. Perhaps handbills and posters mentioned their existence and opportunities for work in them, but the largest number of craftsmen and laborers who moved to the new cities were living not far from them, or, alternatively, from the French seacoast. They must have been astonished to see (or hear about) new cities where none had existed before; this would be a topic for conversation in any era. Long before newspapers, people in one port knew of what occurred in other places because those who traveled spoke of what they saw. And even when newspapers became more common, in the eighteenth century, the traveler remained one of the best sources of news for any editor. So while it is not possible to prove that speech, and not text, transmitted this sort of information, I believe that an oral communications network carried the word.

Population Structure

The new government had tried to encourage immigration to the new cities with tax benefits, grants of municipal liberties, and attractive spatial planning. Although these measures in regard to Brest, Rochefort, and Sète were helpful in setting up each city, they were less important for long-term gains than Sète's dependence on shifts in trade and tax patterns, or Brest's and Rochefort's dependence on naval and political affairs. In fact, Lorient's survival as a small community despite its fragile and temporary aspect shows that government efforts to channel population growth by manipulating city institutions had indirect effects at best. More significant was Rochefort's continued growth, despite its demotion in status after 1672, until royal penury in the early eighteenth century brought an end to employment. Planning did little to stimulate port city growth, but it did help to keep growth orderly and economic activities and port operations efficient when sudden changes in city size occurred. It was unusual for the fortunes of cities to be so closely tied to outside events in the reign of Louis XIV; in this respect the new cities were truly metropolitan colonies, dependent on a remote government, and not on the immediate hinterland.

Trends in population growth and decline are revealed by the numbers of baptisms, burials, and marriages recorded in parish registers.[61] Historical demography is based upon good records; unfortunately, the registers of the new port cities can support only the most elementary study of population. A large percentage of residents may not have passed before clergy during their stay in the port city; the navy chaplains who cared for the sailors kept separate records, which have not survived; and certain aberrancies stand out in the remaining registers, such as an apparent underregistration of infant deaths in Brest, and possibly in Sète as well, in the early eighteenth century. We cannot follow changes in the age structure of the populations, determine whether married life conformed to or varied from patterns in other French cities, or measure the relations between sailors and civilians. Nevertheless, statistics drawn from parish registers provide continuous figures for from four to six decades that cumulatively indicate an increase or decrease in population size, allow for the dating of significant changes in size, and are evidence of the impact of national events on the city.

Brest's figures[62] show that the principal factors in its increase were, first, the government's decision of 1680 to remake it into its leading arsenal base, second, its usefulness in the naval war of the early 1690s, and third, its impor-

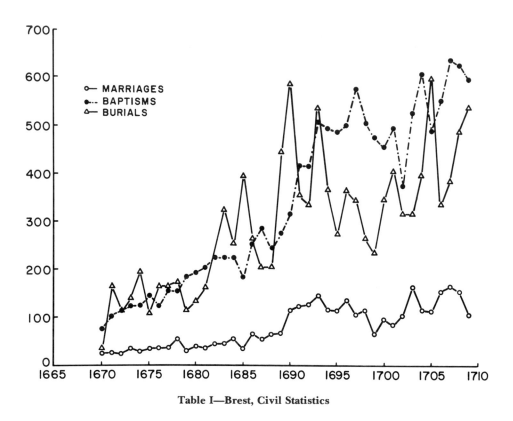

Table I—Brest, Civil Statistics

tance during the War of the Spanish Succession as a prize port. Table I corresponds to these events, and establishes that when naval activity increased, people migrated to Brest. The nearly constant increase in baptisms, burials, and marriages suggests the partial role of natural increase in population growth, although the significant gains over a one or two year period were undoubtedly the result of immigration. The tremendous growth of Brest from 1680 to the 1710s was reflected not only in the ever larger number of baptisms, burials, and marriages, but in the expansion of the arsenal's labor forces, as well: in 1686, 1,275 people were employed in the arsenal; by 1690 the figure had risen to 2,707, suggesting a total population of some 10,000. In 1688, 63 marriages, 247 births, and 207 deaths were recorded; in 1690 those figures had increased to 112, 318, and 587, respectively. In the period from 1696 to 1715, Brest's population may well have averaged 15,000,[63] a significant figure in early modern France. The plans of Seignelay, Sainte-Colombe, and Vauban transformed Brest into a major arsenal city that quickly attracted newcomers, but they also permitted Brest to absorb sudden and significant increases in population when the demands of war attracted additional manpower. Of course Brest lost hundreds of residents during the years of di-

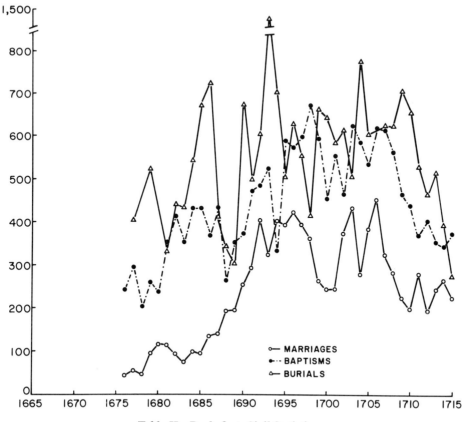

Table II—Rochefort, Civil Statistics

minished activity (1709 to 1714);[64] such an exodus only underscores how important opportunities for work had been for many migrants to Brest. Even in 1714, however, Brest remained a sizeable city: hope as much as despair kept many people there.

Rochefort's population figures also indicate the influence of government initiative on city's growth. In 1667, 31 baptisms were performed in Rochefort; in 1668 there were 73; in 1669, 109; and in 1679, 260. In 1673, the first year for which such figures are available, there were 230 burials; two years later there were 298, and in 1679, 522.

Rochefort's dramatic excess of deaths over births emphasizes the role of immigration in city population growth (see table II). In four of every five years of the reign of Louis XIV, deaths exceeded baptisms, often by two to one. Rochefort was an unhealthy spot, infested by malaria. (In most early modern cities, disease, seasonal work patterns, a sizeable percentage of unmarried adults, or some other circumstance, rendered natural population increase inadequate to sustain urban population growth.) Yet the figures of increased burials—as well as those of increasing numbers of marriages and baptisms—suggest continual, significant patterns of immigration. It was re-

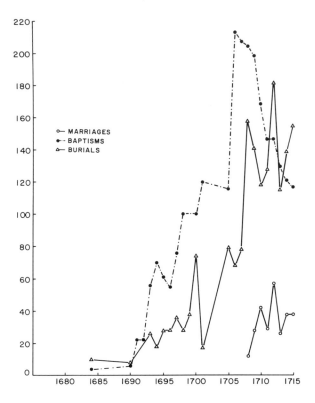

Table III—Lorient, Civil Statistics

markable that Rochefort continued to grow at all, having by the 1680s become an arsenal base of secondary importance. But that, apparently, was no discouragement to the thousands who came there to serve or work. Rochefort grew as long as its workers were paid.

In 1704, however, the government decided to hold off further payments to arsenal workers, and an exodus followed, visible in a striking decline in the numbers of baptisms, burials, and marriages. The decline began gradually, but accelerated during years of bad weather and grain shortages (1709 and 1710) until the numbers of burials, baptisms, and marriages in Rochefort in the last years of Louis's reign were one-third less than they had been at the turn of the century.

Brest and Rochefort became large cities (total population of nearly 15,000 each) in spurts that occurred, cumulatively, for over a generation. The fact that they were completely planned made it possible for them to absorb such increases. One can only wonder if less order in their appearance and institutions would have diminished their desirability. Certainly newcomers were most interested in seeking work, and might well have been indifferent to their surroundings, but of course one cannot be sure of this. Lorient and Sète were smaller, for neither had the activities to support a large working population: around 1700, each was perhaps one-fifth the size of the other two. But

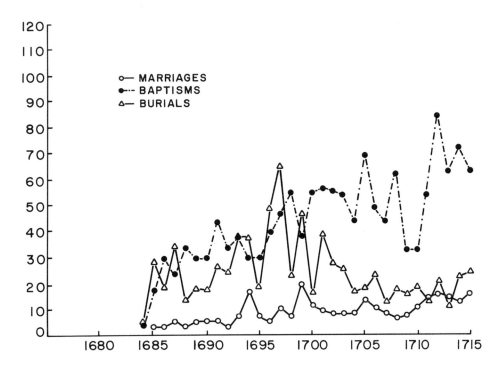

Table IV—Sete, Civil Statistics

just as for Brest and Rochefort, population figures show clearly the critical role of external events in their patterns of growth.

Lorient's parish registers are complete only from 1708, and they illustrate more accurately the ill effects of the royal penury and naval recession of that era than they do the encouragement to growth given by the operation of the arsenal until then (see table III). Nevertheless, some reliable figures indicate the outlines of Lorient's earlier growth. In 1690, for example, only 6 infants were baptized in Lorient; by 1700 the number had risen to 100. This increase continued during part of the War of the Spanish Succession: 205 baptisms were performed there in 1708. Burial statistics tell a similar story: 8 in 1690, 74 in 1700, 108 in 1708. Thereafter the population appears to have declined. Baptisms fell to 199 in 1709, to 117 in 1715. But enough people remained to form a community, as can be seen in the more stable figures for burials.

Sète grew rather slowly from 1670 to 1690, but in the 1690s the expansion of trade to northern Europe encouraged a more rapid rate of settlement.[65] This can be seen in table IV. Even though several epidemics broke out in this period (1687, 1693, 1694, 1696–1697, 1699, 1701), which increased mortality in most Lower Languedoc communities as well as in Sète, the number of marriages and baptisms increased, and baptisms exceeded burials, indicating real growth with steady immigration. The 1695 census listed 199 heads of household; by 1710 the number of property owners alone (many people lived in rented dwellings) was 273.

Where did the residents of these new cities come from? Although the activities in the new cities that attracted newcomers—government operations (arsenal cities) or international trade (Sète)—were extraregional in character, immigrants came from more or less the same places as people in other cities in the same region, cities more completely integrated into an exclusively provincial economic structure. Rochefort, Brest, and Sète (the only three for which this information is available) were composed of roughly the same mixture of people by place of origin as other cities in the same parts of France. Between 1673 and 1680, nearly 55 percent of the newcomers to Sète arrived from Agde and Frontignan, 15 percent arrived from the mountains behind Montpellier, 13 percent from the Rhône valley and the Mediterranean coast as far as Genoa (a source of many sailors and pilots), and 13 percent from the Berre inland sea near Marseille; only 2 percent came from Upper Languedoc. This composition scarcely differed from that of most Lower Languedoc communities.[66]

A similar pattern can be seen for Rochefort. In the years preceeding 1688, nearly 60 percent of Rochefort's inhabitants came from the immediate area of the Aunis and Saintonge, and from Poitou and Angoumois beyond. One-sixth came from Normandy and Brittany, a traditional source of sailors for the Charente region, and the rest came from other areas of France as far inland as Campagne and the Ile de France.[67] Over two-thirds of the men and over 90 percent of the women whose marriages were recorded in Brest came from Brittany, with the overwhelming majority of the rest from other French provinces. The new port cities called to the French seacoast approximately the same people, from the same places, as did other French coastal cities. But that did not make the new cities typically *breton, charentais,* or *languedocien.* As the trends determined by population figures clearly demonstrate, the newcomers knew that only outside their province were the decisions that stimulated each new city's economy made.

Social Structure

In most cities, and certainly in most French seaports, wealth was usually a product of native industry and enterprise as well as outside investment, and it changed according to international and regional business trends, fluctuations in price and production, the fortunes of climate, and business acumen. The new cities imported their income from the Royal Treasury or foreign bankers. A survey of demographic trends has confirmed their existence as metropolitan colonies, recognizably dependent in purpose and fortune upon the French state. This dependence can also be seen in the distribution of the population into professional categories. What people did for a living can be extracted from surviving census and fiscal registers. Even though the way the registers were composed made it likely that in any survey, merchants, professionals, laborers, and craftsmen would occupy roughly similar positions relative to each other in a hierarchy based on fiscal assessments, the strength of each group in the population as a whole differed from city to city.

Most analyses of social structure in the preindustrial city have attempted the description of society for its own sake, in order to make the classification of individuals into groups more rigorous, or as part of an explanation of specific events or circumstances (for example, relating the wealth or influence of social groups to political conflict). These studies have an important heuristic value. Nevertheless, I do not intend to compare Brest, Lorient, Rochefort, and Sète against the social structure of other cities. Their social structure was marked by the characteristic features of European urban societies at that time—the extremely unequal distribution of wealth, limited opportunities for mobility, and the importance of occupational groups in determining the relative position of individuals in a hierarchy. What comparisons among the new cities suggest is that equally characteristic of Europe's urban order was the extent to which a social system that emphasized rigid distinctions between individuals and groups based on wealth, position, and reputation could itself be flexible as to how specific groups and the individuals composing them related to each other in a specific place. Such adaptability must be counted as one of the reasons European cities of the early modern era changed in size so quickly and so often and specialized in and absorbed so many different patterns of economic activity. What the social structure contributed to urbanization during the sixteenth, seventeenth, and eighteenth centuries is still largely unknown: Maurice Garden has noted in his book on eighteenth-century Lyon that the unfinished task of the social historian is to extend the reconstruction of the social structure into a history of *mentalités collectives,* of how the behavior and outlook of individuals and groups conditioned everyday life in an urban milieu.[68] When people settled in one of the new French port cities, they may have found the specific pattern of intergroup relations there to be unfamiliar, but they also appear to have become oriented to it without great difficulty. Throughout this chapter we have seen that the new port cities contained two societies; it is now appropriate to look more closely at the social structure as an expression of the differences between them.

There is nothing surprising in the statement that the professional composition of each new port city differed according to its chief activity; yet on this hinges an understanding of the differences that marked each of the new cities from most others in seventeenth-century France.[69] In Sète, a Mediterranean entrepôt, few people served the king directly (6 percent), but the merchants were numerous (23.5 percent). In Lorient, a military base, the royal officers were more prominent in the population (12 percent) than the merchants (7 percent). In Sète, merchants and officers combined to represent 30 percent of the population, whereas the same groups in Lorient amounted to 19 percent. Of course, it is risky to assume that numbers alone meant influence, as some of the richest persons might belong to a group that was small in size, a condition found in both Sète and Lorient (in Sète, a royal officer; in Lorient, a member of the landholding gentry). Nevertheless, in both, the relative weight of numbers, corresponding to the city's principal economic activity, must have

Table V—Vocational Categories in Sète[a], Lorient[b], and Brest[c]

Categories	Percentage in Sète, 1695	Percentage in Lorient, 1701	Percentage in Brest, 1719
Royal officers	6	12	3
Non-navy artisans	24	10	22
Navy artisans	9	56	22
Laborers	26	9	11
Liberal professionals	0.5	1	2
Merchants	23.5	7	7
Farmers	10	1.5	1
No vocation indicated	3	4.5	22
Servants	—	—	10

[a]Based on AC GG 17 bis, dénombrement
[b]Census, AM B³ 113
[c]Capitation, 1719, AC CCI

helped define each as a "one company town." In fact, in none of the new cities is there a sign of the economic diversity that could have eroded their role in the government's network of cities for sea power.

In Sète, Brest, and Lorient, nearly two-thirds of the people were laborers and craftsmen, but in each city these groups were composed differently. One-fourth (24 percent) of Sète's population were craftsmen unassociated with the navy who worked instead for private concerns; but 56 percent of Lorient's work force were artisans employed by the arsenal, and only 10 percent of the craftsmen worked elsewhere. The figures in table V make Brest appear different from both Lorient and Sète, yet in fact Brest and Lorient had much in common, as the interpretation of fiscal registers illustrates. The non-navy artisans in Brest who appear so numerous (22 percent) were nearly evenly divided among three categories of tradesmen dealing with food, construction, and clothing. In a city the size of Brest (approximately fifteen thousand), a large number of tradesmen were required to meet the needs of the population, so their percentage of all professional categories reflects the city's size more than the nature of its economy. All these figures date from 1719, when the oldest surviving records were made; at that time the navy arsenal in Brest was much less active than it had been earlier, during Louis XIV's reign. This helps explain why navy artisans accounted for only 22 percent of Brest's labor force. In fact, the navy could draw upon an additional 26 percent of the city's workers, those day laborers and unemployed artisans who were classified as without any profession and who paid the minimum tax or a tax sum below average for the city. In Brest, as in Lorient, nearly half the work force could be employed by the navy. While the presence of a separate group of servants is evidence of Brest's prominence, its economy was no less dependent on one activity than was Lorient's or Sète's.

Table VI—Distribution of the Tax Load

Categories	Sète	Rochefort	Brest
Percentage paying average tax or less	77	75	76
Percentage paying more than average tax	23	25	24

In all four cities, well over half the population were laborers or craftsmen of all kinds, and this accounts for the repetitive pattern in the distribution of the tax load (table VI). A further distinction can be made between taxes paid by the members of the same professional category in Brest and in Rochefort (table VII). What is striking in this comparison is the fact that in several categories, people in Brest paid a higher tax than people of Rochefort in the same profession, presumably reflecting a greater capacity to pay, a higher income. (These relations can be seen by expressing the average tax paid by workers in a given category as a multiple greater or smaller than the average tax for the city as a whole, stated as base 100.[70]) Perhaps Brest's more prominent status, greater port activity, and greater growth can explain these differences. If so, the advantages created for Brest by greater government planning and attention after 1680 had an impact on the relative wealth of its residents.

The distribution of professional categories shows the extent to which port activity was a variable in the composition of the population, but the figures on the tax spread shows that this had little impact on basic social structure. The professional differences between Sète and the arsenal cities hardly affected the division between a laboring and artisan majority and a minority composed of officers and merchants, a division common to all four communities. In the absence of more detailed demographic documentation, the most convincing evidence of the influence of professional groups on these communities is in their social geography (see chapter four). Unfortunately it is not possible to say to what extent people who earned barely enough to pay any tax at all or just the average tax (£3 to £5) felt a gap between their standard of living and that of those who paid twice the average tax and more. Even so, it is clear that in the new cities the socially superior persons enjoyed their rank by virtue of their careers. Individuals with high status and incomes but no economic activity were noticeably absent from these cities, for they would not have found everyday life to their taste. There was nothing prestigious about living in Sète when Montpellier was nearby; no one who could afford to live in La Rochelle would settle in Rochefort instead; Quimper, not Brest, was the attractive city of western Brittany; Vannes or Port-Louis were better established than Lorient. This meant that those who were in a position to exercise authority in the new cities did so by virtue of their connections to those persons, located elsewhere, whose decisions could affect what would happen. Given this situation, what were the relations between the new cities and the other, older and more autonomous, cities of their regions?

Table VII—Brest and Rochefort, Comparison of Taxes

Categories	Rochefort	Brest
Average	100	100
Royal officers	(no data)	700
Royal employees	62.5	133
Non-navy artisans	100	100
Navy artisans	62.5	92.5
Carpenters	50	100
Laborers	33.3	33.3
Liberal professionals	200	225
Merchants	175	250

Extraregional Characteristics

The new cities were marked by the government with signs of royal power just as visibly as prostitutes and criminals, who were branded with the fleur-de-lys by Louis's officers. Planning had built into the ports differences that were more decisive for their development than those aspects of their social structure that made them typical of their age and that planning could not affect. Identified by law, defined in part by the privileges and autonomy granted them, and restrained to a single activity, the new cities lacked control over their destiny. They had no history of, and no prospects for, any autonomy or initiative: to the extent that they could not exist as anything else, they remained metropolitan colonies on the seaboard frontiers of France.

Not only were their activities different from those of their regions as a whole; they were not even integrated into preexisting or developing regional trade patterns. The problem of Sète in this regard has already been discussed. It prospered more as an entrepôt of Catalonia, Genoa, and the North Sea countries than as a base for Languedoc, while much of that province's intracoastal trade, which Sète was to have channeled, passed through Agde. It was a part of Languedoc economically only because Montpellier exported wine and spirits through it (cloth passed through Nîmes to Marseille).

Brest was even more clearly isolated from Breton trade. Indeed, Seignelay disapproved of commercial contacts between Brest and Brittany, fearing that the arsenal's efficiency might be compromised.[71] In any case, Bretons reputedly went to Brest in large numbers only at brief moments, and only to marry or to make money;[72] except as a corsair prize port during the periods from 1694 to 1697 and from 1701 to 1713, the city never attained commercial importance for the rest of Brittany.[73] Even as a prize port during the War of the Spanish Succession, it was exploited by Saint-Mâlo shipowners, who took all their profits inland, and Saint-Mâlo, not Brest, continued to dominate traffic in western Brittany.[74] The tremendous growth in wine trade between Bordeaux and Brest, which saw Brest increase its share of Brittany's imports from Bordeaux from one-quarter to one-third during the War of the Spanish

Succession, was exclusively for the sake of the city itself and the naval operations based there.[75]

Lorient, too, was clearly isolated; not only did Hennebont and Plemeur dominate the town's trade through taxation, but whatever permanent local trade there was (in grain, mostly) passed through Hennebont.[76] While some of the profits and spoils from prize ships seized during the War of the Spanish Succession did enter Brittany illegally at Lorient, in theory they were supposed to pass on directly to Nantes. Rochefort was as isolated as the others. La Rochelle dominated trade in the Charente basin, and small ports and cities like La Marennes were more important in regional affairs than Rochefort.

Dependence on the government, which centralized planning fostered and symbolized, kept the new port cities apart from other cities in their regions. They had been planned as extraregional enterprises of the state because existing cities had been judged ill-suited to Louis's ambitions. Thus far in this analysis, discussion of how the new cities were planned and of how they grew and developed has correlated urbanization with *raison d'état.* The context for new city growth, as those who lived there understood, was royal policy; these proto-industrial communities would grow only as long as the French state preserved its ambitions for sea power. They lacked any drive of their own, and as long as they remained tied to the French state, people with other ideas about the exploitation of the sea went elsewhere to live and work. Unlike Brest, Rochefort, and Sète were Saint-Mâlo, Nantes, La Rochelle, Bordeaux, Agde, and Marseille, port cities that were largely free to engage in and pursue maritime opportunities on their own initiative. Clearly, the provincial merchant elites who composed what Edward Fox has called "the other France"[77] preferred to leave the new port cities alone; the methods and goals that the centralized state administration brought to France's maritime frontier were foreign to them. The creation and development of new cities became important events in the history of Brittany, the Charente district, and Languedoc,[78] not only because each provided a secure base for government oppression: Rochefort against the Protestants, Sète against the Camisards, and Brest and Lorient against the Breton peasants in 1675. The new cities were built by and represented new forces in regional life, the intendance, and the military, whose activities and authority limited provincial autonomy and initiative in the nascent French nation-state.[79]

After 1715 Brest, Lorient, Rochefort, and Sète remained metropolitan colonies. Brest, of course, continued to serve as chief Atlantic base for the navy (and still does today); the rhythm of naval activity affected its size after 1715 as directly as before. Its social and demographic structures, too, continue to illustrate Brest's dependence on non-Breton affairs.[80] The other cities lost that direct relation to state maritime policy that had conditioned their pre-1715 development, but they have continued to grow—or decline—as extraregional cities, manifesting a remarkable instance of continuity/discontinuity in urban structures.

Sète demonstrates this clearly. Although Languedoc's merchants replaced foreign traders as its masters for much of the eighteenth century, they misused new opportunities for investment in the nineteenth century, and other business interests from across France came to dominate Sète.[81] The phylloxera blight of the 1870s turned Sète into France's largest wine-importing port, but under non-Languedoc control—today it is the production center for the national vermouth industry, which consumes large quantities of imported wine, even though Languedoc itself produces an excess of wine. Sète was, and remains, a port for hire (during World War One it handled the largest volume of Swiss trade of any European port). There are few commercial offices in Sète today; the decisions affecting its trade are made elsewhere, as they have always been.

Shortly after Louis XIV's death Lorient was reappropriated by a reconstituted Compagnie des Indes under John Law's direction. It became the Compagnie's principal seacoast base. In 1718 and 1719 Langlade completed the plan for a new city that he had begun under Clairambault.[82] By the 1720s the new city was largely laid out and occupied. Lorient has retained its dual character as both commercial and military base: in 1780 the navy returned there, and has not left since, sharing the port with commercial traffic sailing for many non-Breton interests. Today Lorient serves all of France as its largest ocean fishing port and as a submarine base.

Brest, Lorient, and Sète are today larger than they were in the seventeenth or eighteenth centuries, and their futures seem secure. Only Rochefort has suffered decline in the intervening years. In the eighteenth century it gathered supplies that were transported to Brest,[83] and continued to construct boats for the navy. But in the nineteenth century the age of steel and steam brought Rochefort's usefulness to an end. It survives as a town of thirty thousand that somehow cannot die. Since 1715 each of these cities, even Brest, has prospered or declined according to a restricted sense of France's role as a sea power. The ambitions that Louis XIV and his associates preserved until 1715 cannot be traced in the subsequent development of these new port cities; they remained metropolitan colonies only because no one has cared to make anything else of them.

Brest, Lorient, Rochefort, and Sète do not describe a model of the best in early modern port city planning, but rather conditions and situations that, in varying degrees, all Europeans who wanted to benefit from port city planning had to confront. An in-depth analysis of their creation and development illustrates what was at stake wherever seventeenth-century Europeans pursued port city planning, as well as the limits to what it could accomplish. Of course aspects of Louis XIV's France that contributed to or reflected upon the planning process do not resemble in detail those that affected planning in other countries. But one of the purposes of this book is to explain why the planning process differed from country to country, a phenomenon that the French record and the comparative survey preceding it account for by describing the adaptability of urban forms and societies to so many different ideas about how sea power could be sustained and enlarged. Hundreds of Louis's agents were involved in planning and administering France's new port cities and naval affairs, and tens of thousands of French people passed through or settled in those cities, and they all encountered new values, institutions, and patterns of living. Their collective experience composes the most detailed example available of the place of port city planning in the maritime and urban civilizations of early modern Europe.

III

The Decline of Port City Planning

VI

*Port City Planning
after the Seventeenth Century*

The Problem

Only in the seventeenth century did Europeans ever really try to tie the development of commercial and military sea power to an urban context. Of course, not everyone involved with sea power saw a need for port city planning. Mention has already been made of English disregard for Continental planning practices; even the Royal Navy's arsenal ports were temporary stations at a time when Continental navies operated increasingly from permanently established urban bases. Perhaps a better example is the disdain for any city planning schemes that characterized the relations between the merchants of Saint-Mâlo and Marseille and the administrative officers of Louis XIV's government.[1] Operating vast, responsive, and rapidly growing commercial operations, these merchants thought that royal projects for enlarging and beautifying their old and overcrowded cities would diminish the value of their property and increase their tax burden. They would have been content to see their cities prosper with little regard for spatial order; but their protests could not block the will of the king to see executed what were, in fact, some of the most important extensions of seventeenth-century cities. In France, in the Netherlands, and in Scandinavia, governments concerned with the rhythms of commercial traffic and aware of the changing fortunes of war and power thought that port city planning could serve as a matrix for sea power, and hoped that, through it, the cultural, social, economic, and political problems associated with the exercise and extension of sea power might be mitigated.

But in the eighteenth century the relevance of port city planning no longer appeared obvious and compelling, except to a minority who pursued it for its capacity to heighten the monumental and sublime for aesthetic effect. Thanks to their efforts, large-scale planning returned to the cocoon of speculative and largely impractical imagination from which it has not re-emerged. As a result, those who dealt with the space of port cities on a problem-solving basis increasingly relied upon the limited talents, spatial vocabulary, and vision of the surveyor who developed port and city as separate, autonomous entities. Europeans substituted political studies, the fine arts, and literature for port city planning when describing the maritime world and the problems associated with commercial and military sea power.

The decline in importance of port city planning should not be interpreted as meaning that culture and society have evolved a more comprehensive and coherent understanding of the sea. On the contrary; the two societies that shared the same space in Louis XIV's new port cities—one familiar with the exercise of power but not with its extension onto the seas, the other a part of the maritime world but unfamiliar with the workings of the state—*are still two separate groups with two different perspectives on the sea.* To be sure, the record of seventeenth-century port city planning was not one of complete success. But it was sufficiently varied, important, and ambitious to make us want to know, first, why Europeans and Americans in the eighteenth century and after have found port city planning of little importance to their metropolitan and colonial port cities and to their exploitation of sea power, and second, what the consequences of this development have been for the maritime civilization of the West. This story is the real sequel to Brest, Lorient, Rochefort, and Sète as creations of Louis XIV's France. Perhaps the best starting point is the sudden and nearly simultaneous growth of two port cities, St. Petersburg and Liverpool—cities located at opposite ends of the north European world, but both built very much in a seventeenth-century frame of reference.

St. Petersburg

St. Petersburg, founded in 1703, was the last great city planned and established during an unprecedented era of port city development. Peter the Great's ambition was to change Russia and its place in world affairs by importing European commercial, cultural, and political practices through an urban base built on a European, not a Russian, model. As a result, Peter, his successors, and their planners and administrators referred to and were guided by seventeenth-century developments in the Netherlands, France, and Scandinavia. Excellent studies of eighteenth-century St. Petersburg already exist,[2] but their authors have slighted the century-long, continent-wide perspective that gives St. Petersburg its place in this story of maritime urban culture.

For many years the Swedes had been developing forts, cities, and bases along the Russian littoral of the Baltic, which they controlled. Their activities and the seventeenth-century wars between Sweden and Russia had called Peter's attention to the possibility of a prosperous city on the Neva. In fact, several Swedish projects had been proposed for sites that were similar in topographic configuration to St. Petersburg. While it is impossible to know whether the Russians were familiar with any of these projects, it is likely that they became aware of Swedish precedents from former Swedish engineers or from individuals who had worked with the Swedes, from documents captured, stolen, purchased, or copied, and from direct observation of the sites themselves. Moreover, the search for the ideally effective form and the manipulation of waterscape in the city, both characteristics of late-seventeenth-century Swedish planning, probably appealed to the Russians for the same reasons it appealed to the Swedes. The hope that coherent design, symmetry, and perspective might insulate a city against the corrosive effects of changing political and economic fortunes seems to have motivated both Russians and Swedes.

Before looking at some plans for St. Petersburg, it is appropriate to examine some Swedish documents for eastern Baltic locations. For example, plans of and projects for Riga, Nyen, and Narva indicate the variety of solutions to problems of growth and defense considered by the Swedes.[3] For Riga the question was whether or not an extension to the city should be enclosed by a single defense perimeter. But Riga was located on one side of a river, which simplified the problem. Nyen and Narva extended along both sides of a river, and Nyen in particular included a piece of land between two branches of a river—a configuration very close to St. Petersburg's. Swedish planners were undecided whether to impose one scheme on all the land, unifying the city through its topographic form, or whether to compose the city out of distinct elements, each subject to its own historical pattern of development and perhaps related to the others by function or by being enclosed within the same defense works. Implicit in the disagreements among designers were issues of cost, time, and strategic import, but there were differences of vision as well: some of the plans for Nyen reflect concern for how the city would appear to its residents or to travelers arriving by ship. Of course it may only be coincidental that these same issues would dominate disagreement over plans for St. Petersburg in the eighteenth century; even so, it is worthwhile to note that in the second half of the seventeenth century in the same part of the world Swedish planners had already tackled these issues without resolving them.

Peter had traveled to western Europe in 1697, and had visited, among other places, the English naval yard at Deptford and the Zaanstreek district in Holland. He returned to Russia convinced that, with planning, Western conditions and circumstances favorable to the rapid and efficient exploitation of the sea might be replicated in Russia. The succession of plans produced into the nineteenth century shows that Peter and his successors remained committed to this conviction. But the plans also reveal the great paradox of eighteenth-century St. Petersburg: the city developed largely without planning, not only because the government could not control effectively the huge number of people who came there to live, but also because the planners themselves—and their royal patrons—were unable to select a plan they wanted to impose in the first place (to which must be added the difficulty in building on water-logged soil). As the city grew, therefore, each successive plan had to take into account the ever-increasing amount of land that had been put to use without planning.

Between 1700 and 1725, 200 new manufacturing establishments were opened on the banks of the Neva. In 1709 the Russian admiralty employed

900 persons; the next year it added 4,720 more to the payroll; in 1712 another 2,000 were hired. Those figures dropped in peacetime, but even so, some 5,000 individuals probably remained employed by the admiralty. And they produced several hundred ships in the first quarter of the eighteenth century.[4] In 1725 the population approximated 30,000, and by 1750, 95,000. The rhythm of commercial traffic recorded the city's growth, too: 52 vessels called in 1718, 75 in 1720, 114 in 1722, 270 in 1724, and an average of 450 in 1725 and 1726.[5] Apparently, few people reflected on the value of planning because the city was growing well without it. Instead, those responsible for St. Petersburg, no doubt believing that planning could translate the city's activities into a permanent structure and that without such a structure disorder and instability might jeopardize the entire enterprise, preferred to consider plans that emphasized the symbolic and aesthetic qualities of monumental space, and did not search for a pattern of ordered, organic growth that was related to how the city had developed. A sense of the ideal, more than anything else, characterized the plans produced for the city. Whatever Peter may have learned or thought about practical city planning did not survive so far away from the provocative example of the Netherlands; other influences, from France and Scandinavia, proved stronger.

Peter the Great had hoped to create a very un-Russian, well-built modern city with densely spaced brick houses, large gardens, and straight streets. He urged that the river, canals, and channels be incorporated into the general plan, required all buildings to conform to the general plan, suggested that each social group be settled in a separate district, and anticipated committing the management of the city to the care of the commercial and industrial leaders.[6] Peter wanted visiting sailors and merchants to spread the word of St. Petersburg's beauty and industry throughout Europe, but the actual Amsterdam-on-the-Neva, which grew before a satisfactory plan was selected, was a busy and crowded place with little apparent spatial order.[7] Growth by the 1720s suggested that the city was developing in several different, unrelated areas: on the tip of Vasilevski Island, on the left bank of the Neva along both the waterfront and a road leading inland, further downstream along a channel, and on the right bank of the Neva, behind the fort. The site, however, offered many possibilities to anyone with the vision to see them and with the conviction that the city could grow to match them. One plan, circa 1720, showed how the island in the Neva might have been laid out with canals, a dense grid pattern, and a park, and would have abandoned the rest of the city to grow along the lines it had been setting; the island was not integrated into a larger scheme for the city. The Frenchman Leblond, however, had envisioned a way to do that. (He introduced a sense of visual perspective that captured the Russian imagination and led the Russians to call on other Frenchmen in the future.) In 1717 he completed a plan for the city (figure 6.1) that made provision for upstream industrial works, an adjacent suburb, a more ordered growth on the Neva's right bank behind the fort, and the visual and functional unification of Vasilevski Island with at least the left bank of the city. But Leblond did not allow other parts of the city to be related to each other, and his plan isolated the palace from the waterfront.

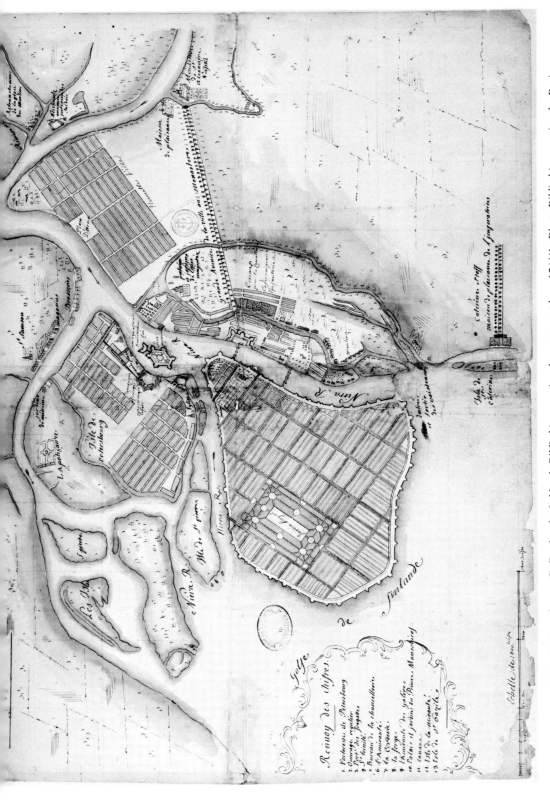

FIGURE 6.1. St. Petersburg, 1717, plan by Leblond. Bibliothèque nationale, cartes et plans 12/4/1. Photo Bibliothèque nationale, Paris.

Leblond's was not the first plan for the city, and others followed his, but his revealed many of the problems others had to face, too: spatial distribution of activities and residences, provision for growth, and concern for the functional and architectonic interrelationship of the parts. Complicating the whole city planning process was the island of Kronstadt at the mouth of the Neva, which protected not only St. Petersburg (from a Baltic-borne invasion) but also large ships that would have difficulty reaching the city (goods were transferred to smaller craft). Plans for Kronstadt are interesting in themselves (figure 6.2). St. Petersburg was a prime candidate for regional planning and development. But of all of Peter's ideas for St. Petersburg, only his prescription for the spatial separation of social groups and industrial activities was consistently implemented; the other ideas were downgraded or modified to better emphasize the city's increasingly aristocratic character.

Iurri Egorov has analyzed these plans (parts of which were translated into reality) and has described the aesthetic and political context in which they were discussed. There is little point in going over the same material here, except to comment by way of conclusion that the difficulties involved in determining which parts of the city (exchange or palace) should be emphasized architectonically and the arguments over whether to isolate a part of the city from or integrate it with the waterfront led to important discussions of political and social significance. From the beginning St. Petersburg had been destined to deliver the wealth of maritime commerce and the power its profits could buy into the hands of the Russian rulers. Like the planners of Copenhagen and Stockholm a century earlier, those who contributed to the planning of eighteenth-century St. Petersburg and wrestled with spatial problems of organization and perspective sought ways to combine the city's functions as courtly capital and commercial entrepôt. In all three cities an expansive aristocracy erected residences in a decorative and grandiose style close to the embankments, canals, and harbor activity belonging to the business world. The cityscape of St. Petersburg is a priceless visual record of how land empires harnessed the open horizons of long-distance commerce to their ascendance.

Liverpool

Liverpool, Defoe wrote, was "one of the wonders of Britain." But Defoe's impressions corresponded to a vision of port cities that few Englishmen of the seventeenth or eighteenth century shared. In Defoe's day, Liverpool was resolutely given over to Atlantic commerce. That this happend at all has excited the curiosity of historians,[8] because until the end of the seventeenth century Liverpool was a minor port that handled traffic with Ireland. The Navigation Acts of the 1660s curbed the trade with Ireland, and when the wars with France imposed a handicap on Britain's eastern and Channel ports, Liverpool merchants seized an opportunity to exploit the shortest and safest route across the Atlantic offered by their city. But Liverpool could not easily handle the ships of the Atlantic trade. Coastal and Irish shipping were handled by small vessels; the law proscribed ships larger than 37 tons from the Irish trade.

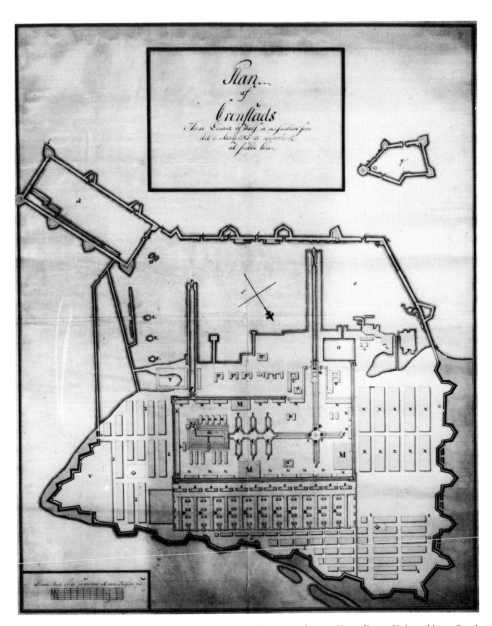

FIGURE **6.2.** *Kronstadt, 1785, no. 13. Stads-och fästningsplaner, Kunglinga Krigsarkivet, Stockholm.*

Atlantic vessels could weigh 200 or 250 tons, but given the twenty- to thirty-foot tidal range of the Mersey River, it was ordinarily difficult to anchor such ships alongside the city. Two common practices were beaching the vessel or taking it into a tidal pool, and neither was particularly safe or easy. Liverpool was, therefore, unequipped for the Atlantic trade, and it was only natural for the city's merchants to propose that a wet dock, a dock facility whose waters were protected from the tide by a lock, be built. The decision to make such a facility was made in 1708; Parliament voted the enabling legislation in 1709; the dock was completed in 1720 (at a cost of £15,000, one-third more than originally estimated); and in 1721 a new customs house was erected along one side of the dock.

Defoe wrote about Liverpool in a *Tour Through England and Wales,* contrasting it favorably with Bristol.[9] According to Defoe, Bristol's merchants were both suspicious of competitors and set in their ways, and their city was overcrowded, lacking in amenities, and locked into a medieval pattern—a reflection of its merchants' mentalities. Liverpool's great new dock and growing commerce would surely enable that city to exceed Bristol's wealth and size, predicted Defoe. Excited by that prospect, Defoe wrote about Liverpool's "exceedingly well built houses" and "straight, clean and spacious" streets. But when Defoe attributed to Liverpool an appearance as splendid as its enterprise, he used poetic license and distorted reality; he was sensitive to city space, and expressed this feeling as if there existed a sublime correspondence between image and reality. Liverpool was just as firmly set into a medieval urban structure, new dock notwithstanding, as Bristol. The merchants Defoe admired lacked his sense of urban beauty. Not until the nineteenth century would they add cultural institutions to their city, and when they did, they placed them far from the port (Liverpool merchants apparently did not believe that a great port called into being a great port city).

The ships that sailed from Liverpool "were among the finest works of man, exquisitely shaped for the seaman's purpose and infinitely more beautiful than any building the town had or would ever build."[10] Most of eighteenth-century Liverpool was built of wood; its streets were sometimes enlarged, but were rarely paved; fires led to constant rebuilding; and the dock basin had to be dredged as sewage and mud flowed into it from the streets. But the merchants preferred to rebuild and clean up rather than reorder the city's space. The only distinguished eighteenth-century additions to the city were schools, churches, almshouses, and hospitals, and these were merely inserted into its fabric. Neither rapid growth nor inconvenience and expense encouraged those responsible for the city to think about it in a new way. The commerce of eighteenth-century Liverpool may have differed radically from what it had been in the seventeenth century, but the city did not. The impact of traffic and population growth had not affected the city's topography except to multiply the number of warehouses, mansions, and tenements. Business remained concentrated in the area immediately adjacent to the port.[11]

Why had no plan to order Liverpool's growth been introduced during the eighteenth century? In the Middle Ages, Englishmen had used planning to establish new towns and to enlarge old ones. Because opportunities to create new towns diminished and because city planning usually represented an increase in the power of civil authorities, after the fifteenth century Englishmen had reduced planning schemes to speculative ventures launched by the crown, important landholders, and capitalists. Even so, such seventeenth-century schemes as those to develop areas of London (Bloomsbury, Covent Gardent, etc.) were beyond the reach or vision of Liverpool's merchants. Although they were in business to make money, they were not yet ready to transfer their profits into land and stone. Typically, speculative land development projects were launched by more established, more moneyed men than merchants engaged in the Atlantic trade for the first time. The City Corporation acquired a lease over land on which the central area and future dock district of Liverpool could be developed as late as 1777, and then it manipulated that lease for profit during the city's second century of growth.

Private property and social order became so closely linked in England that government interference with the former was thought to disrupt the latter. How different this was from the situation on the Continent! The careful observer should not be deceived by the Queen's Palace and Hospital at Greenwich (Jones, 1619–1635 and Wren, 1696–1699), by the great squares of Stuart and Georgian London, by Georgian Bath, or by the New Town of Edinburgh into thinking that the English had ever accepted the Continental spirit: they may have enriched architecture with these and other masterpieces, but architecture cannot be confused with city planning. The great English architectural compositions were not designed to encourage other urban developments, as Continental compositions had often been designed to do since the Renaissance. They were self-sufficient parts that enhanced the rest of a city by the contrast they provoked in it. There was no effort to see the whole as more than the sum of its parts, or any attempt to see in the handling of urban space an opportunity for social or political change. In England debates over change had been detached from the problems of city growth: even though city growth often provoked social and political tensions (as in seventeenth-century London),[12] limits to or a reordering of growth patterns were not among the solutions seriously considered. Liverpool's story in the early eighteenth century can be explained in English terms alone, but that should not blind us to its importance: both Liverpool's unplanned growth and development and planning for St. Petersburg reflected opinions about the contribution city planning could make to maritime expansion.

Maritime Culture in the Age of Enlightenment: The Context for Planning

Both Liverpool merchants and St. Petersburg princes thought of maritime expansion in terms of city space. They arrived at radically different judgments about the relationship of the one to the other while agreeing that the relationship was critical. For this reason both cities belong to a seventeenth-century, and not a distinctively eighteenth-century, frame of reference. What happened in these two cities on the eastern and western frontiers of Europe was literally peripheral to developments in the center, where changes in the Anglo-French maritime world brought on the decline in port city planning. The new eighteenth-century approach called for a decorative, ordered waterfront as a richly evocative by-product of commercial growth and military glory. Planners in London and Bordeaux, for example, no longer thought of the appearance or form of the port city as a critical factor in commercial or military sea power. Their judgment represented a decisive break with seventeenth-century port city planning. That story, which cannot be understood only in terms of the internal history of planning, becomes clear when presented in terms of the role left for planning in the broader maritime culture. For this reason, a study of eighteenth-century maritime culture in England and France precedes here a discussion of planning for London and Bordeaux.

When port city planning emerged in western Europe early in the seventeenth century, existing social, economic, cultural, and political values could neither promote nor sustain an understanding of new patterns of maritime exploitation without modification. Port city planning helped at least one small yet critical group of western Europeans adapt to a new maritime age, but relatively few people contributed to the arguments that port city planning stimulated. Conditioned by the old monolithic view of the sea as a hostile place, contemporaries largely ignored the cultural distance separating their society from the sea and failed to notice that that distance had begun to diminish. They became more conscious of maritime affairs when accumulated knowledge three generations deep began to sweep through French and English culture, riding the high tide of the Enlightenment, replete with its own optimistic outlook on nature and experience. In the eighteenth century conflicts and ambiguities in Western man's understanding of maritime affairs became visible to a much wider circle of Europeans. As changes took place in European arts and letters, some writers and painters did new things with the sea—things that had not been attempted as often or perhaps as well before; they loosened old traditions and gradually elaborated new settings for the sea in a world of man's works and ideas. Once political and economic theory, creative fiction-writing, and art began to absorb port city planning's role as a mediator between society and seafaring, the spatial aspect of port cities no longer seemed relevant to the success of maritime enterprise. Having lost their preeminence in Europe's maritime culture, planners tried to articulate in their own medium a spatial analog to the more innovative, exciting, and provocative attempts to understand the maritime world that others were undertaking: projects for city space became rhetorical, academic exercises in monumentality and impracticality.[13] Engineers inherited the planners' earlier claims to practicality, and they alone became responsible for the urban settings for building, outfitting, and coordinating the movements of large fleets of ships.

Literature

English and French writers began to reevaluate their ideas of the place of the sea in literature, which they had inherited from the Renaissance at least a century after their nations' adventurers and merchants had undertaken the permanent and systematic exploitation of the sea for the first time. Richard Hakluyt had written accounts of voyages in the 1580s so that the English public might know of and be excited about the new nautical age, but in 1724 Defoe could still complain that discovery voyages, commercial trade, and naval encounters were visible in books only "superficially and by halves; [that] the storms and difficulties at sea or on shore have nowhere a full relation; and [that nautical accounts] are generally filled up with directions for sailors coming that way."[14] Tedious logs made dull books, but they are precious evidence of what marked the seventeenth century from previous periods of English and French maritime growth because, like markings on a trail, they indicated that the path of a few pioneers would be repeated routinely. But clearly that was not what men of literary imagination wanted to find in the new nautical age. Seventeenth-century writers used the picturesque or factual evidence of travelers' books to make the sea more real when they bound it into a framework of religious and philosophical ideas.[15] They used the sea as a symbol, and were interested in details about it only to give their expressions the resonance of versimilitude. They saw the seas with the fear of Noah and the conscience of Jonah, the memory of Ulysses and the spirituality of Jesus and his disciples. "Dread Neptune's wild unsocial sea" (Freneau's phrase) was no place for man to stray; its waters would undermine any established community. Writers exploited the sea as a symbol at the expense of the real maritime world around them.

Defoe did not object to the conventional literary use of the sea; rather, he hoped to find in fiction a way to make the new nautical age more interesting to readers. Even though Defoe was a London-based merchant-adventurer who exercised a practical view of affairs, he still asserted the primacy of the imagination over the perceptual environment: he still wanted to submit the sea to his own view of it, which clearly derived from his authority as a writer, and not from his involvement in maritime commerce. Defoe was as yet unready to describe the tasks of seafaring and the accomplishments of seafarers as an important part of a story. His *A New Voyage Round the World* is picaresque, not picturesque; it is disappointing because each storm and each adventure seems identical to all the others, even if it is not. Defoe did not write the first great modern sea story, but his desire to do so is more important than the results he published. His dissatisfaction with existing literary realism pointed to problems that would control literary and artistic production for the next century. How could writers or painters without an intimate knowledge of the sea make a portrait of the sea interesting and plausible? To what ends could a more realistic perception of the sea be directed? Would such a perception help a man better understand himself and his world?

Writers, hesitant to study or describe the sea or to include in their works conditions of life introduced by the new nautical age, continued to apply inherited notions about the sea. Even the central Enlightenment concepts of nature and experience encouraged them to view the sea as a soulless and desolate space, for the sea itself could not yet be included in a concept of nature that made nature rational and open to knowledge through experience.[16] The science of oceanography did not exist at a time when thinking persons were busy organizing, classifying, and conceptualizing the biological, physical, and geological aspects of nature. The point about science is important, because writers replaced the traditional religious view of mountains as ugly and irregular signs of sin for a sublime appreciation of their beauty when Newtonian science and geology made possible an understanding of mountains as part of God's plan. Perhaps the older, traditional, view of the sea as a primeval, original force moved by God since the birth of the world could survive in the Newtonian age, whereas the equally traditional view of mountains as unnatural signs of the fall from grace could not. Joseph Addison was one of the first to grasp that the beauties of mountains and seas were similar,[17] but few writers found it as easy to write about the maritime world as to write about mountains.[18] The natural landscape of eighteenth-century literature was largely terrestrial, whether composed of gardens, of grand vistas, or of precipices.

Two who tried a more documentary approach to the sea were William Falconer and Tobias Smollett. In 1762 Falconer published a long poem, "The Shipwreck," which was popular in its day on both sides of the Atlantic. In it Falconer explored the diction and vocabulary of seafarers (perhaps brought into popular literature for the first time), but he blended it with his own view of the sea as an alien and hostile place: only the seaman's skill and experience could turn the sea to some good use.[19] Falconer's work marked an advance on traditional literary convention, but it still reflected the older judgment that, fundamentally, the sea was alien to man. Such a perspective would encourage those without knowledge of the sea to remain ignorant, and to leave mastery of the sea to seafarers. Smollett's mid-century novels also portrayed the sea as wild and primitive, beyond understanding or praise; their interest for us lies in Smollett's attempt to describe life in the Royal Navy. Both Smollett and Falconer conveyed an appreciation for the seaman's professionalism, but neither could indicate what stake the land-based reader had in what took place at sea. Perhaps because the underdeveloped scientific study of the sea made the sea appear unapproachable and alien, even writers like Smollett and Falconer could not celebrate the maritime world.

Falconer and Smollett were unable to dissolve the established literary formulae regarding the sea; their ventures seemed difficult and tentative. Although the volume of poetic and fictional maritime writings began to increase during the second half of the eighteenth century, most of their creators were unsuccessful at establishing literary reflections of the maritime world that were unbounded by traditional philosophical and religious frameworks. Seafaring was more accurately described, and the sea itself was looked at more closely, but by people with their feet firmly on the ground, who still found the sea on the horizon of man's thoughts. Writers were not yet looking at the land from the sea, nor, really, at the sea itself, but at least their attempts to fit more of the maritime world into literature raised questions about the appropriateness and versimilitude of the older literary conventions, and so helped readers and writers alike become more open to the maritime world. At least this is the tentative conclusion that can be made on the basis of analyses by Stein and Philbrick. But these two researchers have barely skimmed the surface, as they admit. There is much more to be learned about the reasons for the increasing number of literary materials referring to the sea and the meanings they conveyed to their readers.

Writers handled sea materials with ease and ambition at the end of the eighteenth and during the first half of the nineteenth centuries, when a greater understanding of the sea and an intensified search for its relevance to man were channeled into literary expression. The tensions between man and the sea, between society and the maritime world it exploited—tensions that had been a part of the maritime culture ever since the end of the sixteenth century—could be seen in a tremendous literary effort to relate the inner self to the outer world, and to base concepts of identity and existence on perceptions of the environment that were epistemologically and psychologically grounded in the humanism of individual sensibility. The comments that follow do not do justice to either the beauty and strength of numerous stories and poems or the rich body of critical interpretation surrounding them; they are presented in order to document the fact that literature could at last claim for itself an outstanding role in the interpretation of the maritime world.

Poets (Byron in "Childe Harold," Coleridge in "The Rime of the Ancient Mariner") explored the freedom and solitude of those on the sea as good things of themselves.[20] In contrast to a trivial life on shore, time spent at sea could bring on an awareness of eternity, of the unknown, and of one's own destiny. The qualities of being at sea that had encouraged earlier writers only to refer to the sea as a place for the fear of God encouraged these poets to use the sea as a setting for the most profound and revealing experiences of life, but this was still the literary use of the sea for its philosophical values. Novelists, especially in America (Cooper, and, later, Melville), who had an intimate knowledge of seafaring and had a vision of its role in civilization also portrayed the sea as a place where men fought for self-realization and, often, for life itself. Such literary uses of the sea could still reinforce the impression that the sea, and life at sea, were fundamentally divorced from society, which was wholly a terrestrial enterprise: perhaps this explains why eighteenth-century writers stepped back from the shoreline, while romantic authors went on board ship.

There was, however, a tendency among some writers (including Dana, and sometimes Cooper) to demonstrate the contrary, that the effect of sailing on the seaman was like that of farming and hunting on those who worked the land and walked the forests, and that the sea and seafaring were interesting precisely as they revealed parallels to the lives of all men. To be sure, many early-nineteenth-century American writers saw the sea as their country's true frontier, and celebrated America's independence and growth through a fascination with the ocean; the development of maritime novels in the United States was certainly more rapid, intensive, and far-reaching than it was in England or France. Whatever the reason, writers informed their readers about the maritime world in such a way that for the first time the land seemed to support the sea, instead of the other way around. Nevertheless, it would be wrong to magnify the differences between the romantics, who described the sea for metaphysical and aesthetic reasons, and the realists, who described the maritime world in order to make it concrete and approachable. Both groups enlarged the place of the sea in Western literature far beyond what it had ever been before. They may have disagreed about why man should use the sea or pay attention to it; but that disagreement was not new to their day, as the history of seventeenth-century port city planning makes clear. What was new was the fact that that disagreement had become a major issue in the literary world.

For reasons that have not been explained, the great literary interest in the sea did not survive the American Civil War or the Crimean War, even though both wars demonstrated the importance of sea power as much as the engagements of the Napoleonic era had. Writing of the sea since the mid-nineteenth century calls to mind the novels of Joseph Conrad and Jules Verne and poems by Arnold, Baudelaire, Mallarmé, and Valéry, but interest in these writers has had little to do with their uses of the sea. The sea had earlier been a central theme in writing, not peripheral to an understanding of individual and society, but central to it; but then the sea gradually lost that role. In the last century such a theme has attracted neither critics nor audience: Melville has become popular only since the 1920s and the publication of Lewis Mumford's biography, and Cooper's sea novels were neglected altogether until Philbrick's study appeared in 1961. Perhaps now that transoceanic travel has moved into the air few writers will care to ask their readers to become familiar with the richly divergent meanings of seafaring for man. The *Iliad,* the *Odyssey,* and the *Aeniad,* three primal classics of Western literature, are likely to remain the great maritime texts.

Political and Economic Theories

In the early eighteenth century a few writers of fiction saw what the potential for literature might be if the inherited literary nautical conventions were dissolved, but an imaginative mastery over the sea and a vision of the problems associated with contact with the sea came slowly. A "sea change" finally did occur in literature, as we have seen. Nevertheless, new perceptions of the sea and of seafaring did not eliminate stereotypes. Instead, two approaches to the sea unfolded at the same time, one new, the other old. Economic theorists paid attention to the sea long before fictional writers did, yet their knowledge of the sea and their ability to resolve the problems associated with its exploitation were no greater. Why?

The answer, whether for the few seventeenth-century economic writers or the many eighteenth-century ones, is that the nature of the maritime world eluded those who did not belong to it. Writers did not find it hard to realize that the commercial networks of port cities and the traffic carried between them created particular economic and political interests for those involved; contrasts between the maritime and agrarian worlds were easily made. But economic and political theorists made the mistake of trying to assimilate or integrate one world into the other, because they never really discovered that the two worlds were hardly related at all: each writer tried to describe the entire economic system, and somehow failed to comprehend how his view of the whole was distorted by his misunderstanding of how the parts differed. Whereas travelers' books made the topography, society, and economy of, for example, rural France or commercial Holland familiar to outsiders, such books tended to create the impression that every country's rural and commercial economies had more in common with each other than either might have with its homologue elsewhere. Thus, Frenchmen discussed French commerce as it related to French agriculture, and not as it related to English or Dutch commerce.

In the seventeenth century, states had not been masters of the fiscal unity of their territory, and so models of economic interchange and development had not seemed practical. But once that formative period of state-building ended—at around the turn of the eighteenth century—the failure to perceive the autonomy of maritime and agrarian worlds had greater consequences. Debates and controversy about economic and political reforms only heightened the public sense that the issues at stake were real, and that rational comprehension of the issues was possible.[21] The obvious differences between economic models based on the maritime world and models based on the agrarian one only made partisans feel more certain that one of the models was right and the other wrong. Such convictions led many thinking eighteenth-century Europeans to believe that in economic and political studies they had an instrument with which they could gain leverage against the material, natural world. Those who described the maritime world wanted their descriptions to help modify the context in which merchants and smugglers, customs officers and tax ministers, naval officers, suppliers, and administrators operated. But often the habits and activities of seafaring did not conform to their new roles, and the theorists did not bother to explain why this was so.[22]

It is not possible to know whether port city planning became less important because economic and political studies appeared to describe the relations between the land and the sea in terms of taxation and politics, but it is worthwhile to suggest that the very emphasis such writers gave to fiscal and political programs minimized the contributions to economic growth that planned port cities would make. Of course this does not do justice to the richness and originality of writers ranging from Jean Bodin to Adam Smith. Nevertheless, as in the case of literature, I can suggest, though not affirm, what a new reading of economic and political texts demonstrates: I can call attention to the impact such texts may have had on the cultural context for port city planning.

Those most suspicious of the maritime world (Bodin, Montchrétien, Cantillon, the Physiocrats) certainly would have thought that the added investment port city planning called for might exacerbate the harmful influence such cities had on agricultural production and national policy—if they gave the subject any thought at all. Others more favorably disposed to maritime commerce, Englishmen like Mun, Child, Temple, Petty, and Smith, and Continentals such as Laffemas, Boisguilbert, and Galiani, thought that the natural tendency of such commerce to expand was most likely to be influenced by state fiscal policies; mercantilists and free traders alike would have agreed that port city planning absorbed resources and energies best invested in industry

and commerce directly. That port city planning offered ways to emphasize or
deemphasize the maritime world mattered little to writers more concerned
with the circulation of money, the operations of the market place, and the
influence of government policy on trade and production. They were not in a
position to notice that the exploitation of the sea and the cultivation of the
land had separate spatial settings, because they did not see in the differences
in appearance between the great port cities and the trading centers of the
agrarian hinterland the suggestion that each represented a separate social and
economic sphere not paying much attention to the other.[23]

Not until the end of the nineteenth century did English and French
writers begin to emphasize how little the rural hinterland and the ocean
seaboard had in common, politically, socially, or economically. In France
geographers made decisive and rapid progress toward understanding *mentalités,* traditions, values, and lifestyles in terms of social and physical environments. From Vidal de la Blanche to Jean Brunhes, Maximilien Sorre, Lucien
Febvre, and Fernand Braudel, French scholars have given human geography
an analytical framework and historical depth.[24] Their works have endowed
discrete patterns of life with structure, meaning, and visibility, which is what
should concern the social sciences. The French approach, with its emphasis on
a theoretical, generalized, and synthetic scaffolding for articulating the specific, variant identities of differing societies, provides researchers with points
of reference within and outside their own fields.

In contrast is Anglo-American scholarship on the maritime world in the
past century, which has emphasized historical studies. When historical
maritime studies take as a point of reference other, land, events occurring
simultaneously with an event at sea, the result often obscures how the exploitation of commercial and military sea power involves fundamental questions of economic structures and geographic settings: the distinct features of
the maritime world do not become important enough to notice except insofar
as they are linked to the context in which the events being analyzed took place.
Much more is known about the formation of high naval policy now than in
1890, when A. T. Mahan wrote *The Influence of Sea Power upon History,* a work
that had an astonishing impact on the Western world.[25] But Mahan's effort to
associate the fitness of a national culture or political system for sea power with
the evolution of tactics and strategy has not had a sequel. There are dozens of
books on leading statesmen and naval officers and important battles, but they
all tend to make the navy easier to understand in its organizational and
technological dimensions;[26] by inference alone are unique aspects of the
maritime world to be understood as part of a social, cultural, and physical
environment. Only a few authors, Arthur J. Marder and Samuel Eliot
Morison most prominently, have written of sea power with some passionate
sense of what it represents in civilization.[27]

Yet the French approach does not hold all the advantages. As the best
Anglo-American historical writings (and the seventeenth-century evidence in
this book) demonstrate, there is a political and intellectual context in which
maritime affairs are best understood and manipulated. There is a tendency in
the holistic French social geographers' approach to insulate the coastal "men-

tality" against rapid change and to make it appear more autonomous and self-sustaining than it might be. Surely the French and Anglo-American styles of scholarship can complement each other.

Studies of commercial seaborne empires, even more than studies of military sea power, have highlighted the political, social, and economic values carried by those who engage in maritime affairs as well as the impact of their successes and failures on the land-locked society at home.[28] There are also some pioneering works which suggest that a holistic, integrated approach to the seacoast may be valued more in the years to come.[29] Mahan wrote an analysis of naval warfare in civilization in order that his work might have programmatic, prospective value. Few writers since have had such ambition, but now there is reason to anticipate greater demand for conceptual studies of the maritime world.[30] After three quarters of a century of land wars and empires and conquest of the near and far reaches of space, the oceans are becoming the central arena of the 1975 to 2000 period. The importance of navies has only increased since World War Two, whether measured by the strength of the Soviet fleets or by the American resort to blockades of Cuba and Hanoi; in law and in science[31] the oceans are, for the first time, the principal unexplored topic. What this means for the study of society and human achievement remains to be seen.

Painting

Should it be so surprising that the seventeenth-century maritime world developed without making much of an impact on French and English arts and letters? The discovery of new continents and voyages of adventure had their place in European culture, but the practical use of the sea did not represent the culmination of a long-nourished project or the final realization of a cherished dream. Writers, painters, and political theorists in France and England were preoccupied with other problems, and so were largely unconcerned about what was happening on Europe's maritime frontier. And they kept their distance from the sea of commercial routes and naval engagements until those had long lost their novelty. When literature and the study of society finally made room for the experiences and achievements of the new maritime age, they integrated that age into existing cultural patterns without trying to understand it in its own terms. Painting reacted toward the sea in much the same way. The immediacy and color of paintings make them—and their subjects—seem much more accessible than books. But painters came no closer than writers to resolving the choice between creating new forms of thought and symbols for seafaring or refining and updating older ones.[32]

Although the Dutch enthusiastically stimulated marine painting throughout the seventeenth century, the English and French never really cared for the genre or understood why the Dutch liked it so much. Some Frenchmen, such as Pierre Puget, approximated a marine style on their own, especially in drawings of boats, but that aspect of their work went unrewarded and unnoticed. The Van de Veldes lived in England after 1672, painting the naval encounters of England's fleets, but their work had only minimal influence on painting there for quite a while, and was appreciated chiefly for its documentary value. Instead, most artists and their patrons preferred works of art that referred to the sea in symbols (the shell) or in caricature (mythological figures). The works of Claude Gelée were popular in France and England for this reason. Claude's idealized architectural settings by the sea and his natural coastline subjects encouraged viewing the sea according to already determined cultural lines; the sea was included in a composition for the effect it made, for what the painter could do with it, and not for its own sake or interest. The decision of whether or not to paint water, ships, and seashore was an artistic one; these subjects were portrayed to heighten the contrast between the familiar and the exotic, perhaps, or to idealize the sea. For whatever the reasons, Claude, and others who used the sea in the same way, kept the sea firmly fixed in a typology of nature. There was no hint in their works of the new nautical age around them.

This changed somewhat at the turn of the eighteenth century. No one knows why the change in England and France toward a more realistic view of the sea occurred then rather than earlier or later. Painters such as Samuel Scott and the younger Van de Velde in England started out with a new approach to the seashore itself, as if they still had difficulty in leaving the shore for the open sea. Instead of painting an imaginary setting of buildings, rocks, and people in front of a sea that receded evenly toward a golden horizon, they showed a strong interest in seaports as they actually were; they found artistic value in the play of light on the sights of a port; they made the real seem ideal and immediate when they gave artistic dignity to scenes everyone had lived with but had not yet taken seriously as subjects for painting. These artists painted what they saw, freezing a moment in the life of a port city onto canvas. Their paintings, however, never achieved the renown of Canaletto's paintings of the Thames from Somerset House Terrace and Joseph Vernet's unprecedented and unsurpassed sweeping survey of French ports, both executed at mid-eighteenth century. Canaletto and Vernet did not always try to paint an actual scene; instead, they sometimes rearranged what could be noticed on the waterfront for greater variety and interest, placing people, boats, and objects where they wished within the fixed architectural frame. The architectural background was reproduced with fidelity so that the activities represented in the foreground might appear realistic, but this search for effect only heightened the sense of disappointment that cityscapes did not in fact look like pictures of them. Their work implied a criticism of port cities as they actually appeared, as if the changing scenes of life in such places were unintelligible and lacking in beauty until the painter restructured them. From this it was a short step to the design and construction of waterfront ensembles that would transform any quayside into a setting worthy of a picture.

Perhaps the pursuit of the sublime was more difficult in such a familiar and busy place as a port city waterfront than on a remote peninsula or on a mountain road. Efforts to endow the activities of a port city with meaning in visual terms enlarged the artist's subject matter from what it had been in the seventeenth century, but it also called attention to the maritime world for its aesthetic potential rather than for its inherent qualities. This is an important point. Until the nineteenth century true marine painting—ships and the sea—remained the concern only of those officers, merchants, and administrators already possessing a practical knowledge of the sea. Two painters sailed with Cook in 1768 to record his voyage and its discoveries, something no one (except Prince Maurice of Nassau, when he went to Brazil in 1637) had thought to do in previous centuries. If Turner had not grown up near London's docks, it is unlikely that he would have turned to marine subjects so early in life. In 1803 Constable spent a month on a merchant ship and made 130 sketches of ships and weather conditions, but his experience was still extraordinary. By and large the English and French public ready to acquire and appreciate paintings of ships at sea and of their ports of call was as small as the number of artists capable of executing such works. Canaletto and Vernet were successful precisely because they understood that realism alone would not satisfy the aesthetic temper of the age.

Any mention of painting's subsequent uses of the seas must be brief; the nineteenth and twentieth centuries in England and France await their interpreters. Roger B. Stein has shown how a nation's maritime culture can be interpreted from three hundred years of art. His *Seascape and the American Imagination* is not just a catalogue of paintings, for Stein was able to relate the technical aspects of composition and execution of successive themes and styles to changing demands for knowledge of the sea. Similar studies must be carried out for England and France as well. Such studies would perhaps threaten the heroic, isolated position of an artist like Turner, but they would immeasurably enrich our knowledge of painting and its place in an economy of knowledge. Such studies would concentrate on paintings that are currently noticed for their subject matter of ships, seas, men, and battles, and not for their painterly qualities. And such studies would renew the connections between travel and the sea.

In the eighteenth century paintings of the outdoors were often made as souvenirs for tourists on the grand tour. In the late nineteenth century new patterns of resort travel opened the Breton, Norman, and Mediterranean coasts of France to those who lived far away from them. Painting was never the same (as evidenced by works by Cézanne, Monet, Matisse, Boudin, Marquet, Dufy, etc.).[33] How the painters got to the sea has been considered a minor and inconsequential part of the story of modern art. In fact, in cultural terms, France was largely detached from the Mediterranean during most of the nineteenth century. Only since the 1880s has the Mediterranean extended its influence over more aspects of French life—food, fashion, leisure, and politics and economics, too—than at any other time since the sixteenth century. Today Cézanne's view of Marseille from L'Estaque still looks true-to-life, but so much has changed as a result of half a century of urbanization along the coast from the Spanish to the Italian border that it is not easy to reconstruct what life along the French Mediterranean was like before 1914. When the stories of the creation of resort complexes facing the sea in Languedoc, the new industrial center at Fos, and the Côte d'Azur from Cannes to Menton, as well as the story of the fate of the hinterland from the Pyrenees to the Alps are told, the first chapter should belong to the imaginations of painters and tourists.

Decorative Planning in London and Bordeaux

This conceptual framework for understanding the erosion of seventeenth-century port city planning—which had as its function the production of an urban framework suitable for the exploitation of the sea—raises more questions about maritime culture than it answers. Even so, this demonstration of the enlarged capacity of artistic expression for comprehending and describing the maritime world is important to the thesis that the altered cultural climate in which planning operated had more to do with changes in port city planning than the internal evolution of planning and building styles did.

In the seventeenth century the problems of port city growth had been among the most demanding faced by city planners anywhere in the European world, and solutions to those problems must be ranked among the most creative and advanced urban projects of that century. Artist-planners had not tried to conform to or reflect the aesthetic trends of the day, but rather had adopted, rejected, or created styles according to their appropriateness in a given situation, a judgment based on practical considerations of city change and function. Not so in the eighteenth century. Those charged with fostering maritime commerce and naval power then concerned themselves but little with the spatial character and growth patterns of port cities. Planning for port cities derived its formal vocabulary from styles already established in more courtly or rural settings, such as Nancy and Bath. The limited place of port city planning in the history of eighteenth-century architecture and urbanism is a measure of the extent to which Europeans were linking maritime affairs to painting, literature, and political and economic studies. As the problems of sea power and maritime affairs were understood in the eighteenth century, port city planning did not appear to have anything practical to contribute. The erosion of port city planning was not brought about by changes within the architectural world, but by changes without.

Eighteenth-century elites might have followed the example of Liverpool merchants and strenuously avoided any further involvement with port city planning. Instead, they embraced planning for its decorative value alone, and claimed front-row seats in the theater of the waterfront. They fixed upon the very features of the waterfront that made it a working space—light, room, access to water, and concentration of buildings and activities—and tried to orchestrate them into an aesthetic enhancement of the cityscape. The sights, sounds, and spaces associated with maritime affairs were to echo the rhythms of seafaring for the pleasure of those who knew enough to recognize their importance. London and Bordeaux, discussed here, are two cities where such activity occurred.

The thrust toward waterside spatial design for purely decorative ends had been present in the seventeenth century. Scandinavian city designs were often monumental and impractical, but they were not purely decorative, for they were supposed to have an influence on patterns of port city growth. Truly monumental design for aesthetic and decorative purposes only had been limited to the great rural palaces of the rich and powerful. The châteaux at Chantilly and Versailles were set off by moats, canals, and water fountains; Isola Bella of Count Carlo Borromeo and the Villa d'Este in Italy, and Greenwich, Westbury Court, and Chatsworth in England are other seventeenth-century examples.[34] There were also the fanciful and imaginary waterside palaces of Sweden's Erik Dahlberg (published in his *Suecia Antiqua et Hodierna*), complete with pleasure-boating, the view of water from the land and of land from the water, and the play of light by day and night. Such willful and playful ordering of nature was supposed to enhance the status of those who lived and played in such settings; it was supposed to satisfy their sense of their own worth. In the eighteenth century this sort of design was proposed for vast areas of great port cities.

London

One of the first to want to apply this pastoral dream to a city was John Evelyn. His plan for restoring burnt-out London "to far greater Beauty Commodiousness and Magnificence"[35] was flawed by this contradiction: what enhanced the visual aspect of the city often was achieved at the expense of practicality. Thus Evelyn wanted warehouses, if placed along the Thames, to be located beneath beautiful houses on the embankment, but preferred that the warehouses be moved altogether to the south side of the Thames so that the north embankment ("of the noblest aspect") could be given over entirely and uncompromisingly to "palaces." The "deformed" structures lining London Bridge would have to go; they detracted from the bridge's beauty and from the whole city near the river. What Evelyn had in mind was a London of lovely vistas and architectural properties in which the movement and manufacture of goods could be kept to a minimum. Christopher Wren's plan for London also gave prominence to a regular linear embankment along the Thames, and the plans of both men gave prominence to the commercial City at the expense of courtly Westminster. But neither seems to have grasped the fact that merchants would show little interest in grand perspectives and symmetrical alignments. There is an additional damaging criticism of plans by Evelyn and Wren: the appearance of feasibility notwithstanding, neither set of plans would have helped London solve its problems of growth. Those problems required political and financial solutions before a spatial plan for metropolitan expansion would be relevant. Either Evelyn and Wren overlooked this or they presumed that their plans would raise the vision of the City fathers beyond the City's walls—in either case, they were wrong. Evelyn referred with praise to the great variety of cityscapes in Italian stage design; he wanted London to dazzle and impress the spectator; and he would have made the city's appearance into something that could be contemplated aesthetically for its own sake, without reference to political, social, and economic activities that made the space possible and gave it usefulness. Evelyn demanded too much of

London's leaders, but he was not the last person to hope that London might become as beautiful as it was powerful.

Defoe, who hinted that this was his vision as well, imagined the result in different terms than Evelyn. Defoe found the activity and color of the port evocative of London's greatness and vitality. He refused to contrast (as Evelyn had) economic and industrial activity with a quieter, more dignified urban lifestyle—to the port's disadvantage. To Defoe the life of the city—what people did in it—made the city interesting. Defoe described London's markets, trade, and harbor at great length in his *Tour,* and in his concluding survey of the city's prominent features he ranked markets after churches and before palaces. But Defoe was dissatisfied with the London he knew: "It is the disaster of London that it is thus stretched out in buildings, just as the pleasure of every builder or undertaker of buildings, and as the convenience of the people directs, whether for trade or otherwise; and thus has spread the face of it in a most strange line, confus'd manner out of all shape, uncompact and unequal; neither long or broad, round or square."[36] Defoe explicitly included London's waterfront in this criticism. It would be wrong, however, to say that Defoe thought of beauty in conventional terms. His praise of neoclassical, Newtonian symmetry did not refer to spatial, geometric order as a reflection of pure form or as a symbol of absolute political power. Rather, Defoe wanted to order space so that the impression of what occurred in that space would be more easily and pleasurably seen. This objective represented a more complex idea than Evelyn's. Defoe could not articulate or explain this, but could only hint at it. He was in fact invoking the appeal of the sublime, which few others of his day cared to explore.

It is important to take notice of Defoe: he wanted to monumentalize a specific and unique part of the city, its waterfront, that was being spurned because it was of economic interest only, and he wanted to do so for the reason that the activities associated with seafaring were important and interesting enough to deserve an architectonic stone frame. A beautified waterfront would add to London's total impression of orderedness. Defoe's view of ordered space attributed to certain architectural or spatial elements the power to stimulate the imagination by provoking the spectator to notice the activities they contained. Whereas Evelyn had been dismayed by the apparent disorder maritime commerce created in London and had wanted to remove the sight of it as completely as possible, Defoe wanted to make dockside and waterfront activities attractive to see.

Defoe wrote about London early in the eighteenth century, when artists and architects had limited opportunities to act on his or anyone's ideas. By the end of the eighteenth century architects began to rebuild large areas of the city. The planning for Georgian London remains a rich area for research; the work of George Dance the Younger (1768–1825) is representative of the period.[37] Dance confronted London's enormous growth as it approached one million inhabitants. As clerk of the City Works he found government willing, for the first time, to tear down the old walls and take an interest in development beyond. Dance planned a number of residential developments and communications roads, principally for Corporation land, some of which were executed. He also planned major portside works, a double bridge to replace old London Bridge (1786), the Bridgeyard Warehouses (1796), and the Legal Quays (1796–1802), none of which was executed. Dance, who understood the conditions for residential-estate development far better than he did those for waterfront development, emphasized the value of central city land in order to enforce the City's monopoly over customs, taxation, and trade. His Legal Quays project would have lured commodity traffic away from the south and southeast bank to London's center so areas that had a semi-industrial character could become residential areas. Dance must have hoped that the merchants who owned land already given over to commerce and industry outside the City could be lured into approving his schemes by the prospect of profits to be made on the redevelopment of their property. But the merchants must have understood that their cooperation would enhance the City's control over trade and at the same time limit their activities to a monumental structure (adapted from Roman models), which lacked as necessary a feature as a network of streets around it to alleviate the inevitable traffic congestion. There were good reasons why the future users of Dance's warehouses wanted nothing to do with his projects.

The solution that was in fact executed instead of Dance's schemes in the early nineteenth century simply transferred the City's privileges to downstream docks that were privately financed and built by engineers, not by architects.[38] The amount of available land in central London could not have been adequate to match the annual increase in the volume of trade: in the period from 1800 to 1815 the new docks built along the southeastern reaches of London's Thameside totalled 172 acres, and that figure omits warehouses and roadways. Thus Dance's schemes seem poorly adapted to the scale of late-eighteenth-century London. Dance should have tried to regularize and rationalize two centuries of London waterfront development; instead, he tried to undo that pattern with his schemes for docks (truly monumental structures by size alone) to be installed in parts of the city where they did not belong. One can only hypothesize that he was led by the conviction that central London's beauty could be enhanced with the Legal Quays project as a centerpiece in a vast scheme to redevelop the riverfront for residential space, as if the upper classes would enjoy being nearer to a dock than a garden. Dance's projects echo the more absolute, dominating role for architecture in city space typical of the late eighteenth century because he apparently had no sense of the demands seafaring placed on a port city. He seems to have thought of maritime commerce as something that could fit into a building, like a parish into a church; he did not consider whether his projects might enhance or threaten London's commercial and industrial activities. Defoe only wanted to improve the architectural settings in which Londoners worked; Dance wanted to alter the spatial distribution of activities in order to create opportunities for himself to design great buildings. What is important is not the caution of London's government, which failed to approve any of Dance's three port schemes, but Dance's feeling that the schemes should be approved. The re-

FIGURE **6.3.** *Bordeaux, 1785, plan by Victor Louis for the Place Ludovise. Musée des Arts Décoratifs, Bordeaux.*

jected plans for Restoration and Georgian London have more than antiquarian value, for they help illuminate the widening separation of port city planning from an understanding of maritime affairs.

Bordeaux

Helen Rosenau has suggested that Dance might have been influenced by projects for Bordeaux that had been reproduced as engravings and circulated across Europe.[39] From 1726 on, successive intendants and architects had promoted schemes to beautify Bordeaux, a port city that had preserved its traditional role as a wine-exporting base while becoming one of the critical links in the European-African-American trade of manufactured goods, slaves, and sugar. The principal harbor area stretched along the Garonne riverfront of the old city. Most of the projects called for straightening out the city's riverfront facade with new housing and with symmetrically designed formal squares for principal buildings such as the Bourse (construction begun in the 1730s). No overall plan dominated the work of successive architects and administrators. They approached the city instead with a critical sense that so much maritime trade deserved a more flattering harbor than Bordeaux could as yet offer. New structures—houses, the Bourse, a halle for the tax authorities—were assigned a place in the city along the river according to where they might best improve the city's appearance. The number of images of Neptune decorating the new buildings and monuments (statues, arches) must have been truly remarkable.

Two unexecuted projects best represent the spirit that encouraged so much construction. Both date from around 1785 and had as their inception the proposal to tear down the Château-Trompette fort, which stood alongside the river and blocked the city's growth to the southeast. Remodeled (by Mazarin) after the city's mid-seventeenth-century revolt (the Ormée) had been crushed, the fort had come to symbolize political relations between city and state that Louis XVI's enlightened ministers thought anachronistic. (They were obviously unaware that Bordeaux still stood for a different approach to politics than that expressed by the Bourbon centralized state, an approach articulated during the Revolution through the Girondins.) The architect Victor Louis offered a project, sometimes attributed to his subordinate Combes, for a great semicircular place with a statue of the king in its center and thirteen streets radiating inland from it (figure 6.3). The thirteen streets represented the newly independent United States, with which Bordeaux's merchants traded so heavily. This project was accepted in favor of another one by Lhote in 1785. The place was to have carried the name of the sponsoring minister, Calonne, who soon fell from power. Only one building was ever constructed from Louis's plan. Another project for this space was put forward by Dupré de Saint-Maur, intendant for Guyenne from 1776 to 1784, who tried to do much more than plan a place where the Château-Trompette stood. His place was smaller than Louis's and called for only five radiating streets, but he compensated by imagining a bridge across the Garonne, several new streets in Bordeaux, and a long semicircular canal enclosing the entire city beyond its limits.

A Hamburg merchant named Meyer visited late-eighteenth-century Bordeaux, and his impressions reveal why Louis and Saint-Maur conceived such impractical if formally stunning projects: "Along the Garonne and for a league in length stretches a line of great houses . . . the continual coming and going of great and small boats, the tumult of loading and unloading on the banks, what a pleasant painting [this is], ceaselessly renewed by the effects of light which change at all hours of the day!"[40] Meyer's image of Bordeaux related art to life in a way that illuminates the eighteenth-century decline of port city planning. Artist-planners were no longer concerned with making Bordeaux a more permanent or profitable commercial base (they failed to improve the inadequate traffic connections between the quays and the rest of the city); their concern was with satisfying the tastes of all the Meyers of Europe, those who wanted to ennoble commerce by surrounding it with aesthetic symbols that were divorced from the problems and profits of commercial activity. The architectonic harmony of a row of new buildings along the waterfront did nothing for shipping; it could be evaluated only by aesthetic or stylistic criteria that were derived from notions of sensibility and beauty that had nothing to do with maritime affairs.

Ironically, all that remains to be seen of Bordeaux's participation in the open Atlantic world are its eighteenth-century buildings. The city's commercial enterprise did not survive the Revolutionary-Napoleonic era with enough resources and flexibility to prosper in an industrial age. Had Bordeaux been as great a nineteenth-century port as it had been an eighteenth-century one, then it is doubtful if so many of its eighteenth-century buildings would have survived intact to the present. Bordeaux, even more than London, is a symbol of what happened when port city planning, having lost its claim to sustain conditions favorable to commercial expansion and sea power, became a decorative, monumental reflection of the importance of the maritime world. As a survey of American cities illustrates, even monumental planning had so little to offer that it barely survived in the nineteenth century.

Port City Planning
since the Eighteenth Century: The American Example

Neither an in-depth study nor a full survey of American sea and river port cities belongs in this book. What follows are some views of and comments upon the place of American ports in the evolution of port city planning. Mention of American cities is appropriate for two reasons. First, American maritime culture, already referred to in earlier sections of this chapter, can be seen as an integral part of the European-dominated Atlantic world. And second, reference to American cities illustrates, perhaps more graphically than a further discussion of European cities could (given existing research), what happened when monumental planning could do little to alleviate the problems encountered by fast-growing port cities: engineering replaced art and architecture as the principal method of approach for those concerned with the urban spatial dimensions of maritime commerce and sea power.[41]

American eighteenth-century ports, serving as colonial outposts of European empires, had neither the role nor the resources to make use of decorative, monumental planning. This does not mean that the colonial period lacks interest—on the contrary. For example, there were differences between French, Spanish, and English colonial cities that can be traced to the absence or presence of planning.[42] The Spanish Law of the Indies provided for a distinctive colonial checkerboard pattern with an emphasis on the community center. The French were concerned with beautifying their colonial cities by regularizing the street patterns and inserting prominent public structures and spaces into the urban form. English attempts to regulate colonial cityspace were more limited, but occasionally, as in Annapolis, Savannah, and in some New England towns, an appealing spatial form was imposed on the land. The scale of eighteenth-century port cities of America, like that of the new Baltic ports of the seventeenth-century Swedish empire, was too small to make use of highly conceptual and sophisticated planning.

The port city of Halifax, England's response to the French fortress city of Louisbourg, reflects a typical pattern of development and some of the unusual problems planning encountered. In April 1764 Captain Hugh Debbieg, an English engineer, surveyed English possessions in order to provide the cartographic information necessary to the proper placement of fortifications. About Halifax he wrote:

> In the Year 1759 a large careening wharf was begun at Halifax; Lieut. Colonel Meckellar Engineer was there at that time taking a survey and making reports for military works; he represented to the proper officer the impossibility of the works affording the least protection the Wharf and Storehouses . . . before any progress had been made in that expensive work; but no regard was paid to his

remonstrances. The work was continued, large storehouses built, a great space of ground enclosed, and every other convenience provided for heaving down his Majesty's Ships of War. If the Building of the Wharf and Storehouses had been postponed until the Engineers Report and Plans had been considered at home, doubtless a more defendable Situation would have been chosen: where it now stands, it is past the power of Art to cover it with Works; for such is the uncommon Bizarrity of the Ground round Halifax Harbour, that the only spot capable of being Fortified is that on which the Town stands, and the stockaded Fort and line were formerly built. The Memorialist himself sounded the harbour in the most particular manner, and found a greater depth of Water before the Town than where the Dock is now placed; and My Lord Co will assured him many times that there were several places upon the harbour equally fit for the Dock Yard or Careening Wharf.

This last Circumstance alone might be sufficient to convince all Men of the absolute and indispensable necessity of a Co-operation between the Sea Officers and the Engineers, before such important concerns are begun.... The Indiscriminate method of granting Lands at Halifax, and in many other parts of America, where Forts have been Erected, merits the most Serious attention of the Government: It has been already observed how much the Batteries on the Beach are confined by the Wharfs where Houses, and dwellings of the Merchants at Halifax, the purchase of which will cost the Crown Forty or Fifty Thousand pounds; and if it should ever be Resolved to Fortify on that Harbor, the Lands and Tenements which must also in such a case be purchased by the Crown, will amount to half as much more.[43]

The problems facing those who would plan American port cities included more than a lack of cooperation among authorities and lack of control over a local community. These problems alone make us wonder what the French achieved when they regularized the streets of Montreal[44] and saw to it that Louisbourg grew according to plan (figure 6.4); we can also only wonder what they hoped to achieve by a project to add to Quebec's waterfront by extending the city onto land to be reclaimed from the St. Lawrence (figure 6.5). These were to have been monumental cities in the New World, built not according to Old World standards, but according to the colonial norm. Planners who could not overcome these problems—and that most clearly was the situation for those in the English colonies—were confined to small projects of local improvements. Perhaps this was fortunate, because planners who did design complete cities for America often did not take into account how a city and its society would utilize city space. Indeed, it appears that concern for the aesthetic and functional benefits of planned city space were of such low priority in America that the relations between different parts of the city were never really understood. Without such an understanding practical and monumental planning were equally unlikely phenomena. Philadelphia was one of the few cities to receive large-scale planning, and so a look at it might demonstrate how irrelevant port city planning was in the American colonial setting.

Philadelphia was originally laid out by William Penn to fill in all the land between the Delaware and the Schulkyll Rivers, but the city grew into, rather than according to, its plan. In Penn's plan the five principal squares of the city were to sustain a rich social community life looking inward, away from the

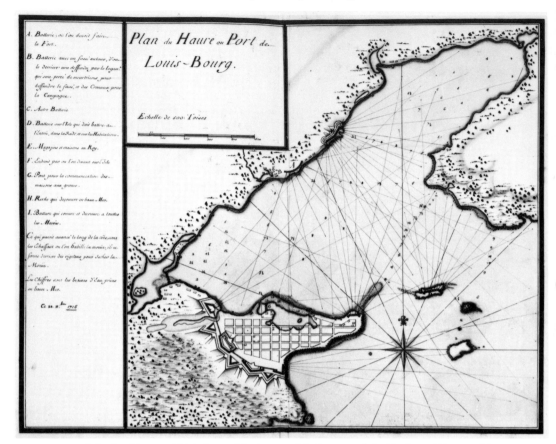

FIGURE **6.4.** *Louisbourg, 1716. Cartes Marines no. 94. Courtesy of the Newberry Library, Chicago.*

rivers, but Philadelphia finally covered the space between the two rivers only in the nineteenth century. Philadelphia first grew north and south along the Delaware; near the river were concentrated its principal buildings and most animated life.[45] The consequences of that pattern of growth on the city's social and political life were enormous. Philadelphia's merchants were located in the middle of the city, and not just at its edge; even as a minority, their influence outweighed that of any other group. This cannot be attributed to spatial geography alone, but clearly Penn's plan was out of proportion to the city's first century and a half of growth, and it clearly failed to provide the structures that could have influenced the city's growth during that period. What can be seen in Philadelphia can also be noticed in many other eighteenth-century American cities (New York and Boston, for example): people worked from the assumption that the waterfront was an adjunct space of a land city, and they did not realize that the reverse, a preponderant influence of the waterfront over the city, was closer to the truth.

Given the circumscribed role and limited value of planning in the New World, Americans had little reason to believe that the growth of their port cities owed anything to urban appearance and spatial patterns. The absence of port city planning, however, did not mean that the waterfront was unimportant, but only that its relation to the larger city did not need to be structured, or even understood. The impact of this development on planning's evolution was the same in the New World as in the Old: neither practical nor ideal port city planning any longer seemed relevant to those concerned with expanding maritime affairs.

Americans appreciated the waterfront and its adjacent district as a place for work and social gathering in a way that they did not care to transform into formal order, a way that owed nothing and taught nothing to the city planner. Port cities with their congestion, noise, and dirt must have appeared to city planners as particularly inauspicious places to set off works of architectural magnificence; planners were interested in beauty in contrast to, not as a functional part of, the material world. At least the inhabitants of the port city could still discover for themselves the singular pleasures of the waterfront. Warehouses, docks, quays, and the movements of men, ships, and cargoes were all close at hand to the pedestrian. The crowds of "water-gazers" fasci-

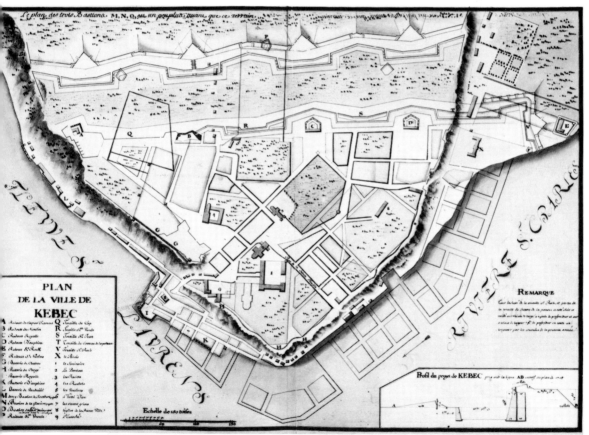

FIGURE 6.5. *Quebec, date unknown. Cartes Marines no. 105. Courtesy of the Newberry Library, Chicago.*

nated Melville, who placed this description of New York at the beginning of
Moby Dick:

> Circumambulate the city of a dreamy Sabbath afternoon. Go from Corlears
> Hook to Coenties Slip, and from thence, by Whitehall, northward. What do you
> see? —Posted like silent sentinels all around the town, stand thousands upon
> thousands of mortal men fixed in ocean reveries. Some leaning against the spikes;
> some seated upon the pier-heads; some looking over the bulwarks of ships from
> China; some high aloft in the rigging, as if striving to get a still better seaward
> peep. But these are all landsmen; of week days pent up in lath and plaster—tied
> to counters, nailed to benches, clinched to desks. How then is this? Are the green
> fields gone? What do they here?
> But look! here come more crowds, pacing straight for the water, and
> seemingly bound for a dive. Strange! Nothing will content them but the extremest
> limit of the land; loitering under the shady lee of yonder warehouses will not
> suffice. No. They must get just as nigh the water as they possibly can without
> falling in. And there they stand—miles of them—leagues. Inlanders all, they
> come from lanes and alleys, streets and avenues—north, east, south, and west. Yet
> here they all unite. Tell me, does the magnetic virtue of the needles of the
> compasses of all those ships attract them thither?[46]

Melville answered that question with a long statement on his idea of the effect
of the sight of water on man: it sets him to thinking, dreaming.

The point is that Melville's New York was similar to Turner's London: in
both cities people found their way to the waterfront without the planner
guiding them there. By the middle of the nineteenth century such access
became increasingly difficult in port cities. The eighteenth-century port city
could survive the introduction of the steamboat, which put few additional
burdens on it, but it could not survive the railroad. Business and government
introduced the railroad onto the land between the waterfront and the city,
and then used it to extend new port facilities beyond the principal areas of
urban growth to places where greater room made economies possible. With
the railroad, the carriage of bulk commodities on land became as practical as
their transport on the sea. The railroad, not the steamship, introduced new
economic requirements and material structures into the port city, and indeed,
made the development of some new port cities possible (Tacoma, for example, and such English seacoast suburbs as Southport and Brighton). The practical considerations of Van Schoonbeke and Colbert of course seem far removed from the industrial age, but it is useful to remember that the distinctive
era of European city-building they nurtured had already come to an end
before the industrial revolution made new demands on port city space.

Because port city planning evolved in the context of Western culture,
only engineers were considered qualified to adjust the port city to the railroad. Usually that process of adjustment put an end to the easy, informal
access of the city dweller to the waterfront because no one cared to find a way
to make urban growth and public access to the waterfront compatible. Historians who assume the task of exploring nineteenth- and twentieth-century
port cities will face the challenge of explaining successive phases of growth

and the subsequent separation of port from city. (Ironically, Manhattan kept its earlier qualities as a port city for a longer period of time than most cities because accidents of nature left the railroads in New Jersey or uptown and inland: the city Melville and Whitman knew could still provide Henry James and Alfred Stieglitz with literary or visual images based on the waterfront.[47]) In the 1968 Report of the President's Council on Recreation and Natural Beauty, *From Sea to Shining Sea*, only 11 of 300 pages refer to the seacoast.[48] "From 1824 to 1966, the federal government invested $22 billion in coastal and Great Lake dredging and other harbor construction to facilitate economic development. How much the government spent to rehabilitate the waterfront . . . is too negligible to have been tabulated."[49]

We should not minimize the inherent aesthetic architectural strength of the structures engineers built in the eighteenth-, nineteenth-, and twentieth-century port city. Engineers created the appropriate spatial settings for the maritime world once artist-planners ceased doing so. Some of their achievements are easy to recognize and appreciate today: nineteenth-century bridges, warehouses, docks, even housing districts, can be assigned cultural and historical value now more than ever before.[50] But we remain dismayed and bewildered when we confront massive railroad staging yards and the precise interweaving of tracks with buildings and piers that set a "maritime style" in the nineteenth-century city as much as or maybe more than anything else. Moreover, we find it easier to pay hommage to the nineteenth-century engineers whose works are close enough to Boston, San Francisco, Bristol, and London to call attention to themselves than to those twentieth-century engineers whose industrial and transportation structures extend between Newark and the Hudson, around San Francisco Bay, or between Rotterdam and the North Sea. There is a potential contradiction in the present-day appreciation and preservation of historical engineering structures in port cities. We now try to preserve and even reuse port structures that, at the time they were built, were praised only for their technical features and commercial value; at the same time, we criticize those contemporary structures that are as strictly utilitarian and devoid of cultural appeal and significance to us as the warehouses and docks of the nineteenth-century were to people then. Is this not another sign that those who operate the maritime world and those who grant cultural significance to its artifacts still belong to two separate cultures, cultures which, apparently, continue to have little to say to one another?

When the railroad became critical to the growth of port cities and the operation of commercial and military maritime affairs, opportunities to embellish port cities with monumental planning diminished greatly. Even today in Bordeaux a railroad track stands between some of the noble facades of the eighteenth century and the Garonne River. Planning for port cities in the nineteenth century bècame indistinguishable from planning for other kinds of cities. Yet the multiplication of railroad lines, the competition among them, and their influence over municipal politics, land-use patterns, and economic growth could create problems of such magnitude that even business interests agreed to help solve them with port city planning. When the Chicago business community, at the beginning of the twentieth century, realized that the prospects for their city's growth were threatened by such problems, they sponsored a master plan for their city. The result, produced by Daniel H. Burnham and Edward H. Bennett and their staff in 1908, is one of the most famous proposals for molding city space ever set forth. It is important to mention this plan here because, for the first time in nearly a century, planners tried to design a city from the shoreline inland. In their ambition to regularize Chicago's transportation, commercial and civic activities, and social development, Burnham and Bennett rediscovered that the imaginative use of waterfronts could have an immense value. How they arrived at that understanding and what they did with it are topics germane to this discussion.[51]

The authors of the plan traced its origins to the World's Columbian Exposition of 1893 in Chicago. This World's Fair did indeed play a decisive role in American urbanism. "For the first time," wrote historian Talbot Hamlin, "hundreds of thousands of Americans saw a large group of buildings harmoniously and powerfully arranged in a plan of great variety, perfect balance and strong climax effect."[52] Water was used to great effect in the exposition. The more informal (from the point of view of architecture and landscape) and the more formal parts were related to each other by means of a waterway between the lagoon and an inner lake, and the broad sweep of Lake Michigan itself was woven into the whole composition, deemed "a stroke of genius."[53] Whether the exposition itself retarded the development and diffusion of the modern architectural idiom remains a point of controversy. From the point of view of port city planning, however, this architectonic use of water represented a decisive break with convention and inherited taste. What made the exposition the point of departure for a plan for Chicago was, as Burnham and Bennett noted, the realization that the "dignity, beauty and convenience" of the fairgrounds "seemed to call for the improvement of the water front of the city." The first plans, initiated in the year after the fair, called for the expansion of Chicago parks to extend the length of the city's South Shore. After that plan was adopted, in 1904, the city passed legislation to permit authorities to acquire the shoreline from private owners. In the final plan (1908), Burnham and Bennett opened the entire shoreline from Evanston to Indiana (23.5 miles long) to recreational use and scenic promenades, with docks for shipping located at the Calumet River and immediately north of the Chicago River. The shoreline was to be divided into two parallel elements, the outer one a succession of peninsulas and narrow islands created by filling along a line following the profile of the shore, the inner a necklace of lagoons protected by the filled areas. The design was scientifically and economically sound, for it was based on the hydrography of Lake Michigan and on the prospect of using the city's waste (then one million cubic yards yearly, enough to raise twenty acres of material seven feet above the water in a depth of twenty feet).[54]

This waterfront plan, with its yacht and commercial harbors, boulevards, beaches, and breakwaters, was not an embellishment, but a central part of Burnham and Bennett's larger vision of Chicago. They saw the city as a commercial center, and understood that its growth would continue. They devoted the rest of their plan to an inland park system, a ring loop of railroad lines, a network of diagonal circulation roads, and a monumental civic center. By providing sufficient room for and connection points between each of these elements, they put together a comprehensive plan, "presenting the city as a complete organism in which all its functions are related one to another in such a manner that it will become a unit."[55] To that end, they protected the shorelines from most commercial uses (having found room for them elsewhere) and opened it up to the large numbers of the city's inhabitants who might otherwise not have access to it. The lakefront became, as they put it, "the great base of Chicago's street circulation." One need only see their plan (figure 6.7) to understand that they located all the other parts of the city in relation to the waterfront.

The planners extended their attention to the waterfront even to the point where the business center straddled the Chicago River. Vehicular traffic over the river was slowed considerably by many bridges, the river itself was polluted, and riparians encroached upon the channel itself. Existing patterns of waterfront use were among the most important problems Burnham and Bennett had to solve. They proposed new lakeside docks to draw most shipping away from the river and to take account of the barge traffic that would then connect river and lake, and they proposed that riverside and surface traffic be separated from each other (figure 6.6). They even arranged the movement of pedestrians and vehicles in such a way that dockside activities would be clearly visible to anyone on his way from one part of the city to another: the utilitarian and aesthetic features of the new Chicago as a water-oriented city could be introduced by similar structures.[56]

Criticism of the Chicago plan is easy: it did not take slums or the automobile into account, and its balanced, axial, geometric design seems removed from more progressive aesthetic trends of the early twentieth century. But serious as such comments are, they do not diminish the importance of that plan in a history of port city planning. For the first time in a century, a plan for the progressive development of a merchant metropolis began at the water's edge. If flaws and contradictions make the Chicago plan seem anachronistic today, we should also remember that few plans or projects since have attempted such an intimate relation between water and land. Does this mean that such plans are impossible, or at least impractical? I believe the answer is "no," but that the need for them will not be strongly felt as long as Western man can increase his exploitation of maritime resources without demanding changes in existing urban forms. New port cities in the 1970s are seen as nothing more than transshipment points for container traffic and bulk cargoes such as oil.[57] In this country, environmental impact studies, now required by law, have prevented government and public alike from allowing anything more than the most limited economic activities at these places. Such studies often fail to identify what standards are to be used to determine environmental impact, and that lack of clarity reflects general confusion about what aspects of development are harmful. The prediction value of environmental impact studies is perhaps less important, however, than their role in encouraging the belief that secondary growth problems (population expansion, intensive land use, pollution, etc.) overwhelm authorities because they

FIGURE **6.6.** *Chicago, c. 1908, in Daniel Burnham and Edward Bennett,* Plan of Chicago *(Chicago: Commercial Club of Chicago, 1909), fig. 137.*

lack adequate planning enforcement mechanisms. So in America it has become easier to limit the scale of a new port project initially than to develop new spatial forms and planning mechanisms appropriate for the creation of new port cities. Things are likely to remain this way until the scale of maritime exploitation compels the pursuit of more radical, innovative alternatives.

There is evidence that this may be happening. The cause of historical preservation in New Orleans produced a plan to protect the Vieux Carré with due concern not only for that area's economic welfare but for the economic and commercial growth of the city as well.[58] In New York the high cost of land has encouraged the development of two housing projects on waterfront land, heretofore despised for housing because of its location (the two projects, one at the Battery, the other on Roosevelt Island, may be compromised by the financial weakness of city and state). In Monte Carlo, Loews has constructed a hotel by the Mediterranean that required the construction of an artificial rock, an indication that many projects of significance can be identified in resort locations. Riverfronts and seafronts may well be the last open space in the city,[59] and new architectural forms may be needed for such sites. An even better example than the Loews Monte Carlo is the new megastructure, Re-

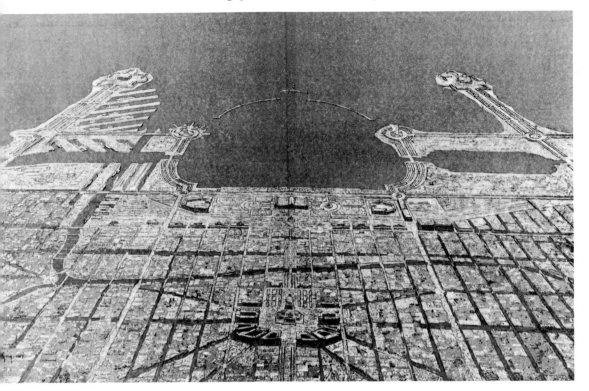

FIGURE **6.7.** *Chicago, c. 1908, in Daniel Burnham and Edward Bennett,* Plan of Chicago *(Chicago: Commercial Club of Chicago, 1909), fig. 107.*

naissance Center, along the Detroit River in downtown Detroit. It stands above railroad tracks, suggesting an effective way to undo the work of the nineteenth century. Combining a hotel, offices, apartments, and shops, the Renaissance Center may well be a civic symbol of an even larger undertaking, the systematic study of the entire Detroit River and the land adjacent to it (the first such study of any industrial American river). Taken together, the Center and the river study suggest the scale of thought and imagination a riverfront metropolis may require for its survival in the late twentieth century.

Approaching the waterfront from the utopian perspective of the mega-structure as the solution to technical and formally aesthetic problems in architecture, several people have already envisaged new forms of urban and social organization to be built along or above the water. Captain Jacques Cousteau's own thinking on artificial islands aptly parallels their work. There is an English project for a sea city "2000." Others are Yona Friedman's "Paris spatial," Kiyonori Kikutake's Marine Civilization, and Kenzo Tange's plan for Tokyo.[60] The Japanese models reflect a particular concern for evolutionary change and flexibility of structure—what had been, in seventeenth-century Europe, the distinguishing feature of all practical city planning. But these architects have relied on new structural forms and technical construction features to allow a city to grow and change, whereas seventeenth-century planners could easily manipulate only the spatial design.

All these examples illustrate the idea that is repeated in every chapter of the Chicago plan, namely, that the survival of a city may depend in part upon man's ability, first, to criticize existing approaches to building near the water, and second, to reformulate the space of the port city in completely new ways. Port city planning and architecture with a nautical style may have a future as individuals and societies, perhaps with little knowledge of or concern for maritime affairs but with a stake in enhancing the opportunities cities provide, perceive the waterfront as a new frontier. The result in cultural terms may be impressive if it allows people to recover access to the water and the activities associated with its exploitation. Of course it is impossible to predict how access to the waterfront would affect the thoughts and actions of city residents. On the basis of the historical record presented in this book, however, it is not unreasonable to suggest that an understanding of present and future uses of the sea will only be deepened by attention to what happens to port city space.

There is more: the Western world is poised at the beginning of a new age of maritime exploitation, one that is expected to be as different from the previous three hundred years of maritime exploitation as the age that began in the seventeenth century was different from its predecessor. The ongoing United Nations Conference on the Law of the Sea derives its importance from that very perception. No one expects the political or legal formulas, the military strategies, or the economic methods developed during the seventeenth century and since to be relevant much longer. Although the current expansion of maritime commerce and naval power has not produced any significant rethinking of the way port cities should be built, the creation of new types of port cities, of new forms for existing ones, and of new models for community living beside the sea may become as important to those concerned with maritime affairs as to those devoted to the growth and welfare of cities. Port city planning is not and has never been a substitute for either the material and technological resources that effective commercial and military sea power commands or the political will to marshall those resources toward specific goals, but it can provide a setting for the development of those resources and for the exercise of that will. If planners and architects are called upon to provide such settings, then the seventeenth-century record of port city planning may give us a point of departure for understanding yet-unimagined ways of building port cities. Even if port city planning plays a minuscule part in the maritime age about to begin, that, too, will be worth noticing. Both the history of planning and the history of the absence of planning bring us a recognition that the urban environment, however men fashion it, conditions and symbolizes how a society approaches the world beyond itself. The effort, which began in seventeenth-century Europe, to place an understanding of maritime affairs at the center of urban civilization may not be over.

Abbreviations

AAE	*Archives des affaires étrangères, Paris*
AC	*Archives communales*
AD	*Archives départementales*
AM	*Archives de la Marine, deposited in Archives nationales unless port archives are mentioned*
AN	*Archives nationales, Paris*
BN	*Bibliothèque nationale, Paris*
Clément	*Pierre Clément, ed.,* Lettres, instructions et mémoires de Colbert *(Paris: Imprimerie nationale, 1861–1873)*
Génie	*Archives du Comité technique du Génie, Paris and Vincennes*
Mel. Colb.	*Mélanges de Colbert, BN Manuscripts*
500 Colbert	*Cinq Cents de Colbert, BN Manuscripts*
NAF	*Nouvelles acquisitions françaises, BN Manuscripts*
SFP	*Stads-och fästningsplaner, Kunglinga Krigsarkivet, Stockholm*

Notes

All quotations from non-English sources have been translated by me, except as otherwise noted.

PREFACE

1. Peter Burke, "Some Reflections on the Pre-Industrial City," in *Urban History Yearbook 1975*, ed. H. J. Dyos (Leicester: Leicester University Press, 1975), pp. 13–21; Hermann Van Der Wee, "Reflections on the Development of the Urban Economy in Western Europe during the Late Middle Ages and Early Modern Times," *Urbanism Past and Present* 1 (Winter 1975–1976): 9–14.
2. There is a rich bibliography on twelfth- to sixteenth-century cities and commerce. One representative study of a port city and its spatial setting is Michel Mollat, "Réflexions sur quelques constantes de l'histoire du Port de Rouen," *Connaître Rouen*, no. 3, pp. 1–19. On the larger question of environmental challenge and social response, see Edward Whiting Fox, *History in Geographic Perspective* (New York: W. W. Norton, 1971), pp. 19–26.
3. For comments on the use of city plans as primary historical sources, see Erwin Anton Gutkind, *International History of City Development*, vol. 3, *Urban Development in Southern Europe: Spain and Portugal* (New York: The Free Press, 1967), pp. 220–91, and specific comments by John Reps, *The Making of Urban America* (Princeton, N.J.: Princeton University Press, 1965), pp. 541–42; John Erichsen, *Københavnske Motiver, 1587–1807* (Copenhagen: Københavns Bymuseum, 1974), pp. 95–102; and Peter C. Bunnell, in *The City: American Experience*, ed. Alan Trachtenberg, Peter Neill, Peter C. Bunnell (New York: Oxford University Press, 1971), pp. xiii, xiv.
4. Robert Eric Dickinson, *The West European City: a Geographical Interpretation* (London: Routledge and Kegan Paul, 1951).
5. Gerhard Eimer, *Die Stadtplanung im Schwedischen Ostseereich* (Stockholm: Svenska Bokförlaget, 1961).
6. Louis Marin, *Utopiques, jeux d'espace* (Paris: Les Editions de Minuit, 1975), pp. 257–90; Françoise Choay, "Urbanism and Semiology," in *Meaning in Architecture*, ed. Charles Jencks and George Baird (London: Barrie and Rockliff, The Cresset Press, 1969), pp. 27–37.
7. Josef Wolf Konvitz, "New Port Cities of Louis XIV's France: Brest, Lorient, Rochefort and Sète, 1660–1720" (Ph.D. diss., Princeton University, 1973).

CHAPTER I

1. The rich and complex folk culture of the sea elaborated by sailors and seacoast peoples is difficult for others to understand. Two good introductions are Horace Beck, *Folklore and the Sea* (Middletown, Conn.: Wesleyan University Press, 1973) and Joseph Conrad, *Mirror of the Sea* (London: Methuen, 1906).
2. Eugenio Garin, "La Cité idéale de la renaissance italienne," in *Les Utopies à la renaissance*, ed. Institut pour l'étude de la Renaissance et de l'Humanisme (Brussels: Presses universitaires de Bruxelles, 1963), pp. 15–16. Mario Morini, *Atlante di Storia dell'Urbanistica* (Milan: Ulrico Hoepple, 1964), p. 191.

3. Hermann Bauer, *Kunst und Utopie, Studien über das Kunst-und Staatsdenken in der Renaissance* (West Berlin: Walter de Gruyter, 1965), p. 62.

4. Pierre Francastel, "Imagination et réalité dans l'architecture civile du Quattrocento," in *Hommage à Lucien Febvre: Eventail de l'histoire vivante*, 2 vols. (Paris: Armand Colin, 1953), 2:197, 199. Kenneth Clark, "Architectural Backgrounds in Italian Painting," *The Arts*, no. 1 (1947), pp. 13–24, 33–42.

5. Joan Kelly Gadol, *Leon Battista Alberti* (Chicago: University of Chicago Press, 1973), and W. E. Eden, "Studies in Urban Theory: The *De Re Aedificatoria* of Leon Battista Alberti," *Town Planning Review* 19 (1943): 10–28.

6. Garin, "La Cité idéale," p. 32.

7. Ivor de Wolfe, *The Italian Townscape* (London: The Architectural Press, 1963), pp. 81–82, 86, 88–103.

8. Garin, "La Cité idéale," p. 23. See also Kurt W. Foster, "From 'Rocca' to 'Civitas': Urban Planning at Sabbioneta," *L'Arte* 1 (1969): 5–40.

9. Lewis Mumford, *The City in History* (New York: Harcourt, Brace and World, 1961), pp. 326–27. Architectural constructions may have modified the character of many cities in the sixteenth century without provoking new ideas about what cities should be made to look like. The loss of creativity in ideal city planning resembles the changes in Florentine letters described by Eric Cochrane in "A Case in Point: The End of the Renaissance in Florence," in *The Late Italian Renaissance, 1525–1630*, ed. Eric Cochrane (New York: Harper and Row, 1970), pp. 58–61.

10. Erwin Anton Gutkind, *International History*, vol. 4, *Urban Development in Southern Europe: Italy and Greece* (New York: The Free Press, 1969), p. 113: "... the great positive value of utopias is that they made people aware of the fact that ... man alone could change the conception and appearance of human communities." A survey of Italian ideal city plans can be found in Morini, *Atlante*, pp. 181–215.

11. This was also characteristic of the baroque plan. Mumford, *City in History*, p. 393.

12. Pierre Lavedan gave a definition of classical urbanism that fits ideal city planning and includes the organic connection of the various parts of the city, the subordination of the parts to the center, monumental perspective, and a program that presupposes overcoming many material obstacles. *Histoire de l'urbanisme*, vol. 2, *Renaissance et temps modernes* (Paris: Henri Laurens, 1941), p. 34.

13. Sybil Moholy-Nagy, *The Matrix of Man* (New York: Praeger, 1968), pp. 187–88.

14. See Mumford, *City in History*, pp. 417 and 420: "Even the building of adequate roads and avenues to connect the port with the city came as an afterthought in most towns, though these facilities often proved congested and impassible." Merchants were usually most reluctant to make investments in land that seemed unlikely to pay off, and so were willing to handicap the trading and industrial activities of their own cities.

15. First steps have been taken by Fernand Braudel, *Civilisation matérielle et capitalisme* (Paris: Armand Colin, 1967), pp. 431–32; Walter Minchinton, "Patterns and Structure of Demand, 1500–1750," in *The Fontana Economic History of Europe: The Sixteenth and Seventeenth Centuries*, ed. Carlo M. Cipolla (London: Collins/Fontana, 1975), pp. 83–177.

16. Because city views until the mid-sixteenth century were stylized, iconographic symbolizations of a city's physical presence, these views are among the oldest surviving attempts at an accurate reproduction of a city's physical appearance. An example of what can be done with such documentation is a work by Cesare De Seta, *Storia della Città di Napoli; dalle origini al settecento* (Rome: Laterza, 1973). De Seta discusses how the two networks of traffic and commerce survived in sixteenth-century Naples without planning.

17. Lavedan, *Renaissance et temps modernes*, pp. 119–37, in a typical statement on this subject, has treated port cities and princely capitals as if the differences between them did not matter very much.

18. Denis Mack Smith, *A History of Sicily*, 2 vols. (London: Chatto and Windus, 1968), 2:193.

19. One of the most magnificent streets for merchants in all of Italy was built in mid-sixteenth-century Genoa. Known as the Strada Nuova, it was only twenty feet wide and less than seven hundred feet long. See Mumford, *City in History*, pp. 349 and 420. See also the information on social geography in Diane Hughes, "Family Structure in Medieval Genoa," *Past and Present*, no. 66 (1975), esp. pp. 6–9 and 26.

20. Smith, *History of Sicily,* 2:190, 193.

21. Mumford, *City in History,* pp. 417, 420.

22. The monumental treatment of harborside districts was proposed for Marseille in the 1680s, for eighteenth-century Bordeaux, and for late-seventeenth- and eighteenth-century London. How this became a phenomenon of port city planning is explained in chapter six.

23. Frederick C. Lane, *Venice, A Maritime Republic* (Baltimore, Md.: The Johns Hopkins University Press, 1973), pp. 11–18.

24. Mumford, *City in History,* p. 323.

25. Lavedan, *Renaissance et temps modernes,* pp. 136–37.

26. Gutkind, *Italy and Greece,* p. 224.

27. Mumford, *City in History,* pp. 321–25. For evidence of how non-Italians esteemed Venice, see Christopher Hill, *Intellectual Origins of the English Revolution* (Oxford: At the Clarendon Press, 1965), pp. 276–78.

28. John Horace Parry, *The Spanish Seaborne Empire* (1966; reprint ed., Harmondsworth: Penguin Books, 1973), pp. 32–34, and 110–14.

29. The new port cities of the sixteenth century were principally in Europe, Leghorn, and Le Havre, and elsewhere they were the imperial creations of Spain. For more information on them see: Giacinto Nudi, *Storia Urbanistica di Livorno, dalle origine al secolo XVI* (Venice: Neri Pozza, 1959), pp. 93–116, and figures 2–9 and 21–38; Fernand Braudel and Ruggiero Romano, *Navires et marchandises à l'entrée du port de Livourne, 1547–1611* (Paris: Armand Colin, 1951); R. Hervé, "Ingénieur siennois en France au 16ᵉ siècle: G. Bellarmati et la création du Havre," *Etudes normandes* 23 (1961):33–43; Reps, *Urban America,* pp. 26–36.

30. Horst de la Croix, "Military Architecture and the Radial City Plan in Sixteenth Century Italy," *Art Bulletin* 42 (December 1960):285.

31. Ibid., pp. 280 and 284.

32. Ibid., p. 290.

33. See studies in cognitive mapping in Roger M. Downs and David Stea, eds., *Image and Environment: Cognitive Mapping and Spatial Behavior* (Chicago: Aldine Publishing, 1973), and Kevin Lynch, *The Image of the City* (Cambridge, Mass.: The MIT Press, 1960).

34. Change had come to the commercial network first: the Bourse was built in 1516, and throughout the century, new market places were introduced into the old city. See Lavedan, *Renaissance et temps modernes,* pp. 158–60.

35. Horst de la Croix, *Military Considerations in City Planning: Fortifications* (New York: George Braziller, 1972), p. 47; Henri Emmanuel Wauwerman, "La Fortification di Nicolo Tartaglia," *Revue belge d'art, de sciences et de technologie militaire* (1876), pp. 1–44; idem, "L'Architecture militaire flamande et italienne au seizième siècle," *Revue belge d'art, de sciences et de technologie militaire* (1878), pp. 36–176.

36. Geoffrey Parker, *The Army of Flanders and the Spanish Road, 1567–1659* (Cambridge: At the University Press, 1972).

37. Charles Ralph Boxer, *The Dutch Seaborne Empire* (New York: Alfred A. Knopf, 1970), pp. 117–58.

38. Simon Stevin, *The Principal Works of Simon Stevin,* ed. Ernest Crone et al., trans. C. Dikshoorn, 5 vols. (Amsterdam: C. V. Swets and Zeitlingen, 1955–1966), vol. 1, *General Introduction, Mechanics,* ed. Eduard Jan Dijksterhuis (1955), pp. 6–8.

39. Gutkind's explanation that the grid plan and the buildings designed for it represented "Calvinist dogmatism and democratic equalitarianism" is insufficient, as is his judgment that Stevin displayed a "lack of inventiveness." See *International History,* vol. 6, *Urban Development in Western Europe: The Netherlands and Great Britain* (New York: The Free Press, 1970), p. 35.

40. Peter Anson, *Fisher Folk Lore* (London: Faith Press, 1965).

41. Marjorie Hope Nicolson, *Mountain Gloom and Mountain Glory: The Development of the Aesthetics of the Infinite* (Ithaca, N.Y.: Cornell University Press, 1959).

42. Stevin, *Works of Simon Stevin,* vol. 5, *Engineering, Music, Civic Life,* ed. R. J. Forbes (1966), p. 205.

43. Paolo Rossi, *Philosophy, Technology and the Arts in the Early Modern Era* (New York: Harper and Row, 1970).

44. D. Alan Stevenson, *The World's Lighthouses before 1820* (London: Oxford University Press,

1959); René Faille, "Les Phares et la signalisation au 17e siècle," *Dix-Septième Siècle*, no. 86–87 (1970), pp. 39–81.

45. Bruegel, in his painting "Tower of Babel," situated the tower along the seacoast and adjacent to a seaport. The painting is in the Museum Boymans-van Beuningen, Rotterdam.

46. Stevenson, *World's Lighthouses*, p. 8, figure 28; H. Wallon, *Les Phares établis sur les côtes maritimes de la Normandie par la Chambre de Commerce de Rouen et administrées par elle de 1773 à 1791 et leurs transformations au 19e siècle* (Rouen: Agniard, 1900), pp. 57, 64, 84.

47. Eighteenth-century pre-Romantic painters captured the ambiguous role of the lighthouse when they placed one in a painting to heighten the portrayal of the forces of nature. Artists such as Ozanne and Vernet located a lighthouse above or beyond a rocky coast, thus emphasizing the terrible crash of sea on shore. The sea appeared more savage because of the lighthouse, yet that structure, erect and intact, was as worthy of admiration as the stormy sea to which it pointed. Many of these paintings showed travelers absorbed in what they saw. Indeed, lighthouses commonly were visited as tourist sites. The painters of these scenes were interpreters of the sea to those who were unable to visit the coast.

48. Boxer, *Dutch Seaborne Empire*, pp. 20–21.

49. Theodore K. Rabb, *Enterprise and Empire: Merchant and Gentry Investment in the Expansion of England, 1575–1630* (Cambridge, Mass.: Harvard University Press, 1967). Georges Duby referred to the often neglected problem of acculturation: "History of Systems of Value," in *The Ethnologist and the Futurologist*, ed. J. Dumoulin and D. Morisi (Paris: Mouton, 1973), pp. 217–19. John U. Nef dealt at length with the linkages between "what happened in the temporal world of positive experience" and organized violence at the end of the sixteenth century in reference to the writings of Grotius and Cruce, in *War and Human Progress* (Cambridge, Mass.: Harvard University Press, 1950), pp. 140–44.

50. Harold F. Watson, *The Sailor in English Fiction and Drama, 1550–1880* (New York: Columbia University Press, 1931); Anne Turner, *The Sea in English Literature from Beowulf to Donne* (Liverpool: University of Liverpool Press, 1926); Jean-Pierre Chauveau, "La Mer et l'imagination des poètes au 17e siècle," *Dix-Septième Siècle*, no. 86–87 (1970), pp. 107–34.

R. R. Cawley presented a strong case for writers making "full use of the material which the sea afforded" in *Unpathed Waters: Studies in the Influence of the Voyagers on Elizabethan Literature* (Princeton, N.J.: Princeton University Press, 1940), but he overstated his case. The first part of his book is about the myths, allegories, and taste for the picturesque that characterized map illustrations and literature during the sixteenth century. To be sure, a change took place under Elizabeth when writers (really only a few) began to refer to and discuss the voyages of discovery of that age. But stereotype and exaggeration continued to suppress the observable maritime world because writers used the sea and seafaring to create images of splendor and terror for their own ends.

There is, of course, little record of whether people traveled to the seaside. If England was at all typical (and there is little reason to suppose that it was not), then, during most of the seventeenth century, Europeans did not visit the seashore for pleasure—did not travel to the coast, swim in fresh or salt water, or sail on the sea for fun—without feeling that somehow this was wrong. See Reginald Lennard, *Englishmen at Rest and Play* (Oxford: At The Clarendon Press, 1931), pp. 67–78. S. C. McIntyre, in a work I have not seen, mentioned the impact of sea-bathing on two resort towns when its popularity spread. "Towns as Health and Pleasure Resorts: Bath, Scarborough and Weymouth, 1700–1815" (D. Phil. diss., University of Oxford, 1973), cited by H. J. Dyos in *Urban History Yearbook 1976*, ed. H. J. Dyos (Leicester: Leicester University Press, 1976), p. 159.

51. David W. Waters, *The Art of Navigation in England in Elizabethan and Early Stuart Times* (New Haven, Conn.: Yale University Press, 1958); Margaret Deacon, *Scientists and the Sea, 1650–1900* (New York: Academic Press, 1971).

52. John Parker, *Books to Build an Empire* (Amsterdam: N. Israel, 1965). John Smith, in *A Sea Grammar* (1627), wrote that he had "seen many books of the Art of Warre by Land and never any for the Sea." Quoted by Beck, *Folklore and the Sea*, p. 316.

53. Daniel Defoe, in *A Tour through England and Wales*, 2 vols (1725; reprint ed., London: J. M. Dent and Sons, 1927), included many observations about actual port cities and the seacoast. His was not the first such journal, but only in his day did such journals become widely known and appreciated. For more information, see chapter six.

CHAPTER II

1. Lavedan, *Renaissance et temps modernes,* pp. 278–81.

2. Moholy-Nagy, *Matrix of Man,* p. 215.

3. Rockefeller Center in twentieth-century New York, like the Place Dauphine, stands as a monument to alternate patterns of city growth, options that were never elected.

4. Of the entire seventeenth century, John Nef wrote, "Each of the major European countries was learning from the economic experiences of others and was assimilating the experiences into its own ways of farming, mining, manufacturing and trading." *War and Human Progress,* p. 154. On patterns of acculturation and communication, see William H. McNeill, *The Shape of European History* (New York: Oxford University Press, 1974), pp. 31–42.

5. Helge Gamrath, "Christianshavns Grundlaeggelse og Aedlste Bybygningsmaessige Udvikling," *Historiske Meddelelser Om København, 1968* (Copenhagen: Københavns Kommunalbestyrelse, 1968), pp. 7–117. Christianshavn was legally independent of Copenhagen until 1674, when the two were united. See also Joakim A. Skovgaard, *A King's Architecture: Christian IV and His Buildings* (London: Hugh Evelyn, 1973).

6. For the eighteenth century, see Christian Elling and Viggo Sten Möller, *Holmens Bygningshistorie, 1680–1930* (Copenhagen: Henrik Koppel, 1932); Erichsen, *Københavnske Motiver.*

7. This illustration is not unique in containing a mixture of fiction and truth. Here an actual attack on the city is depicted as if the new fortifications had been completed. A more accurate version of that battle appeared in a print by Dahlberg (figure 2.7), but that print shows other fictions, in the form of suburban projects. See Erichsen, *Københavnske Motiver,* pp. 97–99.

8. John Erichsen, *Frederiksstaden, Grundlaeggelsen af en Københansk Bybel, 1749–1760* (Copenhagen, 1972). The space and refinement of Frederiksstad were derived from eighteenth-century French and German ideal aesthetics, not from seventeenth-century Dutch examples.

9. Skovgaard, *A King's Architecture,* pp. 102–13.

10. Gerald Breese has written, "For persons familiar with the scale and nature of planning problems in newly developing countries it is axiomatic that the greater the growth problems, and the more limited the resources to cope with them, the more logical—and essential—it is to plan for maximizing whatever effective action is possible. Problems of urban development can be effectively dealt with best by planning." Yet Breese noted that urban planning remains a low priority item in the national planning process of such countries. In seventeenth-century Sweden city planning was considered essential to other programs of national development. *Urbanization in Newly Developing Countries* (Englewood Cliffs, N.J.: Prentice Hall, 1966), p. 128.

11. For a historical geographer's approach, see Lennart Améen, *Stadsbebylgelse och Domänstruktur* (Lund: C. W. K. Gleerup, 1964). This is a study of urban morphology and urban development in Sweden in relation to property rights and administrative limits. Améen developed categories of analysis for Sweden's early modern and modern cities; see pp. 236ff. and the lists on p. 26.

12. Michael Roberts, *Gustavus Adolphus: A History of Sweden, 1611 1632,* 2 vols. (London: Longmans, 1953–1958), esp. 2:120–47; idem, *Essays in Swedish History* (London: Weidenfeld and Nicolson, 1967); Eli Hecksher, *An Economic History of Sweden* (Cambridge, Mass.: Harvard University Press, 1954); idem, "Den Ekonomiska inneborden av 1500 och 1600 talens svenska stadsgrundningar," *Historisk Tidskrift* (1923); Eimer, *Stadtplanung;* Pierre Jeannin, *L'Europe du Nord-Ouest et du Nord* (Paris: Presses universitaires de France, 1969), esp. pp. 318–35.

13. See the multivolume publication on Gothenburg, *Skrifter utgivna till Göteborg stads trehundråårsjubileum,* ed. Jubileumsutställningens publikationskommitté (Gothenburg: W. Zachrisson, 1928), vol. 7, *Stadsbildningar och Stadsplanen I Götaälvs mynningsområde från äldsta tider till omkring aderthundra,* ed. Albert Lilienberg. The Swedish crown provided the land for new city settlement; see Améen, *Stadsbebylgelse och Domänstruktur,* p. 240.

14. See the maps of Gothenburg by Classon, Lantmäteristylrelsens arkiv (Stockholm) 31:1 (1644); anon, SFP 690 (c. 1680); anon., SFP 2 (c. 1682).

15. Anne-Marie Fällström, "Befolknings sociala och ekonomiska structur i Göteborg, 1800–1840," *Historisk Tidskrift* (1974).

16. See the maps of Jönköping, all anonymous: SFP 2 (1611), SFP 7 (c. 1617), SFP 8 (c. 1617), SFP 9 (c. 1617), SFP 14 (c. 1620), and SFP 42 (c. 1620).

17. In the period from 1650 to 1700, two-thirds to three-quarters of Sweden's foreign trade still passed via Stockholm. Even in 1800 Stockholm had a population of only seventy-five thousand; around 1680 Gothenburg and Karlskrona had approximately twelve thousand inhabitants each, Landskrona and Kalmar, only three to five thousand. Marie Nisser, "Stadsplanering i det Svenska niket, 1700–1809," *Ars Suetica* (1970).

18. Eimer, *Stadtplanung.*

19. See the maps of Kalmar: anon., Uppsala University Library no. 995 (1647, copied 1763); Tessin the Elder, SFP 53a and 53b (1648); anon., SFP 57b (c. 1651, copied c. 1750); Dahlberg, SFP 66a (1683).

20. See the maps of Landskrona: Tessin the Elder, SFP 107 and 741 (1659); H. Janssen, SFP 745, no. 2 (c. 1669); Dahlberg, SFP 109a (1679).

21. Eimer, *Stadtplanung,* pp. 466–82.

22. See the maps of Karlskrona: anon., SFP 138 (1683); P. Leijonsparre, SFP 30a (1693); anon., SFP 147 (1718).

23. Eimer, *Stadtplanung,* pp. 444–65.

24. Ibid., p. 263.

25. Ibid., pp. 541–62.

26. Frans Andrée Jozef Vermeulen, *Handbook tot de geschiedenis der Nederlandsche bouwkunst,* 3 vols. (The Hague: Martinus Nijhoff, 1928–1944), 3:1–101, 408–10, 417–33. Vermeulen emphasized the limited impact of architectural styles on Dutch city planning; indeed, the Dutch planning tradition muted Italian influence on the urban environment.

27. Aris van Braam, *Bloei en verval van het economisch-sociale level aan de Zaan in de 17ᵉ en 18ᵉ eeuw* (Wormerveer, 1944); Aris van Braam et al., *Historische Atlas van de Zaanlanden, twentig eeuwen landschapsontwikkeling* (Amsterdam: Meijer, 1970); P. Boorsma, *Duizend Zaanse Molens* (Wormerveer, 1950). Jan de Vries has provided many useful suggestions on this subject.

28. Van Braam et al., *Historische Atlas,* p. 54. Peter the Great worked there in 1697; Audrey M. Lambert, *The Making of the Dutch Landscape* (London: Seminar Press, 1971), p. 197.

29. Van Braam et al., *Historische Atlas,* p. 35, and Boxer, *Dutch Seaborne Empire,* p. 287.

30. Van Braam et al., *Historische Atlas.*

31. The example of Amsterdam can be contrasted with mid-seventeenth-century London, where the city's rapid growth was the subject of profound political and social disagreement. See Valerie Pearl, *London and the Outbreak of the Puritan Revolution* (London: Oxford University Press, 1961); Norman G. Brett-James, *The Growth of Stuart London* (London: G. Allen and Unwin, 1935).

32. Moholy-Nagy, *Matrix of Man,* pp. 113 and 224–26; Reps, *Urban America,* pp. 147–54; Fred Roy Frank, "The Development of New York City, 1600–1900" (Master's thesis, Cornell University, 1955).

33. Writers' Program of the Works Projects Administration, *A Maritime History of New York* (New York: Doubleday, Doran and Co., 1941), p. 41.

34. Sam Bass Warner, Jr., *The Urban Wilderness* (New York: Harper and Row, 1972).

35. Carl Bridenbaugh, *Cities in the Wilderness* (New York: Ronald Press, 1938), p. 328.

36. In seventeenth-century England a few new port communities developed, but without planning. Whitehaven became an export base for Cumberland coal when the Lowther family paternalistically encouraged its growth (and demonstrated as well some concern for the town's appearance). Deal grew gradually, after the 1640s, as a Kent coastal town. Portsea, on farming land outside the Portsmouth dockyards, took shape during the War of the Spanish Succession. At first naval authorities were afraid that building outside Portsmouth would weaken the area's defenses; they preferred to concentrate the growing population in the existing town rather than attempt controlled development. In the end Portsea grew as farmers sold their land piecemeal to arsenal employees and Portsmouth residents. There was no plan—and so no church, no market, no control over land uses, housing, or urban character. C. W. Chalklin, "The Making of Some New Towns, c. 1600–1720," in *Rural Change and Urban Growth, 1500–1800, Essays in English Regional History in Honour of W.*

G. *Hoskins,* ed. C. W. Chalklin and M. A. Havinden (New York: Longmans, 1974), pp. 228–52.

37. Charles W. Cole, *Colbert and a Century of French Mercantilism,* 2 vols. (New York: Columbia University Press, 1939); Charles de la Roncière, *Histoire de la marine française,* vol. 5 (Paris: Plon, 1920).

CHAPTER III

1. Jean Meuvret, "La France au temps de Louis XIV," republished in Jean Meuvret, *Etudes d'histoire économique,* Cahiers des Annales, no. 32 (Paris: Armand Colin, 1972), pp. 17–37.

2. Etienne Taillemite, "Royal Glories," in *Great Age of Sail,* ed. Joseph Jobe (New York: Viking Press, 1971), p. 73.

3. On France see René Mémain, *La Marine de guerre sous Louis XIV: Rochefort, arsenal modèle de Colbert* (Paris: Hachette, 1938); Daniel Dessert, "La Flotte française, constructions, 1661–72" and Jean-Louis Journet, "Approvisionnements de la Marine de guerre, 1661–72" (thèses de maîtrise, Université de Nanterre, 1968). On England see Daniel Baugh, *British Naval Administration in the Age of Walpole* (Princeton, N.J.: Princeton University Press, 1965); John Ehrman, *The Navy in the War of William III* (Cambridge: At the University Press, 1953).

4. Lavedan, *Renaissance et temps modernes,* pp. 210–24; Erwin Anton Gutkind, *International History,* vol. 5, *Urban Development in Western Europe: France and Belgium* (New York: The Free Press, 1970), pp. 127–30.

5. Local historians have been concerned to portray the uniqueness of a city. By contrast, here all four cities are studied together, not because they were all alike, which they were not, but because the differences and similarities among them can be best explained in terms of how each was planned to play its role as part of the monarchy's maritime strategy. The local histories are: P. Levot, *Histoire de la ville et du port de Brest,* 2 vols. (Brest: Anner, 1864); Mémain, *Rochefort;* Henri-François Buffet, *Lorient sous Louis XIV* (Rennes: Oberthur, 1937); Louis Dermigny, "Esquisse d'une histoire de Sète," *Sète* (Sète, 1966).

6. Thorough treatments of Louis's reign are: John B. Wolf, *Louis XIV* (New York: W. W. Norton, 1968); Pierre Goubert, *Louis XIV et vingt millions de français* (Paris: Arthème Fayard, 1966); John Rule, ed., *Louis XIV and the Craft of Kingship* (Columbus: Ohio State University Press, 1969); Robert Mandrou, *Louis XIV en son temps* (Paris: Presses universitaires de France, 1973); Herbert H. Rowen, "L'Etat c'est à moi: Louis XIV and the State," *French Historical Studies* 2 (Spring 1961):83 98. Bibliographic essays have been written by John B. Wolf, "The Reign of Louis XIV: A Selected Bibliography of Writings since the War of 1914–1918," *Journal of Modern History* 36 (June 1964):127–44, and by Ragnhild Hatton, "Louis XIV: Recent Gains in Historical Knowledge," *Journal of Modern History* 45 (June 1973):277–91.

7. In addition to the works cited in note 6, see: Eugene L. Asher, *The Resistance to the Maritime Classes* (Berkeley: University of California Press, 1960); Orest Ranum, *Paris in the Age of Absolutism* (New York: John Wiley and Sons, 1968); Fernand Braudel and Ernest Labrousse, eds. *Histoire économique et sociale de la France,* vol. 2, *Des derniers temps de l'âge seigneurial aux préludes de l'âge industriel (1660–1789),* ed. Ernest Labrousse et al. (Paris: Presses universitaires de France, 1970); Leon Bernard, "French Society and Popular Uprisings under Louis XIV," *French Historical Studies* 3 (Fall 1964):454–74; Jean Meuvret, "Comment les Français du 17ᵉ siècle voyaient l'impôt," reprinted in Meuvret, *Etudes d'histoire,* pp. 295–308.

8. Meuvret, "La France au temps de Louis XIV," p. 34.

9. Clément, vol. 2, part 1, p. cclxiii, 3 August 1661, "Mémoire sur le commerce."

10. Because Colbert wanted to silence his enemies, who had discovered that he, his friends, and his family had become the principal contractors for naval supplies, he needed to demonstrate that Louis's naval investment was worthwhile, so in 1672 he strongly supported a war against the Dutch. (Ironically, the minister had to rely on an Anglo-French naval coalition [created in 1670] and on France's superiority on land to make up for the weakness of the

French Navy.) He hoped to compel the Dutch to yield to the French at the conference table those commercial maritime advantages that appeared to be still beyond France's grasp.

11. The organization by which the French state fashioned sea power was greatly admired by many English contemporaries. No English king could have raised similar sums for such an enterprise with confidence that he could sustain it in the years to come. A different pattern of sovereignty and executive power in England made such initiatives subject to Parliament's control. See John Ehrman, *Navy in the War of William III*, p. 172.

The differences between the English and French political systems could produce only short-term advantages for the French. When a war started, the French were in a position to send a prepared fleet into action sooner than the English, but once Parliament began to spend large sums of money, that French lead quickly vanished. See Donald Pilgrim, "The Colbert-Seignelay Naval Reforms and the Beginnings of the War of the League of Augsburg," *French Historical Studies* 9 (Fall 1975):235–62.

A different relationship between maritime provinces and peoples and central government existed in the two countries, as well, one that worked to England's advantage. There the regions upon which the navy relied the most for manpower, bases, and supplies were historically close to the crown; in France, the navy had to operate in areas with a long history of autonomy from the French state. Indeed, during the long wars at the end of Louis's reign, the French were afraid that the seacoast peoples of the west would welcome an English invasion. I am indebted to T. K. Rabb for this comparison.

12. Sir George Clark, "New Social Foundations of States," in *The New Cambridge Modern History*, vol. 5, *The Ascendancy of France, 1648–88*, ed. F. L. Carsten (Cambridge: At the University Press, 1961), p. 180.

13. La Roncière, *Histoire de la marine française*, vol. 5, pp. 325, 331.

14. Mémain, *Rochefort*, p. 89.

15. Michel Parent and Jacques Verroust, *Vauban* (Paris: J. Fréal, 1971), p. 62.

16. AAE 1725, f. 208, 8 February 1660, de Clerville to Mazarin, and Mel. Colb. 103, fos. 87, 189.

17. Mel. Colb. 108, f. 847, 30 May 1663, de Clerville to Colbert.

18. Mel. Colb. 109 bis. f. 857, 18 July 1663, de Clerville to Colbert; Bezons and de Clerville on Port Vendres, see AM 3JJ 206, 13 April 1666.

19. AM G 184, 1663, Colbert to de Clerville.

20. 500 Colbert 202, f. 255, "Mémoire du Ch. de Clerville sur . . . le canal projecté entre Narbonne et Thoulouze."

21. Ibid., f. 144, Avis des Commissaux du Languedoc sur le canal, 19 January 1665, Sète: ". . . le plus avantageux qui fut le long de la côte pour y faire un port capable d'y contenir des vaisseaux marchands et même quelques escadres de gallères."

22. Ibid., f. 133.

23. Mel. Colb. 137, f. 140, 10 April 1666, de Clerville to Bezons.

24. *Atlas des Places de Languedoc, Louis XV*, vol. 2, f. 414, Bibliothèque du Génie, Paris.

25. Génie, Sète 8/1/1/4, 13 April 1681, by Niquet.

26. Bezons and Tubeuf to Colbert, 8 September 1665, in *Correspondance administrative sous le règne de Louis XIV*, 4 vols. Guillaume Depping, ed. (Paris: Imprimerie nationale, 1861–1873), 1:36, doc. 9.

27. 500 Colbert 202, f. 133.

28. AM B³2, f. 188, Arrêt of 20 August 1668.

29. Génie, Sète 8/1/1/4, 13 April 1681, by Niquet.

30. NAF 9479, f. 226, June 1666.

31. Mel. Colb. 103, f. 301, 23 July 1661, Jansse to Colbert.

32. Placide Mauclaire and Charles Vigoureux, *Blondel* (Laon: Imprimerie de l'Aisne, 1938), pp. 86–87.

33. Mel. Colb. 106, f. 145, 14 September 1661, de Terron to Colbert.

34. Mel. Colb. 106, f. 373, 26 December 1661, de Terron to Colbert.

35. Mel. Colb. 106, f. 482, 17 May 1662, de Terron to Colbert.

36. Mel. Colb. 118 bis, f. 605, 25 November 1663, de Terron to Colbert.

37. Mel. Colb. 120 bis., f. 1089, 23 May 1664, de Terron to Colbert.

38. Mel. Colb. 106. f. 357, 9 March 1663, de Terron to Colbert.

39. Mel. Colb. 119 bis, f. 917, 16 March 1664, de Terron to Colbert.
40. Colbert de Terron at Saint-Mâlo, 1 December 1664, in Depping, *Correspondance administrative*, 1:13, doc. 4.
41. Mel. Colb. 127, f. 21, 1 January 1665. De Terron added to his criticism of Brest on 11 January 1665, Mel. Colb. 127, f. 112.
42. 500 Colbert 202, fos. 122–291, 1664, "Rapport que faict le Chevalier de Clerville."
43. Compare the seventeenth-century experience with current searches for deepwater ports on the North Atlantic and elsewhere: Committee on Interior and Insular Affairs, United States Senate, "Deepwater Port Policy Issues" (Washington, D.C.: U.S. Government Printing Office, Serial no. 93–42 [92–77], 1974).
44. In 1663 the cost of developing Le Plomb was estimated at £800,000; Mel. Colb. 118 bis, f. 605, 25 November 1663, de Terron to Colbert.
45. Génie, ports 4/2/1/7, 4 April 1665.
46. Mel. Colb. 130 bis, f. 146, 11 June 1665, de Terron to Colbert.
47. Mémain, *Rochefort*, p. 41.
48. Mel. Colb. 129, f. 248, 8 May 1665, de Terron to Colbert.
49. Mel. Colb. 130 bis, f. 146, 11 June 1665, and f. 850, 20 July 1665, de Terron to Colbert.
50. Mémain, *Rochefort*, p. 44, n. 2; Mel. Colb. 130, 11 June 1665, and 131, 10 August 1665, Colbert to de Terron.
51. Mel. Colb. 130 bis, f. 850, 20 July 1665, de Terron to Colbert.
52. Mel. Colb. 133, f. 362, 16 November 1665, de Terron to Colbert.
53. Mel. Colb. 131, fos. 305-6, 10 August 1665, de Terron to Colbert.
54. Mémain, *Rochefort*, p. 45, n. 2; Mel. Colb. 133, f. 262, 12 November 1665, and f. 364, 16 November 1665, de Terron to Colbert.
    In 1671 Blondel wrote of having known about Rochefort's defects, but commented that a port still could be built there. His statement only reinforces the impression that de Terron deliberately did not speak of the port's defects in his letters to Colbert. François Blondel, *Cours d'architecture enseigné dans l'académie royale d'architecture* (Paris, 1675), p. 656.
55. Mel. Colb. 133, f. 754, 30 November 1665, de Terron to Colbert.
56. Mémain, *Rochefort*, p. 50, n. 1.
57. Mel. Colb. 134 bis, 13 and 20 December 1665, de Terron to Colbert.
58. AM 3JJ 168, f. 3, 26 January 1666, Copy of a letter written by the Marquis Martel to Colbert.
59. It is not possible to know if Colbert himself invested financially in any of the port sites or if he wanted particularly to do so in Rochefort.
60. In 1666 de Clerville wrote a "Mémoire pour augmenter le nombre de matelots en Bretagne." NAF 9479, f. 20.
61. Quoted by La Roncière, *Histoire de la marine française*, vol. 5, p. 401.
62. For more on private exploitation of royal affairs under Colbert, see Daniel Dessert and Jean-Louis Journet, "Le Lobby Colbert: un royaume ou une affaire de famille?", *Annales ESC* 30 (November–December 1975):1303–36.

CHAPTER IV

1. AM 3JJ 168, 18 May 1667, "Mémoire sur l'éstablissement de la Marine proposé à faire au lieu de Rochefort," Duc de Beaufort, de Terron, de Clerville, etc.
2. NAF 4872 vol. 30, 21 August 1671, Colbert to François le Vau.
3. AM B²9, f. 132, 11 May 1669, Colbert to de Terron.
4. AM B³8, f. 133, 12 February 1669, "Mémoire pour de Clerville par Colbert."
5. AM B²9, 4 April 1669, Colbert to de Terron, in Mémain, *Rochefort*, p. 180. Sardam is today Zaandam, a port near Amsterdam active in shipbuilding since the sixteenth century; see chapter two.
6. Mémain, *Rochefort*, p. 180, cites AM B²9, 4 April 1669, Colbert to de Terron.
7. AM B²10, f. 57, 7 February 1670, Colbert to de Terron.
8. Mel. Colb. 165, f. 86, 6 July 1973, Colbert, "Mémoire pour mon fils." AM G 184, f. 72, 30 September 1673, Colbert to the navy.

9. AM D²24, f. 282, 1667, "Rapport que le Chevalier de Clerville faict au Roy de l'estat du port de Brest."
10. Ibid., f. 33, October 1670, by de Seuil.
11. AM B²14, f. 131, 13 March 1671, and f. 177, 27 March 1671, Colbert to de Seuil.
12. "Le nombre de 50 gros vaisseaux de guerre placez de distance en distance rendent ce lieu d'une magnificence à laquelle il n'y a rien de comparable en ce genre." AM G 184, f. 86, 13 May 1681, Seignelay to Colbert.
13. Buffet, *Lorient*, p. 12.
14. Ibid., p. 13.
15. AN Colonies C²279, 1679, sur Lorient.
16. Wolf, *Louis XIV,* p. 446.
17. AM Lorient 1E⁵6, fos. 165-66, 22 June 1700, Pontchartrain to Mauclerc.
18. Clément, vol. 4, p. 340, early 1670, Colbert to Sr. La Feuille.
19. Génie, Sète 5/5/1/2, 3 June 1669, contract to Riquet; Clément, vol. 4, p. 336, 13 October 1669, Colbert; Colbert to La Feuille, Ibid., p. 340, early 1670, and Ibid., p. 303, 31 October 1671.
20. 500 Colbert 123, f. 54, 16 June 1669, and f. 88, 29 July 1669, de Clerville to Colbert.
21. Clément, vol. 4, p. 336, 12 October 1669, Colbert to Riquet.
22. AM B⁷53, f. 56, 30 January 1671, Colbert to Bezons.
23. Henri Pirenne, *Medieval Cities* (1925; reprint ed., Garden City, N.Y.: Doubleday, 1956), p. 521; Maurice Beresford, *New Towns of the Middle Ages* (New York: Praeger, 1967), p. 198. In the sixteenth century the English granted some declining ports new charters (with more favorable terms) to revive them; Roger Manning, *Religion and Society in Elizabethan Sussex* (Leicester: Leicester University Press, 1969), p. 71.
24. Lorient: NAF 9479, f. 226, June 1669; Rochefort: AM D²34, fos. 2-5, 18 March 1669; Sète: AC AA1, 30 September 1673; and Brest: Levot, *Brest,* vol. 1, p. 177, doc. of July 1681.
25. To date, there have been no studies devoted to the fiscal regime of seventeenth-century French cities.
26. Jean Brissaud, *A History of French Public Law* (Boston: Little, Brown and Co., 1915), pp. 419, n. 3, and p. 501.
27. Marcel Marion, *Dictionnaire des institutions de la France aux 17ᵉ et 18ᵉ siècles* (Paris: Picard, 1923), p. 402.
28. Brissaud, *History of French Public Law,* p. 418; NAF 21329, f. 157, 21 May 1683, Déclaration du Roy concernant les dettes des communautés.
29. Fox, *History in Geographic Perspective,* pp. 61-63.
30. Braudel and Labrousse, eds., *Histoire économique et sociale de la France,* p. 268; Pierre Chaunu, *La civilisation de l'Europe classique* (Paris: Arthaud, 1966), p. 606.
31. AN G⁷337, 16 November 1692, Bégon to controller general.
32. AN G⁷533, dossier 4, 22 August 1703; and AM D²34, f. 35, 18 November 1703, Bégon to Pontchartrain.
33. AM Brest 1E4, f. 82, 15 March 1684; f. 105, 30 July 1685, by Seignelay; f. 89, 15 April 1684, by Seignelay; AM Brest 1E5, f. 55, 24 October 1681, by Seignelay.
34. AM Brest 1E414, f. 200, 4 January 1686, by Seignelay.
35. AN G⁷178, untitled and undated document.
36. AM B³79, f. 338, 31 July 1693, Lavardin to Phélypeaux; and AN G⁷180, 4 September 1695, Ville de Brest.
37. AN G⁷175, 17 August 1692, Nointel to controller general.
38. AN Q¹121; AN G⁷174, 1 June 1691.
39. AM B³176, f. 72, 13 July 1697, Phélypeaux to Desclouzeaux, and f. 157, 27 July 1697, Pontchartrain to Nointel.
40. AM B²109, f. 5, 9 July 1700, and B²148, f. 189, 21 July 1700, Pontchartrain to Desclouzeaux.
41. AN G⁷184, Prévoté de Nantes.
42. AM B²113, f. 222, Extrait du Registre du Controlle de la Marine . . . [à] Lorient; AM B³65, f. 45, 21 October 1691, Beaujeu to Phélypeaux, and f. 465, 21 December 1691, Céberet to Phélypeaux.
43. AM B³222, fos. 78-79, 12 March 1714, Clairambault to Pontchartrain.

44. AN G⁷188, 14 July 1708, Avis de Ferrand; and AM B³198, f. 40, 2 February 1711, Clairambault to Pontchartrain.

45. AM Lorient 1E⁴6, fos. 165–66, 23 June 1700, Pontchartrain to Mauclerc, is typical of the government's position throughout this period.

46. AM B³137, f. 254, 13 April 1706, Clairambault to Pontchartrain; AM B²206, f. 472, 8 February 1708, Pontchartrain to Chamillart; AN G⁷189, 6 August 1709, Ferrand to controller general; AM B²214, f. 489, Pontchartrain to Desmaretz, 8 May 1708; Pontchartrain to Ferrand, 13 February and 13 June 1709, in Arthur Boislisle, ed., *Correspondance des contrôlleurs-généraux des finances,* 3 vols. (Paris: Imprimerie nationale, 1874–1897), 3:91; AM B³222, f. 72, 29 January 1714, Clairambault to Pontchartrain; AN G⁷196, 15 September 1714, memo of controller general; and AM B³222, f. 374, 8 October 1714, Clairambault to Pontchartrain.

47. AM B³198, f. 40, 2 February 1711, Clairambault to Pontchartrain.

48. AN G⁷196, 15 September 1714, memo of controller general.

49. AD Hérault C 4830; and AD Hérault C 4829, 27 January 1714; AN G⁷320, 5 September 1713.

50. Gaston Rambert, ed., *Histoire du Commerce de Marseille,* vol. 4, *De 1660 à 1789,* by Gaston Rambert (Paris: Plon, 1954), p. 207.

51. Louis Dermigny, "Armement languedocien et trafic du Levant et de Barbarie, 1681–1795," *Provence historique* 5–6 (1955–1956):248–61; Mireille Zarb, *Les Privilèges de la ville de Marseille* (Paris: Picard, 1961), p. 331.

52. Dermigny, "Armement languedocien," p. 261.

53. L.-J. Cazalet, "Cette et son commerce des vins, 1666–1920," (Thèse de doctorat en droit, Université de Montpellier, 1920), p. 32.

54. Dermigny, "Histoire de Sète."

55. AD Hérault C 1157; Clément, vol. 2, p. 718, f. 310, 8 May 1681, Colbert to Daguesseau; AM B³87, 27 June 1681; and Dermigny, "Histoire de Sète."

56. Guillaume Girard-Perracha, "Le Commerce des vins et des eaux-de-vie en Languedoc sous l'ancien régime" (Thèse de doctorat en droit, Université de Montpellier, 1955), p. 110.

57. Dermigny, "Armement languedocien," p. 361.

58. AD Hérault C 4833; AD Hérault A34, 10 October 1698.

59. AD Hérault A87, 21 October 1710.

60. Ibid.

61. Guy Chaussinand-Nogaret, *Les Finances de Languedoc au 18ᵉ siècle* (Paris: SEVPEN, 1970).

62. Meuvret, "La France au temps de Louis XIV," pp. 36–37; Minchınton, "Patterns and Structure of Demand," presents an overview of economic conditions across Europe, and highlights rural/urban dichotomies. For France, see Braudel and Labrousse, eds., *Histoire économique et sociale de la France:* for information on population, pp. 12–13; rural production, p. 80; commerce, pp. 166–200; and the structure of the French economy, pp. 351–65.

63. Blondel, *Cours d'architecture,* épitre; John S. Bromley, "Decline of Absolute Monarchy, 1683–1774," in *French Society and Government,* ed. J. M. Wallace-Hadrill and John McManners (London: Methuen and Co., 1957), p. 147.

64. Rudolph Wittkower, *Architectural Principles in the Age of Humanism* (London: A. Tiranti, 1952), pp. 125–26.

65. Leon Bernard, *The Emerging City: Paris in the Age of Louis XIV* (Durham, N.C.: Duke University Press, 1970), pp. 26–27.

66. Anthony Blunt, *Art and Architecture in France, 1500–1700* (Harmondsworth: Penguin, 1953), p. 241.

67. Blondel, *Cours d'architecture,* p. 784.

68. René Descartes, *Discours de la méthode,* ed. E. Gilson (Paris: Vrin, 1964), p. 59-60.

69. Wittkower, *Architectural Principles,* pp. 4, 7, 8, 16, 22–57.

70. Ibid., p. 8.

71. Mauclaire and Vigoureux, in *Blondel,* pp. 94–100, neglecting the evidence of de Clerville's sketch, state that Blondel was the first to give Rochefort its form. In *Cours d'architecture,* Blondel claimed that honor, but there are no authenticating documents. The rivalry be-

tween de Clerville and Blondel was intense in the 1660s. Blondel's plan would have to date either from 1666, since by the fall of that year he was sent to the Antilles (returning only in 1668), or from 1668.

72. For the story of Richelieu, see Lavedan, *Renaissance et temps modernes,* pp. 228–32.

73. Mel. Colb. 147, f. 48, 2 January 1668, De Terron to Colbert.

74. Colbert was in constant communication with his agents, especially those working on Rochefort. In his correspondence with de Terron, which has been largely preserved, Colbert made frequent reference to his letters to and from de Clerville, which have been lost. I am assuming that Colbert presented his view to de Clerville in words or drawings and that de Clerville incorporated the minister's opinions into each successive drawing until one met Colbert's approval.

75. This Le Vau was the brother of the famed Louis Le Vau, who was the architect of Vaux-le-Vicomte and who helped design parts of the Louvre and Versailles. François never achieved the stature or reputation of Louis.

76. AM D²33, port. III, fos. 13 and 45, 20 August 1672, Le Vau to Colbert.

77. AM D²33, port. III, f. 42, 15 November 1671, Le Vau to Colbert.

78. Le Vau's attempt to give Rochefort an impressive-looking waterfront is more important than Colbert's rejection of it might indicate. To be sure, Le Vau's project highlights Colbert's own understanding of planning, and was mentioned for that reason. But Le Vau's project was strikingly different from de Clerville's proposals for Rochefort in one important respect. De Clerville had concentrated on how the arsenal complex might appear from the rest of the city, whereas Le Vau designed the arsenal complex as it would appear from the waterfront. Le Vau's plan suggested that the most important aspect of a port city should be visible from the water. De Clerville all but ignored the waterfront in his plans for Rochefort; Le Vau emphasized it. The differences between these two approaches can also be seen in the proposals for rebuilding portside districts in Marseille, Bordeaux, Toulon, Le Havre, and Nantes late in the seventeenth and eighteenth centuries. Such proposals to render waterfronts handsome and impressive to city dwellers and to travelers and traders alike aroused the same concerns as Le Vau's ideas for Rochefort: Is it necessary, desirable, or appropriate that a given city appear handsome from the perspective of the waterfront? Is such a handsome portside district an encouragement to the commercial activities vitai to a city's prosperity, or is it superfluous? What have such projects to do with the king's *gloire?* See my article "Grandeur in French City Planning under Louis XIV: Rochefort and Marseille," *Journal of Urban History* 2 (November 1975):3–42, for further discussion.

79. Colbert to d'Infreville, 14 July 1669, cited by L. Lagrange in *Pierre Puget* (Paris: Didier, 1868), p. 123.

80. AM B²12, f. 612, 16 November 1670, Colbert to Matharel.

81. Lemonnier, ed., *Procès-Verbaux de l'Académie royale d'architecture,* vol. 2 (Paris: 1911), statement by Blondel, 2 July 1674, p. 79; AAE 1477, f. 205, 1698, Bégon "Mémoire sur la généralité de la Rochelle." Some officers moved outside Rochefort for their health or to live on their estates despite orders from Louis that they reside in the city: AM Rochefort 1E39, fos. 470–71, 1 May 1697.

82. Mel. Colb. 102, f. 603, 17 May 1674, de Terron to Colbert.

83. Mel. Colb. 162, f. 383, 20 November 1671, de Terron to Colbert.

84. AM B⁴44, f. 332–33, 19 August 1681, Arrêt de conseil.

85. AM B²61, f. 21, 13 January 1687, Seignelay to Arnoul; on Louis's land ownership, see the map of Rochefort made in 1681, Maps 144–167, Manuscript Collection, Service historique de la Marine.

86. AM D²33, port. III, f. 65, 27 January 1682, Demuin to Colbert.

87. Ibid., f. 116, 18 August 1700, Pontchartrain to Bégon.

88. AM Rochefort, 1E37, f. 217, 28 April 1696, Phélypeaux to Bégon. See the map of Rochefort made in 1696, Génie 8/1/13.

89. AM B²189, fos. 520–21, 26 May 1706, Pontchartrain to Bégon.

90. AM B²188, f. 174, 10 March 1706, and f. 541, 24 March 1706, Pontchartrain to Bégon.

91. AM B²189, f. 170, 12 May 1707, Pontchartrain to Bégon.
92. AM D²24, f. 33, October 1670, de Seuil, Mémoire sur Brest.
93. AM B²60, f. 535, 4 December 1690, Céberet to Phélypeaux.
94. AM B²9, f. 132, 11 May 1669, Colbert to de Terron.
95. AN G⁷174, 6 December 1691, document on Brest housing.
96. AM B³113, f. 81, 9 May 1701, Mauclerc to Pontchartrain.
97. AM B³61, f. 166, 12 February 1691; B³65, f. 123, 12 March 1691, letters by Céberet to Phélypeaux.
98. AM B³69, f. 230, 14 June 1692, Céberet to Phélypeaux.
99. Ibid., f. 349, 7 July 1692, Céberet to Phélypeaux.
100. Génie, Vauban letters, Brest: fos. 167, 170, 9 May 1683.
101. AM Brest 1E414, f. 131, 12 September 1687, Vauban.
102. Génie, Lorient 8/1/1/5.
103. AM B³109, f. 56, 15 December 1700, and fos. 59–60, 1 March 1700, Mauclerc to Pontchartrain.
104. AN Colonies C²279, 1700.
105. AM D²33, f. 52, 13 May 1681, by Seignelay.
106. NAF 9479, f. 236, 7 September 1685, Vauban to Seignelay.
107. Ibid., f. 255, 4 December 1689.
108. AM D²41, f. 297, 14 September 1679, anon. to Seignelay.
109. AD Finistère B 2404, Robelin to Chateaurenault.
110. AM B²84, f. 135, to Nointel, 12 April 1692.
111. AN G⁷176, 1 June 1691.
112. AN G⁷184, 23 May 1704, to Pontchartrain.
113. AM B³113, list of 1701.
114. AN Colonies, C²279, 22 November 1719.
115. AM B³129, f. 289, 15 June 1705, Clairambault to Pontchartrain.
116. AM Lorient, 1E⁴11, f. 233, 10 June 1705; f. 255, 21 June 1705; f. 273, 28 October 1705, Clairambault to Pontchartrain.
117. AM B³183, f. 686, 9 December 1705, Pontchartrain to Langlade.
118. AM B³147, f. 103, 31 January 1707 and B³148, fos. 304–6, 14 November 1707, Clairambault to Pontchartrain; AM B³159, fos. 202–5, 27 February 1708, Clairambault to Pontchartrain; and AM B³159, f. 322, 16 April 1708, and fos. 346–47, 14 May 1708, Clairambault to Pontchartrain.
119. AM B³129, f. 289, 15 June 1705, Clairambault to Pontchartrain.
120. Génie, Lorient 8/1/1/13, 10 March 1707, by Robelin.
121. AM B²137, f. 219, 27 January 1706, Pontchartrain to Clairambault; AM Lorient 1P300, liasse 46, f. 1, 1 February 1706, Chateaurenault to Clairambault; AM B²187, f. 395, 10 February 1706, Pontchartrain to Clairambault; AN Colonies, C²279, 30 November 1706, Robelin; AM B³159, f. 119, 16 January 1708, Clairambault to Pontchartrain.
122. AM B³160, f. 62, 23 July 1708, Clairambault to Pontchartrain.
123. Ibid., f. 122, 17 August 1708, Clairambault to Pontchartrain.
124. Ibid., f. 347, 26 November 1708, Clairambault to Pontchartrain; AM Lorient 1 E⁴14, f. 833, 21 November 1708, Pontchartrain to Clairambault.
125. AC Brest CC I Capitation 1719.
126. AD Charente-Maritime C71, f. 7.
127. NAF 21329, f. 283, 28 October 1683.
128. AC Sète, Compoix of Sète, 1705. Using this register, I composed a map locating all landowners on which my conclusions are based.
129. Michael Couturier, *Structures sociales de Chateaudun, 1525–1789* (Paris: SEVPEN, 1969) p. 272. "... les familles ont tendance à se grouper en des maisons voisines, les habitants de même genre de vie à occuper, les mêmes portions de rue. Cette ségrégation spontanée résulte des mêmes concours complexes de circonstances qui expliquent la formation et l'existence des groupes sociaux. Elle contribue à assurer leur cohésion et leur survie."·

CHAPTER V

1. Mel. Colb. 153, f. 627, 20 June 1669, de Terron to Colbert.
2. Victor-Louis Tapié, "Comment les français voyaient la France: la patrie," *Dix-Septième Siècle,* nos. 25–26 (1955).
3. Georges Livet, "Louis XIV et les provinces conquises," *Dix-Septième Siècle* no. 16 (1951).
4. Lorient: AM B²79, fos. 395–96, 1 September 1691, Pomereu to Céberet: Brest: AM B²47, f. 262, 20 June 1682, Colbert to de Seuil.
5. Lorient: AM B³77, f. 315, 24 October 1693, and B²92, f. 348, 7 November 1693, by Céberet to Phélypeaux; Rochefort: AM B²57, f. 118, 20 February 1686, and NAF 21333, fos. 426, 454, 4 July 1686, Seignelay to Arnoul.
6. AM B²50, f. 131, 4 March 1684, Seignelay to Arnoul.
7. AM B²170, f. 114, 10 October 1713, Pontchartrain to de Bedoye; B²46, f. 302, 13 June 1682, Colbert to de Seuil; B²83, f. 293, 24 February 1694, Phélypeaux to de Richebourg.
8. NAF 21334, f. 313, 26 August 1687, Desclouzeaux to Seignelay; AM B²51, f. 461, 7 November 1684, Seignelay to Desclouzeaux.
9. AM B²57, f. 118, 20 February 1686, Seignelay to Desclouzeaux.
10. NAF 21333, f. 426, 4 July 1686, Arnoul to Seignelay.
11. AM B²55, f. 621, 21 December 1685, Seignelay to Desclouzeaux; also B²73, f. 279, 10 March 1690.
12. AD Finistère B 2425, 1691.
13. AM B³69, f. 107, 1692, Céberet to Phélypeaux.
14. AM B³70, f. 108, 22 September 1692, Phélypeaux to M. de Campagnolles.
15. AM B³129. f. 24, 1705, Céberet to Pontchartrain.
16. AN Colonies C²279, 1700, by Bazin.
17. François Jégou, *Marine militaire et corsaires sous le règne de Louis XIV, histoire de Lorient, port de Guerre (1690–1720)* (Vannes: E. Lafolye, 1887), p. 82, doc. of 17 March 1694; AM Lorient 1E⁴14, f. 664, 12 September 1708.
18. AM B³230, f. 523, 16 December 1715, Clairambault to Pontchartrain.
19. AM B²89, fos. 495, 461, November 1695, and B²109, f. 300, 2 November 1695, Phélypeaux to Campagnolles.
20. AM B²155, f. 116, 20 July 1701, Pontchartrain to Louvigny. See also Bourde de la Roguerie, "Introduction," *Inventaire des Archives départementales de Finistère antérieure à 1790,* Finistère, Archives civiles series B, vol. 3, B4160–4670 (Quimper, 1913), p. lxii, for an explanation of the role of foreign consuls in Brest.
21. AM B³69, f. 13, 11 February 1692, and f. 212, 9 March 1692, Beaujeu to Phélypeaux.
22. Lorient: AM B³109, f. 171, 6 November 1700, and AN Colonies C²279, 6 February 1700, Mauclerc to Pontchartrain. Rochefort: Mel. Colb. 158, f. 426, 28 March 1672, de Terron to Colbert; Clément, vol. 6, p. 132, 11 June 1680, Seignelay to Louis XIV; ibid., vol. 3, part 2, p. 383, 9 May 1680, to Demuin.
23. Brest: AM Brest 1E17, f. 47, 19 July 1690, by Seignelay; AM B³50, fos. 39–42, 1685, Mémoire sur les Jésuites; AM Brest 1E4, f. 176, 12 October 1685. Rochefort: AM B²43, f. 331, 3 July 1680, Colbert to Demuin. Lorient: AM B²149, f. 235, 17 November 1700, Pontchartrain to Bishop of Vannes.
24. AM B²55, f. 442, 2 October 1685, Seignelay to Desclouzeaux.
25. Génie, Vauban letters, Brest, f. 170, 9 May 1683; AN K⁷1152, f. 1, 1702, Poirier, etc., to King.
26. François de Dainville, *Les Jésuites et l'éducation de la société française* (Paris: Beauchesne, 1930), p. 436; and Génie, Vauban letters, Brest, f. 170, 9 May 1683; AN K⁷1152, f. 1, 1702, Poirier, etc., to king.
27. AN G⁷172, 27 June 1685, by controller general; AM Brest 1E4, f. 94, 4 September 1687.
28. AM B²55, f. 442, 2 October 1685, Seignelay to Desclouzeaux.
29. There is a long correspondence. Important pieces are: AM B³111, f. 113, 29 May 1699, rector of Jesuits to Phélypeaux; B³105, f. 292, 8 June 1699, Desclouzeaux to Phélypeaux; B²146, f. 217, 17 February 1700, Pontchartrain to Pomereu.
30. AM B²190, f. 500, 28 July 1706, to Pontchartrain.
31. Mémain, *Rochefort,* p. 125.

32. Mel. Colb. 166, f. 174, 22 October 1673, de Terron to Colbert.
33. Mémain, *Rochefort,* p. 125.
34. NAF 21329, f. 246, 24 July 1683, by Seignelay; Clément, vol. 6, p. 132, 11 June 1680.
35. AM D²33, f. 356, 15 October 1683, Colbert to Jolly.
36. AM Rochefort 1E44, fos. 97–102, 25 April 1701.
37. AM Rochefort 1E56, f. 877, 16 April 1700, Pontchartrain to Bégon.
38. AM B²149, f. 166, 2 November 1700, Pontchartrain to Mauclerc.
39. AM B²161, f. 211, 26 April 1702, Pontchartrain to Mauclerc.
40. Buffet, *Lorient,* pp. 59–62.
41. AM B²214, f. 733, 13 March 1709, Clairambault to Pontchartrain.
42. He left because the demands were too great. AM B³207, fos. 269–70, 27 July 1712, to Pontchartrain.
43. Marcel Giraud, "Tendances humanitaires à la fin du règne de Louis XIV," *Revue historique* 77 (April–June 1953):217–37; idem, "Crise de conscience et d'autorité à la fin du règne de Louis XIV," *Annales ESC* 7 (April–June 1952), pp. 172–73.
44. AM B²133, f. 240, 20 August 1698, Pontchartrain to Bégon.
45. AN G⁷533, dossier 4, January 1703, Pontchartrain to Desmaretz.
46. AM B²180, fos. 17–18, 7 January 1705, Pontchartrain to Robert, and B²182, fos. 100–101 and 131, 15 July 1705, to Bégon and Chamillart.
47. AN G⁷533, 20 January 1706, Pontchartrain to Chamillart; AM B²191, f. 388, 22 September 1706, Pontchartrain to Robert.
48. Marcel Giraud, "Marins et ouvriers des ports devant la crise à la fin du règne de Louis XIV," in *Hommage à Lucien Febvre: Eventail de l'histoire vivante,* 2 vols. (Paris: Armand Colin, 1953), 2:347–52.
49. Giraud, "Tendances humanitaires," pp. 217–19.
50. AM B³124, f. 335, 28 July 1704, Lusançay to Pontchartrain.
51. AM B²180, f. 18, 7 January 1705, Pontchartrain to Robert.
52. AM B²206, f. 186, 18 January 1708, Pontchartrain to Bégon; AM Rochefort 1E67, f. 736, 22 September 1709; AM B³175, f. 235, 21 March 1709, Chotier to Pontchartrain.
53. Giraud, "Tendances humanitaires," pp. 219–20.
54. Bourde de la Roguerie, "Introduction," pp. lxxiii, liv.
55. NAF 21329, f. 227, 3 July 1683, Seignelay to Arnoul.
56. NAF 21333, f. 3, 2 January 1686, Arnoul to Seignelay
57. AN G⁷338, 17 and 27 January 1699, Bégon to controller general.
58. Boislisle, *Correspondance des contrôleurs-généraux,* 2:421, July 1709, Bégon to controller general; AN Q¹121 and 122, Rochefort, 1709.
59. Clément, vol. 3, part 2, pp. 53–59, 1671, Colbert to Seignelay; see also Clément, vol. 3, part 1, p. 285, 1670, Colbert. See also Edward P. Thompson's suggestive article on adjustment to industrial life, "Time, Work, Discipline and Industrial Capitalism," *Past and Present,* no. 38 (1968), pp. 56–97.
60. Robert Mandrou, *De la culture populaire aux 17ᵉ et 18ᵉ siècles, la bibliothèque bleue de Troyes* (Paris: Stock, 1964).
61. Demographic and fiscal data: Sète: Capitation, AC CC 189, 28 April 1705; Compoix, AC CC 188, 1713; Dénombrement, AC GG 16 bis, 8 February 1695; Etat civil, GG 18, 19, 20. Lorient: Census by the Compagnie, AM B³113, 1701; Parish registers, AD Morbihan. Brest: Tax roles, 3 April 1686, AM Brest 1E414, fos. 220–21; Capitation, AC CCI, 1719; "Extrait du nombre des ouvriers," 12 July 1692, AM Brest Library, Mss 164; Parish registers, AC. Rochefort: Capitation, AC 315, September 1708; Etat civil, AC. Data compiled with assistance from Susan Erenburg and my wife.
62. The data are relevant only to that part of the city always known as Brest, which was the more populous sector where much of the city's growth was concentrated.
63. Roger Le Prouhon, "La Démographie léonarde de 1600 à 1715," *Bulletin de la Société archéologique de Finistère* 99 (1972/3):727.
64. AN G⁷535, dossier 3, 20 February 1715, Pontchartrain to Desmaretz.
65. Dermigny, "Histoire de Sète."
66. Ibid.

67. Fontaine, "Les Origines de la population [de Rochefort], 1665–1688," in *Mélanges historiques publiés à l'occasion du tricentenaire de la fondation de Rochefort* (Rochefort, 1966), pp. 39–69.

68. Maurice Garden, *Lyon et les Lyonnais au 18ᵉ siècle* (Paris: Les Belles lettres, 1970), pp. 401–3.

69. Selection of groupings based on Adeline Daumard, "Une référence pour l'étude des sociétés urbaines en France aux 18ᵉ et 19ᵉ siècles, projet de code socioprofessionnel," *Revue d'histoire moderne et contemporaine* 10 (1963):185–210.

70. Method adapted from Régine Robin, *La Société française en 1789: Saumur en Auxois* (Paris: Plon, 1970), and J. Dupaquier, "Problèmes de mesure et de représentation graphique en histoire sociale," *Actes du 89ᵉ Congrès des sociétés savantes*, vol. 3 (Lyon, 1964); Christopher Friedrichs gave me useful assistance on this issue.

71. AM G184, f. 86, 13 May 1681, Seignelay to Colbert.

72. Bourde de la Roguerie, "Introduction," pp. clv, clxii.

73. Ibid., pp. xlix, clxxiv; AN KK⁷1104, 1704, "Mémoire sur le province de Bretagne."

74. J. Munar, "Activité maritime et commerciale du port de Morlaix dans la première moitié du 18ᵉ siècle" (Thèse de maîtrise for U.E.R.-Bretagne occidentale, Brest, 1971); and AN G⁷184, 18 November 1704, Robert to Pontchartrain.

75. Christian Huetz de Lenps, "Le Commerce maritime des vins d'Aquitaine de 1698 à 1716," *Revue d'histoire de Bordeaux et de la Gironde*, n.s. 14 (January–June 1965), p. 36.

76. Bourde de la Roguerie, "Introduction," p. clxxv, and John S. Bromley, "Le Commerce de la France de l'Ouest et de la guerre maritime, 1702–12," *Annales du Midi* 65 (1953):53.

77. Fox, *History in Geographic Perspective,* pp. 65ff.

78. Jean Delumeau, ed., *Histoire de la Bretagne* (Toulouse: Privat, 1969), pp. 304–7.

79. By contrast, when Napoleon I established La Roche-sur-Yon in 1804 to serve as a new administrative center for the government in the politically difficult area of western France, he designed it as a metropolitan colony that would be a part of its region. More recently (in the last fifteen years) several new cities have been established by the French government to serve as high-density regional centers and as nodes for commerce, industry, and civic life in areas designated for rapid development—Toulouse, the Seine Valley, the Lyon-Grenoble (Rhône-Alps) region, Marseille-Languedoc and Lille—because existing cities cannot play this role without becoming overpopulated. New and wholly unorthodox urban forms are being created for these cities, whose functions are to regenerate the regions and create new activities in them. Meanwhile the large-scale contemporary exploitation of Le Havre, Dunkerque, and Fos-Marseille can be sustained by financial and industrial structures established at an earlier stage of industrial development. The most striking urban configurations by the sea in France are the dramatic leisure environments presently found along the portions of the Atlantic and Mediterranean coasts that have no other economic or urban attractions. If current urban developments in France generate greater regional autonomy in economic and social affairs, the government may later be faced with the sort of challenges to its political leadership that Louis's new cities, by their very existence, helped to prevent.

80. Based on research completed by Mellouef and Ragnerry under the direction of Yves Tanguy at the Université de Bretagne occidentale, Brest; Yves Le Gallo, *Brest et sa bourgeoisie sous la Monarchie de Juillet,* vol. 1 (Paris: Presses universitaires de France, 1968), p. 56.

81. Dermigny, "Histoire de Sète."

82. Colonies C²279, 1717.

83. Paul Roger, "La Vie économique du port de Brest au 18ᵉ siècle," *Revue maritime* 184 (January 1962):69.

CHAPTER VI

1. The complete story of the enlargement of Saint-Mâlo and Marseille has not yet been recounted. Louis's interest in Marseille was evident in the early 1660s, when Fort St. Nicolas was erected at the entrance to the harbor. Arnoul, the intendant, may have reflected court opinion when he remarked that the Marseillais have always been involved in uprisings against the crown—actions that he attributed as much to the meridional temper as to legitimate grievances. (Mel. Colb. 143, fos. 89–90, 18 January 1667, letter by Arnoul to

Colbert.) The fort symbolized Louis's victory over the Frondeurs in Marseille. Significant changes came when Louis and Arnoul undertook the enlargement of the entire city in 1666, perhaps to lower housing costs for newcomers, perhaps to relieve pressure on the overcrowded galley arsenal, perhaps to provide room for new institutions and social areas, perhaps for all these reasons. (Gaston Rambert, *Marseille, la formation d'une grande cité moderne* [Marseille: S. A. du Sémaphore de Marseille, 1934]; idem, *Nicolas Arnoul, Intendant des galères à Marseille* [Marseille: Provincia, 1931]; and Charles Carriére and René Pillorget, *Histoire de Marseille* [Toulouse: Privat, 1973]. On the galley base in particular, see Paul Bamford, *Fighting Ships and Prisons* [Minneapolis: University of Minnesota Press, 1973].) From the 1660s until the late 1680s, arguments over the beautification of Marseille marked the different perspectives on the city's social and economic development that separated Louis XIV and the city fathers. One artist in particular (Pierre Puget) tried to please both parties in the hope of winning commissions. His work and these controversies are explored in my article "Grandeur in French City Planning under Louis XIV: Rochefort and Marseille."

Material on Saint-Mâlo can be found in Delumeau, *Histoire de Bretagne,* and in the documents of the Dépôt général des fortifications, Vincennes (Saint-Mâlo, art. 8, sec. 1, carton 2, pieces 6^2, 5^3, 9^2, among others). The city fathers presumed that enlarging Saint-Mâlo would absorb a large portion of the merchants' liquid money; they strongly disliked the prospect of a large garrison for the new fort protecting the newly settled land; and they suggested that in an enlarged city merchants would be far apart from one another, a disadvantage to a commercial community. To these and to other criticisms, Vauban replied that the defense of the city and the traffic of its merchants fully justified the enlargement scheme. While Vauban talked mostly of how easy an attack on Saint-Mâlo would be to execute unless the enlargement (and fortifications around it) were completed, he clearly found the merchants' point of view petty and anachronistic. In fact, the merchants and the state were indicating to each other how little each cared for the other's sense of priorities: the enlargement project is one way to see how the integration of the maritime, merchant world into the superstructure of the nascent nation-state was accomplished. See Fox, *History in Geographic Perspective,* pp. 61–64.

2. Iurri Alekseevich Egorov, *The Architectural Planning of St. Petersburg* (Athens: Ohio University Press, 1969); M. P. Vyatkin, ed., *Ocherki Istorii Leningrada, tom pervyy, period feodalizma (1703–1861)* (Moscow and Leningrad: Isdatel'stvo Akedemii Nauk SSR, 1955); James H. Bater, *St. Petersburg, Industrialization and Change* (London: Edward Arnold, 1976); Gilbert Rozman, *Urban Networks in Russia, 1750–1800, and Premodern Periodization* (Princeton, N.J.: Princeton University Press, 1976).

3. Eimer, *Stadtplanung,* pp. 290–303, 435–43, and city maps. SFP series.

4. Vyatkin, *Leningrada,* pp. 53, 58, 62, 63, 86, 102.

5. Egorov, *Planning of St. Petersburg,* p. xx.

6. Ibid., p. 11.

7. Ibid., p. 20. See the anonymous map of St. Petersburg from 1710–1711, SFP 52.

8. Francis Hyde, *Liverpool and the Mersey* (London: David and Charles, 1971); C. Northcote Parkinson, *The Rise of the Port of Liverpool* (Liverpool: Liverpool University Press, 1952); the collection of photographs edited by Quentin Hughes, *Seaport: Architecture and Townscape in Liverpool* (London: L. Humphries, 1969); Henry Peet, "Thomas Steers, The Engineer of Liverpool's First Dock: A Memoir," *Transactions of the Historic Society of Lancashire and Cheshire* 82 (1930):163–241; Eric Midwinter, *Old Liverpool* (London: David and Charles, 1971).

9. Defoe, *Tour through England and Wales,* vol. 2, pp. 255–57.

10. Parkinson, *Rise of the Port of Liverpool,* p. 4.

11. For more information on how Liverpool's housing was increased to match population growth, see C. W. Chalklin, *The Provincial Towns of Georgian England* (London: Edward Arnold, 1974), pp. 97–112. Liverpool docks were increased and enlarged at a rate that matched but did not exceed the rate of growth of trade. See D. Swann, "The Pace and Progress of Port Investment in England, 1660–1830," *Yorkshire Bulletin of Economic and Social Research* 12 (1960):36, n. 1.

12. Brett-James, *Growth of Stuart London,* and Pearl, *London and the Outbreak of the Puritan Revolution.*

13. During the long years of peace, from 1713 until mid-century, port cities had been changing little, adding buildings and projects within an established schema. The masterpieces of early- to mid-eighteenth-century planning and architecture were land-and-court places such as Nancy, Paris, Strasbourg, Bath, and Edinburgh; they were designed, moreover, as the terrestrial coordinates of that brilliant new constellation, neoclassical Newtonian rationalism. By the last part of the eighteenth century established and growing port cities began to look out of step with the times, and so were ripe for planners' schemes. But that may only have determined an interest in planning, not the content of the plans produced. Why plans were solicited, and by whom, are questions that further research must answer. In any case, this pattern does not altogether correspond to J. C. Perrot's statement (based on Caen) that in the second half of the eighteenth century the city was thought of in terms more reflective of actual patterns of growth and less bound to cautious literary imagery, as if concepts of the city were finally catching up with the city itself. See Jean-Claude Perrot, "Rapports sociaux et villes au 18ᵉ siècle," *Annales ESC* 23 (March–April 1968):241–67.

14. Daniel Defoe, *A New Voyage Round the World by a Course Never Sailed* (1724; reprint ed., New York: Crowell, 1903–1904), p. 2.

15. Watson, *Sailor in English Fiction and Drama;* Turner, *Sea in English Literature;* Roger Stein, "Pulled out of the Bay: American Fiction in the Eighteenth Century," *Studies in American Fiction* 2 (1974):13–36; and idem, "Seascape and the American Imagination: The Puritan Seventeenth Century," *Early American Literature* 7 (1972):17–37.

16. I have avoided popular or folk literature because of the additional problems such sources pose and because the record of literature for the élites as an expressive medium of ideas is more significant to the changing role of port city planning. Nicolson, *Mountain Gloom and Mountain Glory.*

17. Ibid., pp. 279, 304–7. Addison had written of his pleasure in arriving at Genoa after having been at sea during a storm, but he had also written that the sea had affected his imagination even more when stormy than when calm. In *Spectator 489,* Addison wrote: "A troubled ocean, to a man who sails upon it, is, I think, the biggest object he can see in motion, and consequently gives his imagination one of the highest kinds of pleasure that can arrive from greatness. I must confess, it is impossible for me to survey this world of fluid matter, without thinking on the hand that first poured it out, and made a proper channel for its reception. Such an object naturally raises in my thoughts the idea of an Almighty Being, and convinces me of his existence as much as a metaphysical demonstration. The imagination prompts the understanding and by the greatness of the sensible objects, produces in it the idea of a being who is neither circumscribed by time nor space." What is remarkable about this passage is the writer's interest in analyzing how the sea produced impressions. Addison was willing to undergo travel in mountain ranges and on the seas in order to have these sorts of experiences, but mountain travel proved more popular in the eighteenth century—and more stimulating to the literary imagination—than ocean voyages or channel crossings. Comfort and safety had little to do with it, for writers often commented on the danger of mountain travel as an important part of their experiences. I believe that the place of the sea in the broader culture still inhibited most from intimate contact with it.

18. Thomas Philbrick, *James Fenimore Cooper and the Development of American Sea Fiction* (Cambridge, Mass.: Harvard University Press, 1961), pp. 12–13.

19. Ibid., pp. 4–5.

20. W. H. Auden, *The Enchafèd Flood* (1950; reprint ed., New York: Vintage, 1967), pp. 15ff. Philbrick, *Cooper and American Sea Fiction,* p. 165. An example of the best modern nonfictional writing on the sea that has the metaphysical sweep of great fiction is John C. Van Dyke, *The Opal Sea, Continued Studies in Impressions and Appearances* (New York: Charles Scribners Sons, 1917).

21. John Bosher, *French Finances, 1770–1795* (Cambridge: At the University Press, 1967).

22. ". . . commerce tends to create its own society. It need not, therefore, appear impossible that Atlantic commerce also developed a discrete social structure independently of and radi-

cally different from the great administrative states. . . . To move directly to a pivotal case, was Bordeaux Atlantic or French?" Fox, *History in Geographic Perspective*, pp. 63ff., answers this question by studying the economic and political formulas of Bodin, Montesquieu, and Smith to make the point that at least two totally different social systems were competing for position and survival in the territorial body of France. But the differences were discrete and self-contained to the point that it never occurred to either set that its dealings with the other were with a radically different society. Pierre Dockès offers a detailed evaluation of the role of geography in economic and political thought in *L'Espace dans la pensée économique du 17ᵉ et 18ᵉ siècles* (Paris: Flammarion, 1971). See also Jean Meuvret, "Les idées économiques en France au 17ᵉ siècle," in *Etudes d'histoire économique*, and Joseph Spengler, *French Predecessors of Malthus* (Durham, N.C.: Duke University Press, 1942). I am not aware of anything written on Hugo Grotius in this context, yet his legal theories were a form of descriptive and prescriptive economic and political analysis. There has not been a full study of the impact of economic and political theory on the financial and commercial enterprise of the seventeenth and eighteenth centuries, either. Lionel Rothkrug's *Opposition to Louis XIV* (Princeton, N.J.: Princeton University Press, 1965) was an unsuccessful attempt to link theory to political reform. T. S. Willan, in *River Navigation in England, 1600–1750* (London: Frank Cass, 1964), p. 135, suggested that English promoters of river improvement and canal schemes rarely referred to concepts and arguments elaborated in economists' pamphlets, whereas continental canal builders often made such references.

23. At least one recent book on America demonstrates that seacoast/hinterland conflicts were very important right down to the end of the nineteenth century. Harold B. Schonberger, in *Transportation to the Seaboard* (Westport, Conn.: Greenwood Publishing Co., 1971), wrote of how rural interests and farm product exporters often rightly assumed that the railroad interests of the great seacoast cities approached questions of tariffs and transport costs from a point of view inimical to the interior. Today's questions of overseas agricultural sales and transportation regulation show that such issues are not being handled very differently than they were in the nineteenth century.

24. Anne Buttimer, *Society and Milieu in the French Geographic Tradition*, Monograph Series no. 6, Association of American Geographers (Chicago: Rand McNally, 1971).

25. Margaret Tuttle Sprout, "Mahan: Evangelist of Sea Power," in *Makers of Modern Strategy*, ed. Edward Mead Earle (1941; reprint ed., New York: Atheneum, 1967), pp. 415–45; and in the same book, Theodore Ropp, "Continental Doctrines of Sea Power," pp. 446–56. On the limitation of the validity of Mahan's conceptual framework to the modern Anglo-American world, see John F. Guilmartin, Jr., *Gunpowder and Galleys* (Cambridge: At the University Press, 1975), esp. ch. 1. Guilmartin observes (p. 18, n. 2) that in World War Two Anglo-American intelligence failed to understand Japanese naval tactics and strategy because they did not lend themselves to Mahanian analysis.

26. For the pre-1800 era, see these important works: John Ehrman, *Navy in the War of William III;* Daniel Baugh, *British Naval Administration in the Age of Walpole;* Jean Meyer, *L'Armement nantais dans la deuxième moitié du dix-huitième siècle* (Paris: SEVPEN, 1966); and Pierre Dardel, *Commerce, industrie et navigation à Rouen et au Havre au 18ᵉ siècle* (Rouen: Société libre d'émulation de la Seine-Maritime, 1966). On the post-1800 period, see such diverse works as Donald W. Mitchell, *A History of Russian and Soviet Sea Power* (New York: Macmillan, 1974); David Trask, *Captains and Cabinets: Anglo-American Naval Relations, 1917–1918* (Columbia: University of Missouri Press, 1972); Bernard Brodie, *Sea Power in the Machine Age* (London: Oxford University Press, 1941); Emanuel Raymond Lewis, *Seacoast Fortifications of the United States* (Washington, D.C.: Smithsonian Institution Press, 1970).

27. Arthur J. Marder, *The Anatomy of British Sea Power* (London: Cass, 1974); idem, *From the Dreadnought to Scapa Flow*, 5 vols. (London: Oxford University Press, 1961–1970); Samuel Eliot Morison, *The European Discovery of America*, 2 vols. (New York: Oxford University Press, 1971–1974); idem, *History of United States Naval Operations in World War II*, 15 vols. (Boston: Little, Brown and Co., 1947–1962); idem, *The Maritime History of Massachusetts, 1783–1864* (Boston: Houghton Mifflin 1921).

28. Francis Hyde, *Far Eastern Trade, 1860–1914* (London: Adam and Charles Black, 1973);

Charles Ralph Boxer, *Dutch Seaborne Empire;* idem, *The Portuguese Seaborne Empire, 1415–1825* (London: Hutchinson, 1963); John Horace Parry, *Spanish Seaborne Empire;* idem, *The Age of Reconnaissance* (Cleveland: World Publishing, 1963).

29. Notice must be taken of contemporary guides for travel along seacoasts, such as Serge Bertino, ed., *Guide de la mer mystérieuse,* Les Guides Noirs Series (Paris: Tchon/Emom, 1970), and the Automobile Association, *Book of the Seaside* (London, 1972).

30. Edgar Augustus Jerome Johnson, in *The Organization of Space in Developing Countries* (Cambridge, Mass.: Harvard University Press, 1970), has some fascinating things to say about intellectual creativity and the capacity to posit ideas and discrete facts in spatial terms (pp. 399–419). His statement is especially relevant to what I have to say at the end of this chapter about the likelihood of a return to port city planning in the late twentieth century.

31. On law, see Evan Luard, *The Control of the Sea-Bed* (London: Heinemann, 1974); Ludwik A. Teclaff, *The River Basin in History and Law* (The Hague: Martinus Nijhoff, 1967); and especially Edward Wenk, Jr., *The Politics of the Ocean* (Seattle: University of Washington Press, 1974), for evidence of how difficult the formulation of ocean policy seems when the problems of maritime affairs are barely visible to the government. See also Daniel Patrick O'Connell, *The Influence of Law on Sea Power* (Manchester: Manchester University Press, 1975); John Robert Victor Prescott, *The Political Geography of the Oceans* (New York: John Wiley and Sons, 1975). On science, see Margaret Deacon, *Scientists and the Sea, 1650–1900;* Vincent Ponko, Jr., *Ships, Seas and Scientists* (Annapolis, Md.: Naval Institute Press, 1974); Susan Schlee, *The Edge of an Unfamiliar World: A History of Oceanography* (New York: Sutton, 1973); and Rachel Carson, *The Sea Around Us* (New York: Oxford University Press, 1951). The Canadian government, through the Department Environment Canada, began in 1975 the publication of a yearbook *Canada Water Year Book* (Ottawa: Information Canada, 1975). The United States, it may be added, has no such publication. Bostwick H. Ketchum, ed., *The Water's Edge: Critical Problems of the Coastal Zone* (Cambridge, Mass.: The MIT Press, 1972), gives a science perspective on land-use problems.

32. Lauren J. Bol, *Die Holländische Marinemalerei des 17 Jahrhunderts* (Braunschweig: Klinhardt and Bienmann, 1973); David Cordingly, *Marine Painting in England, 1700–1900* (London: Studio Vista, 1974); Arts Council of Britain, *Shock of Recognition: The Landscape of English Romanticism and the Dutch Seventeenth School* (London: 1971); Luke Herrman, *British Landscape Painting of the Eighteenth Century* (London: Faber and Faber, 1973); and Roger Stein, *Seascape and the American Imagination* (New York: Clarkson N. Peter, Inc., and the Whitney Museum of American Art, 1975). On the Van de Veldes see Charles Ralph Boxer, *The Anglo-Dutch Wars of the 17th Century, 1653–1674* (London: HMSO, 1975).

33. Mention should also be made of the influence of Japanese printmakers, whose water scenes were openly imitated in nineteenth-century France.

34. These and other places are illustrated and discussed by Susan and Geoffrey Jellicoe, *Water: The Use of Water in Landscape Architecture* (London: Adam and Charles Black, 1971).

35. John Evelyn, *London Revived* (1666; reprint ed., Oxford: At the Clarendon Press, 1938); Michael Hanson, *2000 Years of London* (London: Country Life, 1967); Kerry Downes, "John Evelyn and Architecture: A First Inquiry," in *Essays on Architectural Writers and Writing Presented to Nikolaus Pevsner,* ed. John Summerson (London: Allen Lane the Penguin Press, 1968).

36. Defoe, *Tour through England and Wales,* vol. 1, pp. 315f.

37. John Summerson, *Georgian London* (London: Barrie and Jenkins, 1970); H. Kalman, "The Architecture of Mercantilism: Commercial Buildings by George Dance the Younger," in *The Triumph of Culture: 18th Century Perspectives,* ed. Paul Fritz and David Williams (Toronto: A. M. Hakkert, 1972), pp. 69–96; M. Hugo-Brunt, "George Dance, the Younger, as Town Planner (1768–1814)," *Journal of the Society of Architectural Historians* 14 (1955), pp. 13–23.

38. D. Swann, "The Pace and Progress of Port Investment in England, 1660–1830," p. 39. For a utilitarian harbor scheme without pretense, see F. M. Eden's project for *Porto-Bello* (published in 1798), as referred to in Helen Rosenau, *Social Purpose in Architecture* (London: Studio Vista, 1970), p. 43. Joseph Conrad, in *Mirror of the Sea,* described the result of

London's nineteenth-century waterfront growth in terms remarkably relevant to this study.

39. Rosenau, *Social Purpose in Architecture,* p. 43; François-Georges Pariset, "Les Beaux-Arts de l'âge d'or," in his *Bordeaux au 18ᵉ siècle,* vol. 5, *Histoire de Bordeaux,* ed. Charles Higounet (Bordeaux: Fédération historique du Sud-Ouest, 1968), pp. 523–707.

40. Quoted by Pariset, "Les Beaux-Arts de l'âge d'or," p. 703.

41. John R. Kellett's *The Impact of Railways on Victorian Cities* (London: Routledge and Kegan Paul, 1969) is an example of what needs to be attempted for nineteenth-century continental Europe. In this regard, see also James Bird, *The Major Seaports of the United Kingdom* (London: Hutchinson, 1963).

42. Reps, *Urban America;* Douglas Marshall, "The City in the New World: The Military Contribution," a guide to an exhibition at the William L. Clements Library, University of Michigan (Ann Arbor, 1973). See also the interpretive, analytic, and nearly encyclopedic treatment of how and why the English colonial ports grew (only reference to uses of urban space appears to go without mention) in Jacob Price, "Economic Function and the Growth of American Port Towns in the Eighteenth Century," *Perspectives in American History* 8 (Cambridge, Mass.: Harvard University Press, 1974), pp. 23–86.

43. Shelburne MS. 86–1, copy of ms. submitted by H. Debbieg to Board of Ordnance, in Clements Library, University of Michigan. I am indebted to Douglas Marshall of the Clements Library for the reference.

44. Reps, *Urban America,* p. 71.

45. Sam Bass Warner, Jr., *The Private City: Philadelphia in Three Periods of Its Growth* (Philadelphia: University of Pennsylvania Press, 1968), esp. ch. 1 and p. 54.

46. Herman Melville, *Moby Dick or The Whale* (1846: reprint ed., New York: The Modern Library, 1944), p. 2.

47. One of the results in New York was that great ocean liners could berth not far from the center of the city, to the delight of travelers and sightseers alike.

48. Wenk, *Politics of the Ocean,* p. 168.

49. Ibid., p. 172.

50. Eric de Maré, *The Nautical Style* (London: Architectural Press, 1973).

51. Daniel H. Burnham and Edward H. Bennett, *Plan of Chicago* (Chicago: Commercial Club, 1909). See also "Project for Lakefront Development of the City of Chicago," by Eliel Saarinen, *The American Architect* 124, no. 2434 (5 December 1923):487–514, and Carl Condit, *Chicago, 1910–19* (Chicago: University of Chicago Press, 1973).

52. Hamlin, quoted by Condit, *Chicago,* pp. 59–60.

53. Burnham and Bennett, *Plan of Chicago,* p. 6.

54. Ibid., legend to illustration cx.

55. Ibid., p. 100.

56. Eugène Hénard was probably the first to provide for the separation of vehicular and pedestrian traffic in the modern city; see Peter M. Wolf, *Eugène Hénard and the Beginning of Urbanism in Paris, 1900–1914* (The Hague: Ando, for the International Federation for Housing and Planning and the Centre de recherche d'urbanisme, 1968). Burnham and Bennett's achievement can be ranked with Hénard's. Wolf mentions on page 71 that Jaussely used Hénard's unique three-cornered building blocks in his plan for Barcelona in order to provide a direct view to the sea from every house along a new street.

In 1910 the city of Antwerp held an international competition for urban improvements. Henri Prost submitted the plan awarded the first prize. It included an elevated park and walkway along the passenger quay and astride railroad and commercial traffic. It was to be built in reinforced concrete because that material could produce a simplicity of line that would echo the qualities of naval architecture. (Was this not a prefiguration of what Le Corbusier wanted?) Prost hoped this construction would be as important to the people of Antwerp as the Pincio was to the people of Rome: it would be the city's principal promenade. See *L'Oeuvre de Henri Prost, architecture et urbanisme* (Paris: Académie d'architecture, 1960). Prost also designed a regional plan for the coastline of the Var in the 1930s.

57. Committee on Interior and Insular Affairs, "Deepwater Port Policy Issues," pp. 66–90.
58. *Plan and Program for the Preservation of the Vieux Carré,* Historic District Demonstration Study conducted by Bureau of Governmental Research, City of New Orleans, 1968.
59. Roy Mann, *Rivers in the City* (New York: Praeger, 1973), p. 20.

The Greater London Council's Docklands Joint Committee has recently proposed a plan for developing the economically depressed Thameside districts southeast of London (the same areas Dance wanted to convert from industry to housing in the eighteenth century). A new subway line, four centers of industrial development, over twenty thousand new housing units, five shopping centers, and public access to the river compose this £2 billion scheme, but the different perspectives of the interested parties and the problems of mixed public/private funding may make long-range, large-scale planning impossible. (*The Economist,* April 10, 1976, p. 38.)

Since the 1960s the City of Vancouver has engaged in waterfront planning. Citing a likely increase in harbor activity and implying that without planning the character of the entire city may be altered by the ways private interests expand their uses of the waterfront, planning studies have sought to create a new setting for commercial and industrial uses of the seafront by providing for increased public use and enjoyment of Vancouver's waterfront: "The essence of the planning problem is to ensure optimum interaction between maritime activity and urban life." Planners propose to "link the waterfront, physically and socially, with the adjacent Downtown Peninsula" once they relocate the CP Railyards, which permit only three pedestrian access points to the waterfront. Then they plan to use continuous landscaping, "appropriately selected for the salt air environment," to create a "sea-side urbanity," mixing private, community, and public spaces: "Create a variety of experiences along the waterfront walk by varying the treatment of the water's edge, by changing the walk's direction, width and elevation, by pulling the walk back from the water occasionally and by changing vistas along it. Encourage a variety of facilities and activities to develop along the walk that are sympathetic to the water's edge." "Waterfront walkway connections and public viewing platforms shall be incorporated into new and existing industrial developments, thereby allowing for visual access while maintaining any necessary physical separation of industrial and public uses." In the Waterfront Planning Study prepared by Richard C. Mann and submitted to the City of Vancouver in November 1974, there is in fact little evidence of how such planning will affect the land-use demands of maritime commerce. Permeating the document is the assumption that shipping and industry can work out for themselves the best ways to use the land assigned them in the plan. Rather, the planner's ambition seems to be to extend the border between the city and its harbor to the water's edge. Perhaps the plan stops short of reconsidering more of the city's space for political reasons. I am indebted to Arthur Phillips, Mayor of Vancouver, for providing me with copies of several waterfront planning studies.

60. Edouard Albert and Jacques Cousteau, "Projet d'île artificielle au large de Monaco," *L'Architecture d'Aujourd'hui* 38 (April–May 1967); Arthur Nettleton, "Cities in the Sea," *Oceans* 5 (March–April 1972):71–75; John Lear, "Cities on the Sea?", *Saturday Review* (4 December 1971), pp. 80–90; J. Gordon Hammer, "Ocean Installations: State of Technology," in *Coastal Zone Management, Multiple Use with Conservation,* ed. John F. Brahtz (New York: Wiley-Interscience, 1972), esp. pp. 271–85; Jürgen Joedicke, *Architecture since 1945* (New York: Praeger, 1969), pp. 154–57; the seaside resort projects illustrated in *L'Architecture d'Aujourd'hui* 33 (June–July 1962); and above all, the articles on the theme "Living in the Sea," *L'Architecture d'Aujourd'hui* 46 (September–October 1974).

Bibliography

UNPUBLISHED SOURCES

Written Records in France

The most extensive archival sources for the new port cities of Louis XIV's France are the Archives de la Marine deposited at the Archives nationales, Paris. The relevant series are B^2, dispatches and orders, B^3, papers sent to the court, B^7, foreign countries, commerce, and consulates, D^2 (pre 1789) and DD^2 (post 1789), hydraulic works and civil buildings, G, miscellaneous, and 3JJ, naval hydrographic service. The Archives de la Marine deposited at the ports of Brest, Lorient, and Rochefort should in theory match the papers in the B^2 and B^3 series in Paris, but destruction by war, the elements, and human neglect have substantially reduced the size of the archives in these ports. Even so, there are some documents in the port archives that do not exist in Paris. Other government papers can be found in the Paris manuscript collections of the Archives des affaires étrangères, and of the Bibliothèque nationale; at the latter: Cinq Cents de Colbert, Nouvelles acquisitions françaises, Mélanges de Colbert, Fonds Clairambault, and the Fonds Anisson. The Bibliothèque and Archives du Comité technique du Génie are especially useful for topographic, spatial analysis. There are a few relevant series in the Archives nationales; these are: Colonies, G^7, correspondence with the controller general, H^* 748, the Languedoc Estates, K, royal property, and Q^1, taxation. Archives départementales de Finistère at Quimper, de la Charente-Maritime at La Rochelle, de l'Hérault at Montpellier, and de Morbihan at Vannes, and the Archives communales of Brest, Lorient, Rochefort, and Sète complement state papers with civil registers, tax documents, and the records of city government. All of these archives have been catalogued. I will be happy to correspond with any reader who is interested in a more detailed accounting of French archival materials.

Maps and Plans

Because map collections have been systematically catalogued, it is unnecessary for me to cite the individual reference numbers for what would be nearly eighty maps in France and several times that number in other countries. The legends accompanying illustrations provide full bibliographic references for the maps and plans presented in this book. I have annotated the following list of institutions to indicate the scope and value of their collections.

France

Paris. Bibliothèque nationale. Manuscripts; Estampes; Cartes et Plans, including the special depository of maps from the Service hydrographique de la Marine. Perhaps the most comprehensive collection of pre-1900 maps and atlases in the world; the widest possible coverage of cartography and graphics.

———. Génie, archives deposited at Vincennes. Although limited to primary sources relating to fortifications, its records touch upon most aspects of early modern French cities.

_____. Musée de la Marine. A large archive of original and secondary materials, cross-indexed, and covering the full range of graphics production in France.

_____. Service historique de la Marine, Ministère de la Marine. A general collection of all navy materials not at the Bibliothèque nationale.

Europe, Excepting France

Copenhagen. Bymuseum. A rich city-history museum and study center.

_____. Forsvarets Bygningstienst. Materials relating to fortifications and military engineering and, thus, to early modern city form.

_____. Harensarkiv.

_____. Kongelige Bibliotek. A general archive for areas formerly under Danish rule as well as for Denmark.

Gothenburg. Landsarkivet.

_____. Stadsarkiv.

Haarlem. Rijksarchief Noordholland. Compared to those from France or Sweden, the number of surviving city plans from seventeenth-century Netherlands is surprisingly small; that country's prominence in printing and cartography had little to do with the production of city plans.

Helsinki. National Architectural Museum.

Stockholm. Kunglinga Krigsarkiv, SFP Collection (Carlsburg, Gävle, Gothenburg, Jönköping, Kalmar, Karlshamn, Karlskrona, Kronstadt, Landskrona, Narva, Nyen, Riga, St. Petersburg, Stettin, Stockholm). An encyclopedic survey of cities in Sweden and its empire can be found in this military archive.

_____. Kunglinga Bibliotek. Especially valuable for engravings and printed materials.

_____. Lantmäteristyrelsens arkiv (Gothenburg, Kalmar, Karlshamn, Lidköping, Norrköping, Uddevalla). The Archive of the royal surveyors.

_____. National Museum. Includes a large number of prints and drawings of Continental, especially French, places and topics sent back to Sweden during the seventeenth, eighteenth, and nineteenth centuries.

Uppsala. University Library (Eskilstuna, Gothenburg, Kalmar, Norrköping, Stockholm). By virtue of its age alone, this library has a distinguished collection in cartography and graphic arts.

United States

Ann Arbor. William Clements Library at the University of Michigan. Excellent for European atlases and original maps of eighteenth-century America.

Chicago. The Newberry Library, Hermon Dunlap Smith Center for the History of Cartography. The Sack and Cartes Marines Collections cover a variety of topics in Europe and America. The Novacco Collection is the best source for sixteenth-century Italian cities because it includes most of the oldest surviving maps and plans.

New York. The New York Public Library, Stokes Collection. The history of New York.

Washington, D.C. Library of Congress Map Division. Valuable for its European atlases, and for nineteenth- and twentieth-century sheet maps.

Dissertations

Cazalet, L.-J. "Cette et son commerce des vins, 1666–1920." Thèse de doctorat en droit, Université de Montpellier, 1920.

Cestain, Camille. "La Ville de Lorient et les classes sociales au 18e siècle selon les roles de capitation." Mémoire DES, Université de Poitiers, 1967.

Dessert, Daniel. "La Flotte française, constructions, 1661–72." Thèse de maîtrise, Université de Nanterre, 1968.

Frank, Fred Roy. "The Development of New York City, 1600–1900." Master's thesis, Cornell University, Ithaca, N.Y., 1955.

Girard-Perracha, Guillaume. "Le Commerce des vins et des eaux-de-vie en Languedoc sous l'ancien régime." Thèse de doctorat en droit, Université de Montpellier, 1955.

Journet, Jean-Louis. "Approvisionnements de la Marine de guerre, 1661–72." Thèse de maîtrise, Université de Nanterre, 1968.

Konvitz, Josef Wolf. "New Port Cities of Louis XIV's France: Brest, Lorient, Rochefort and Sète, 1660–1720." Ph.D. dissertation, Princeton University, Princeton, N.J., 1973.

Maistre, André. "Le Canal des Deux-Mers ou Canal royal de Languedoc, 1666–1810." Thèse de doctorat en droit, Université de Toulouse, 1962.

Munar, J. "Activité maritime et commerciale du port de Morlaix dans la première moitié du 18ᵉ siècle." Thèse de maîtrise, U.E.R.-Bretagne occidentale, Brest, 1971.

Tudez, M. "Le Développement de la vigne dans la région de Montpellier du XVIIᵉ siècle à nos jours." Thèse de doctorat en droit, Université de Montpellier, 1934.

ARTICLES AND BOOKS

Collected Documents

Boislisle, Arthur, ed. *Correspondance des Controlleurs-Généraux des Finances.* 3 vols. Paris: Imprimerie nationale, 1874–1897.

Clément, Pierre, ed. *Lettres, instructions et mémoires de Colbert.* 10 vols. Paris: Imprimerie nationale, 1861–1883.

Depping, Guillaume, ed. *Correspondance administrative sous le règne de Louis XIV.* 4 vols. Paris: Imprimerie nationale, 1850–1855.

Devic, Claude, and Vaissette, Joseph, ed. *Histoire générale de Languedoc.* Toulouse: Privat, 1872–1892.

Lemonnier, ed. *Procès-Verbaux de l'Académie royale d'architecture.* Vol. 2. Paris, 1911.

Lorenzen, V. *Handtegnede Kort over København.* Vol. 1, *1600–1660.* Copenhagen: Henrik Koppels Verlag, 1930. Vol. 2, *1660–1757.* Copenhagen: Einar Murrksgaads Forlag, 1942.

Maritime and Urban History

This listing provides partial, not exhaustive, coverage of maritime and urban history. Because maritime affairs is a specialized, well-defined topic that has interested a small circle of able scholars, it has a better bibliographic core than urban history, a larger and newer field. The established English language source is Robert C. Albion, *Naval and Maritime History, an Annotated Bibliography,* 4th ed. revised and expanded (Mystic, Conn.: Munson Institute of American Maritime History, 1972). Bibliographies in urban history are all too often arranged as an aspect of a nation's local history, and are best utilized by scholars who are interested in a particular locality rather than in a particular problem. The Commission internationale pour l'histoire des villes is publishing a series of national urban history bibliographies. The best interpretive statements on urban history research can be found in *Urban History Yearbook,* ed. H. J. Dyos (Leicester: Leicester University Press, 1974–).

General Studies in Maritime Culture and Affairs

Anson, Peter. *Fisher Folk Lore.* London: Faith Press, 1965.

Arts Council of Britain. *Shock of Recognition: The Landscape of English Romanticism and the Dutch Seventeenth School.* London, 1971.

Auden, W. H. *The Enchafèd·Flood.* 1950. Reprint. New York: Vintage, 1967.

Automobile Association. *Book of the Seaside.* London, 1972.

Beck, Horace. *Folklore and the Sea.* Middletown, Conn.: Wesleyan University Press, 1973.

Bertino, Serge, ed. *Guide de la mer mystérieuse.* Les Guides Noirs Series. Paris: Tchon/Emom, 1970.

Bol, Lauren J. *Die Holländische Marinemalerei des 17 Jahrhunderts.* Braunschweig: Klinhardt and Bienmann, 1973.

Boxer, Charles Ralph. *The Dutch Seaborne Empire.* New York: Alfred A. Knopf, 1970.

_____. *The Portuguese Seaborne Empire, 1415–1825*. London: Hutchinson, 1963.

_____. *The Anglo-Dutch Wars of the 17th Century, 1653–1674*. London: HMSO, 1975.

Brodie, Bernard. *Sea Power in the Machine Age*. London: Oxford University Press, 1941.

Buttimer, Anne. *Society and Milieu in the French Geographic Tradition*. Monograph Series no. 6, Association of American Geographers, Chicago: Rand McNally, 1971.

Carson, Rachel. *The Sea Around Us*. New York: Oxford University Press, 1951.

Cawley, R. R. *Unpathed Waters: Studies in the Influence of the Voyagers on Elizabethan Literature*. Princeton, N.J.: Princeton University Press, 1940.

Conrad, Joseph. *Mirror of the Sea*. London: Methuen, 1906.

Cordingly, David. *Marine Painting in England, 1700–1900*. London: Studio Vista, 1974.

Deacon, Margaret. *Scientists and the Sea, 1650–1900*. New York: Academic Press, 1971.

Defoe, Daniel. *A New Voyage Round the World by a Course Never Sailed*. 1724. Reprint. New York: Crowell, 1903–1904.

Dockès, Pierre, *L'Espace dans la pensée économique du 17ᵉ et 18ᵉ siècles*. Paris: Flammarion, 1971.

Environment Canada. *Canada Water Year Book*. Ottawa: Information Canada, 1975.

Guilmartin, John F., Jr. *Gunpowder and Galleys*. Cambridge: At the University Press, 1975.

Herrman, Luke. *British Landscape Painting of the Eighteenth Century*. London: Faber and Faber, 1973.

Hyde, Francis. *Far Eastern Trade, 1860–1914*. London: Adam and Charles Black, 1973.

Ketchum, Bostwick, H., ed. *The Water's Edge: Critical Problems of the Coastal Zone*. Cambridge, Mass.: The MIT Press, 1972.

Lennard, Reginald. *Englishmen at Rest and Play*. Oxford: At the Clarendon Press, 1931.

Luard, Evan. *The Control of the Sea-Bed*. London: Heinemann, 1974.

Mahan, Alfred Thayer. *The Influence of Sea Power upon History, 1660–1783*. 1890. Reprint. New York: Hill and Wang, 1957.

Marder, Arthur J. *The Anatomy of British Sea Power*. London: Cass, 1974.

_____. *From the Dreadnought to Scapa Flow*. 5 vols. London: Oxford University Press, 1961–1970.

Melville, Herman. *Moby Dick or The Whale*. 1846. Reprint. New York: The Modern Library, 1944.

Mitchell, Donald W. *A History of Russian and Soviet Sea Power*. New York: Macmillan, 1974.

Morison, Samuel Eliot. *The European Discovery of America*. 2 vols. New York: Oxford University Press, 1971–1974.

_____. *History of United States Naval Operations in World War II*. 15 vols. Boston: Little, Brown and Co., 1947–1962.

_____. *The Maritime History of Massachusetts, 1783–1860*. Boston: Houghton Mifflin, 1921.

Nicolson, Marjorie Hope. *Mountain Gloom and Mountain Glory: The Development of the Aesthetics of the Infinite*. Ithaca, N.Y.: Cornell University Press, 1959.

O'Connell, Daniel Patrick. *The Influence of Law on Sea Power*. Manchester: Manchester University Press, 1975.

Parry, John Horace. *The Spanish Seaborne Empire*. 1966. Reprint. Harmondsworth: Penguin Books, 1973.

_____. *The Age of Reconnaissance*. Cleveland: World Publishing, 1963.

Philbrick, Thomas. *James Fenimore Cooper and the Development of American Sea Fiction*. Cambridge, Mass.: Harvard University Press, 1961.

Ponko, Vincent, J. *Ships, Seas and Scientists*. Annapolis, Md.: Naval Institute Press, 1974.

Prescott, John Robert Victor. *The Political Geography of the Oceans*. New York: John Wiley and Sons, 1975.

Ropp, Theodore. "Continental Doctrines of Sea Power." In *Makers of Modern Strategy*. Edited by Edward Mead Earle. 1941. Reprint. New York: Atheneum, 1967.

Rossi, Paolo. *Philosophy, Technology and the Arts in the Early Modern Era*. New York: Harper and Row, 1970.

Schlee, Susan. *The Edge of an Unfamiliar World: A History of Oceanography*. New York: Sutton, 1973.

Sprout, Margaret Tuttle. "Mahan: Evangelist of Sea Power." In *Makers of Modern Strategy*. Edited by Edward Mead Earle. 1941. Reprint. New York: Atheneum, 1967.

Stein, Roger. "Pulled out of the Bay: American Fiction in the Eighteenth Century." *Studies in American Fiction* 2 (1974).

_____. "Seascape and the American Imagination: The Puritan Seventeenth Century." *Early American Literature* 7 (1972).

_____. *Seascape and the American Imagination.* New York: Clarkson N. Peter, Inc., and the Whitney Museum of American Art, 1975.

Stevenson, D. Alan. *The World's Lighthouses before 1820.* London: Oxford University Press, 1959.

Teclaff, Ludwik A. *The River Basin in History and Law.* The Hague: Martinus Nijhoff, 1967.

Trask, David. *Captains and Cabinets: Anglo-American Naval Relations 1917–1918.* Columbia: University of Missouri Press, 1972.

Turner, Anne. *The Sea in English Literature from Beowulf to Donne.* Liverpool: University of Liverpool Press, 1926.

Van Dyke, John C. *The Opal Sea, Continued Studies in Impressions and Appearances.* New York: Charles Scribners Sons, 1917.

Watson, Harold F. *The Sailor in English Fiction and Drama, 1550–1880.* New York: Columbia University Press, 1931.

Wenk, Edward, Jr. *The Politics of the Ocean.* Seattle: University of Washington Press, 1974.

General Studies in Urban Development

Albert, Edouard, and Cousteau, Jacques. "Projet d'île artificielle au large de Monaco." *L'Architecture d'Aujourd'hui* 38 (April–May 1967).

L'Architecture d'Aujourd'hui. Seaside resort projects. 33 (June–July 1962). Living in the Sea. 46 (September–October 1974).

Beresford, Maurice. *New Towns of the Middle Ages.* New York: Praeger, 1967.

Braudel, Fernand. *Civilisation matérielle et capitalisme.* Paris: Armand Colin, 1967.

Breese, Gerald. *Urbanization in Newly Developing Countries.* Englewood Cliffs, N.J. Prentice Hall, 1966.

Burke, Peter. "Some Reflections on the Pre-Industrial City." In *Urban History Yearbook 1975.* Edited by H. J. Dyos. Leicester: Leicester University Press, 1975.

Choay, Françoise. "Urbanism and Semiology." In *Meaning in Architecture.* Edited by Charles Jencks and George Baird. London: Barrie and Rockcliff, The Cresset Press, 1969.

Croix, Horst de la. *Military Considerations in City Planning: Fortifications.* New York: George Braziller, 1972.

Dickinson, Robert Eric. *The West European City: A Geographical Interpretation.* London: Routledge and Kegan Paul, 1951.

Downs, Roger M., and Stea, David, Eds. *Image and Environment: Cognitive Mapping and Spatial Behavior.* Chicago: Aldine Publishing, 1973.

Duby, Georges. "History of Systems of Value." In *The Ethnologist and the Futurologist.* Edited by J. Dumoulin and D. Morisi. Paris: Mouton, 1973.

Foucault, Michel. *Les Mots et les choses.* Paris: Gallimard, 1966.

Fox, Edward Whiting. *History in Geographic Perspective.* New York: W. W. Norton, 1971.

Francastel, Pierre. "Art et sociologie." *L'Année sociologique,* 3rd ser. 2 (1940–1948).

_____. *La Figure et le lieu.* Paris: Gallimard, 1967.

_____. *Peinture et société.* Paris: Gallimard, 1950.

Francastel, Pierre, ed. *L'Urbanisme de Paris et l'Europe, 1600–1680.* Paris: Klincksieck, 1969.

Gutkind, Erwin Anton. *International History of City Development.* Vol. 3, *Urban Development in Southern Europe: Spain and Portugal.* New York: The Free Press, 1967.

_____. *International History of City Development.* Vol. 4, *Urban Development in Southern Europe: Italy and Greece.* New York: The Free Press, 1969.

_____. *International History of City Development.* Vol. 5, *Urban Development in Western Europe: France and Belgium.* New York: The Free Press, 1970.

_____. *International History of City Development.* Vol. 6, *Urban Development in Western Europe: The Netherlands and Great Britain.* New York: The Free Press, 1970.

Jacobs, Jane. *The Economy of Cities.* New York: Random House, 1969.

Joedicke, Jürgen. *Architecture since 1945.* New York: Praeger, 1969.

Johnson, Edgar Augustus Jerome. *The Organization of Space in Developing Countries.* Cambridge, Mass.: Harvard University Press, 1970.

Lavedan, Pierre. *Histoire de l'urbanisme.* Vol. 2, *Renaissance et temps modernes.* Paris: Henri Laurens, 1941.

_____. *Les Villes françaises.* Paris: Vincent, 1960.

Lynch, Kevin. *The Image of the City.* Cambridge, Mass.: The MIT Press, 1960.

McNeill, William H. *The Shape of European History.* New York: Oxford University Press, 1974.

Marin, Louis. *Utopiques, jeux d'espace.* Paris: Les Editions de Minuit, 1975.

Minchinton, Walter. "Patterns and Structure of Demand, 1500–1750." In *The Fontana Economic History of Europe: The Sixteenth and Seventeenth Centuries.* Edited by Carlo M. Cipolla. London: Collins/Fontana, 1975.

Moholy-Nagy, Sybil. *The Matrix of Man.* New York: Praeger, 1968.

Mols, Roger. *Introduction à la démographie historique des villes d'Europe du 14e au 18e siècles.* 3 vols. Louvain: Université catholique, 1954–1956.

Morini, Mario. *Atlante di Storia dell'Urbanistica.* Milan: Ulrico Hoepple, 1964.

Mumford, Lewis. *The City in History.* New York: Harcourt, Brace and World, 1961.

Nef, John U. *War and Human Progress.* Cambridge, Mass.: Harvard University Press, 1950.

L'Oeuvre de Henri Prost, architecture et urbanisme. Paris: Académie d'architecture, 1960.

Perrot, Jean-Claude. "Rapports sociaux et villes au 18e siècle." *Annales ESC* 23 (March–April 1968).

Pirenne, Henri. *Medieval Cities.* 1925. Reprint. Garden City, N.Y.: Doubleday, 1956.

Van Der Wee, Hermann. "Reflections on the Development of the Urban Economy in Western Europe during the Late Middle Ages and Early Modern Times." *Urbanism Past and Present* 1 (Winter 1975–1976).

Wolf, Peter M. *Eugène Hénard and the Beginning of Urbanism in Paris, 1900–1914.* The Hague: Ando, for the International Federation for Housing and Planning and the Centre de recherche d'urbanisme, 1968.

**Specialized Studies in European Urban
and Maritime History, Excepting France**

Améen, Lennart. *Stadsbebylgelse och Domänstruktur.* Lund: C. W. K. Gleerup, 1964.

Argan Giulio C. *The Renaissance City.* New York: George Braziller, 1969.

Bater, James H. *St. Petersburg, Industrialization and Change.* London: Edward Arnold, 1976.

Bauer, Hermann. *Kunst und Utopie, Studien über das Kunst und Staatsdenken in der Renaissance.* West Berlin: Walter de Gruyter, 1965.

Baugh, Daniel. *British Naval Administration in the Age of Walpole.* Princeton, N.J.: Princeton University Press, 1965.

Bird, James. *The Major Seaports of the United Kingdom.* London: Hutchinson, 1963.

Boorsma, P. *Duizend Zaanse Molens.* Wormerveer, 1950.

Braam, Aris van. *Bloei en verval van het economisch-sociale level aan de Zaan in de 17e en 18e eeuw.* Wormerveer: 1944.

Braam, Aris van; Groesbeck, J. W.; Hart, S.; and Verkade, M. A. *Historische Atlas van de Zaanlanden, twentig eeuwen landschapsontwikkeling.* Amsterdam: Meijer, 1970.

Braudel, Fernand, and Romano, Ruggiero. *Navires et marchandises à l'entrée du port de Livourne, 1547–1611.* Paris: Armand Colin, 1951.

Brett-James, Norman G. *The Growth of Stuart London.* London: G. Allen and Unwin, 1935.

Burke, Gerald. *The Making of Dutch Towns.* London: Cleaver-Hulme, 1956.

———. *Towns in the Making.* London: Edward Arnold, 1971.

Chalklin, C. W. "The Making of Some New Towns, c. 1600–1720." In *Rural Change and Urban Growth, 1500–1800, Essays in English Regional History in Honour of W. G. Hoskins.* Edited by C. W. Chalklin and M. A. Havinden. New York: Longmans, 1974.

———. *The Provincial Towns of Georgian England.* London: Edward Arnold, 1974.

Clark, Kenneth. "Architectural Backgrounds in Italian Painting." *The Arts,* no. 1 (1947).

Cochrane, Eric. "A Case in Point: The End of the Renaissance in Florence." In *The Late Italian Renaissance, 1525–1630.* Edited by Eric Cochrane. New York: Harper and Row, 1970.

Croix, Horst de la. "Military Architecture and the Radial City Plan in Sixteenth Century Italy." *Art Bulletin* 42 (December 1960).

Defoe, Daniel. *A Tour through England and Wales.* 2 vols. 1725. Reprint. London: J. M. Dent and Sons, 1927.

De Seta, Cesare. *Storia della Città di Napoli; dalle origini al settecento.* Rome: Laterza, 1973.

Downes, Kerry. "John Evelyn and Architecture: A First Inquiry." In *Essays on Architectural Writers and Writing Presented to Nikolaus Pevsner*. Edited by John Summerson. London: Allen Lane the Penguin Press, 1968.

Eden, W. E. "Studies in Urban Theory: The *De Re Aedificatoria* of Leon Battista Alberti." *Town Planning Review* 19 (1943).

Egorov, Iurri Alekseevich. *The Architectural Planning of St. Petersburg*. Athens: Ohio University Press, 1969.

Ehrman, John. *The Navy in the War of William III*. Cambridge: At the University Press, 1953.

Eimer, Gerhard. *Die Stadtplanung im Schwedischen Ostseereich*. Stockholm: Svenska Bokförlaget, 1961.

Elling, Christian, and Möller, Viggo Sten. *Holmens Bygningshistorie, 1680-1930*. Copenhagen: Henrik Koppel, 1932.

Erichsen, John. *Frederiksstaden, Grundlaeggelsen af en Københansk Bybel, 1749-1760*. Copenhagen, 1972.

_____. *Københavnske Motiver, 1587-1807*. Copenhagen: Københavns Bymuseum, 1974.

Evelyn, John. *London Revived*. 1666. Reprint. Oxford: At the Clarendon Press, 1938.

Fällström, Anne-Marie. "Befolknings sociala och ekonomiska structur i Göteborg, 1800-1840." *Historisk Tidskrift* (1974).

Foster, Kurt W. "From 'Rocca' to 'Civitas': Urban Planning at Sabbioneta." *L'Arte* 1 (1969).

Francastel, Pierre. "Imagination et réalité dans l'architecture civile du Quattrocento." In *Hommage à Lucien Febvre: Eventail de l'histoire vivante*. Vol. 2. Paris: Armand Colin, 1953.

Gadol, Joan Kelley. *Leon Battista Alberti*. Chicago: University of Chicago Press, 1973.

Gamrath, Helge. "Christianshavns Grundlaeggelse og Aedlste Bybygningsmaessige Udvikling." In *Historiske Meddelelser Om København, 1968*. Copenhagen: Københavns Kommunalbestyrelse, 1968.

Garin, Eugenio. "La Cité idéale de la renaissance italienne." In *Les Utopies à la Renaissance*. Edited by Institut pour l'étude de la Renaissance et de l'Humanisme. Brussels: Presses universitaires de Bruxelles, 1963.

Hanson, Michael. *2000 Years of London*. London: Country Life, 1967.

Hecksher, Eli. *An Economic History of Sweden*. Cambridge: Mass.: Harvard University Press, 1954.

_____. "Den Ekonomiska inneborden av 1500 och 1600 talens svenska stadsgrundningar." *Historisk Tidskrift* (1923).

Hill, Christopher. *Intellectual Origins of the English Revolution*. Oxford: At the Clarendon Press, 1965.

Hughes, Diane. "Family Structure in Mcdieval Genoa." *Past and Present*, no. 66 (1975).

Hughes, Quentin. *Seaport: Architecture and Townscape in Liverpool*. London: L. Humphries, 1969.

Hugo-Brunt, M. "George Dance, the Younger, as Town Planner (1768-1814)." *Journal of the Society of Architectural Historians* 14 (1955).

Hyde, Francis. *Liverpool and the Mersey*. London: David and Charles, 1971.

Jeannin, Pierre. *L'Europe du Nord-Ouest et du Nord*. Paris: Presses universitaires de France, 1969.

Jellicoe, Susan, and Jellicoe, Geoffrey. *Water: The Use of Water in Landscape Architecture*. London: Adam and Charles Black, 1971.

Kalman, H. "The Architecture of Mercantilism: Commercial Buildings by George Dance the Younger." In *The Triumph of Culture: 18th Century Perspectives*. Edited by Paul Fritz and David Williams. Toronto: A. M. Hakkert, 1972.

Kellett, John R. *The Impact of Railways on Victorian Cities*. London: Routledge and Kegan Paul, 1969.

Lambert, Audrey M. *The Making of the Dutch Landscape*. London: Seminar Press, 1971.

Lane, Frederick C. *Venice, A Maritime Republic*. Baltimore, Md.: The Johns Hopkins University Press, 1973.

Lilienberg, Albert, ed. *Stadsbildningar och Stadsplanen I Götaälvs mynningsområde från äldsta tider till omkring aderthundra*. Vol. 7 of *Skrifter utgivna till Göteborg stads trehundråarsjubileum*, edited by Jubileumsutställningens publikationskommitté. Gothenburg: W. Zachrisson, 1928.

Manning, Roger. *Religion and Society in Elizabethan Sussex*. Leicester: Leicester University Press, 1969.

Maré, Eric de. *The Nautical Style*. London: Architectural Press, 1973.

Midwinter, Eric. *Old Liverpool.* London: David and Charles, 1971.

Nisser, Marie. "Stadsplanering i det Svenska niket, 1700–1809." *Ars Suetica* (1970).

Nudi, Giacinto. *Storia Urbanistica di Livorno, dalle origine al secolo XVI.* Venice: Neri Pozza, 1959.

Parker, Geoffrey. *The Army of Flanders and the Spanish Road, 1567–1659.* Cambridge: At the University Press, 1972.

Parker, John. *Books to Build an Empire.* Amsterdam: N. Israel, 1965.

Parkinson, C. Northcote. *The Rise of the Port of Liverpool.* Liverpool: Liverpool University Press, 1952.

Pearl, Valerie. *London and the Outbreak of the Puritan Revolution.* London: Oxford University Press, 1961.

Peet, Henry. "Thomas Steers, The Engineer of Liverpool's First Dock: A Memoir." *Transactions of the Historic Society of Lancashire and Cheshire* 82 (1930).

Rabb, Theodore K. *Enterprise and Empire: Merchant and Gentry Investment in the Expansion of England, 1575–1630.* Cambridge, Mass.: Harvard University Press, 1967.

Rasmussen, Steen Eiler. *København.* Copenhagen: GEC Gads Forlag, 1969.

Roberts, Michael. *Essays in Swedish History.* London: Weidenfeld and Nicolson, 1967.

———. *Gustavus Adolphus: A History of Sweden, 1611–1632.* 2 vols. London: Longmans, 1953–1958.

Rosenau, Helen. *Social Purpose in Architecture.* London: Studio Vista, 1970.

Rozman, Gilbert. *Urban Networks in Russia, 1750–1800, and Premodern Periodization.* Princeton, N.J.: Princeton University Press, 1976.

Skovgaard, Joakim A. *A King's Architecture: Christian IV and His Buildings.* London: Hugh Evelyn, 1973.

Smith, Denis Mack. *A History of Sicily.* 2 vols. London: Chatto and Windus, 1968.

Stevin, Simon. *The Principal Works of Simon Stevin.* 5 vols. Edited by Ernst Crone, E. J. Dijksterhuis, D. J. Struik, A. Pannekoek, W. H. Schukking, R. J. Forbes, A. D. Fokker, and A. Romein-Verschoor. Translated by C. Dikshoorn. Amsterdam: C. V. Swets and Zeitlingen, 1955–1966.

Summerson, John. *Georgian London.* London: Barrie and Jenkins, 1970.

Swann, D. "The Pace and Progress of Port Investment in England, 1660–1830." *Yorkshire Bulletin of Economic and Social Research* 12 (1960).

Thompson, Edward P. "Time, Work, Discipline and Industrial Capitalism." *Past and Present,* no. 38 (1968).

Vermeulen, Frans Andrée Jozef. *Handbook tot de geschiedenis der Nederlandsche bouwkunst.* 3 vols. The Hague: Martinus Nijhoff, 1928–1944.

Vyatkin, M. P., ed. *Ocherki Istorii Leningrada, tom pervyy, period feodalizma (1703–1861).* Moscow and Leningrad: Isdatel'stvo Akedemii Nauk SSR, 1955.

Waters, David W. *The Art of Navigation in England in Elizabethan and Early Stuart Times.* New Haven, Conn.: Yale University Press, 1958.

Wauwerman, Henri Emmanuel. "La Fortification di Nicolo Tartaglia." *Revue belge d'art, de sciences et de technologie militaire* (1876).

———. "L'Architecture militaire flamande et italienne au seizieme siècle." *Revue belge d'art, de sciences et de technologie militaire* (1878).

William, T. S. *River Navigation in England, 1600–1750.* London: Frank Cass, 1964.

Wittkower, Rudolph. *Architectural Principles in the Age of Humanism.* London: Tiranti, 1952.

Wolfe, Ivor de. *The Italian Townscape.* London: The Architectural Press, 1963.

Studies in French Urban and Maritime History

Asher, Eugene L. *The Resistance to the Maritime Classes.* Berkeley: University of California Press, 1960.

Augoyat, Antoine-Marie. *Aperçu sur les fortifications, les ingénieurs, et sur les corps du génie en France.* 3 vols. Paris: Tanera, 1864.

Babelon, Jean-Pierre. *Demeures parisiennes sous Henri IV et Louis XIII.* Paris: Les Editions du temps, 1965.

Bamford, Paul. *Fighting Ships and Prisons.* Minneapolis: University of Minnesota Press, 1973.

_____. *French Forests and Sea Power, 1660–1789.* Toronto: University of Toronto Press, 1956.

Beauchesne, Geneviève. "Les Sources de l'histoire du port de Lorient et des trois compagnies des Indes." *Revue d'histoire des Colonies* 42 (1955).

Bernard, Leon. "French Society and Popular Uprisings under Louis XIV." *French Historical Studies* 3 (Fall 1964).

_____. *The Emerging City: Paris in the Age of Louis XIV.* Durham, N.C.: Duke University Press, 1970.

Bézard, Y. *Fonctionnaires maritimes et coloniales sous Louis XIV.* Paris: Albin Michel, 1933.

Blois, P. Théodore de. *Histoire de Rochefort, contenant l'établissement de cette ville, de son port et arsenal de Marine, et les antiquités de son château.* Paris and Blois: 1733.

Blondel, François. *Cours d'architecture enseigné dans l'académie royale d'architecture.* Paris, 1675.

Blunt, Anthony. *Art and Architecture in France, 1500–1700.* Harmondsworth: Penguin, 1953.

Bois, Paul. *Les Paysans de l'Ouest.* Paris: Mouton, 1960.

Boissonnade, Pierre. "Colbert, son système et les entreprises industrielles d'état en Languedoc, 1661–1683." *Annales du Midi* (1902).

_____. "L'Essai de restauration des ports et de la vie maritime en Languedoc de 1593 à 1661 et son échec." *Annales du Midi* (1934).

_____. "La Production et le commerce des céréales, des vins et des eaux-de-vie en Languedoc dans la seconde moitié du 17ᵉ siècle." *Annales du Midi* (1905).

_____. "La Restauration et le développement de l'industrie en Languedoc au temps de Colbert." *Annales du Midi* (1906).

Bosher, John. *French Finances, 1770–1795.* Cambridge: At the University Press, 1967.

Bourde de la Roguerie. "Introduction." *Inventaire des Archives départementales de Finistère antérieure à 1790.* Finistère, Archives civiles series B, v. 3, B4160–4670. Quimper, 1913.

Brissaud, Jean. *A History of French Public Law.* Boston: Little, Brown and Co., 1915.

Bromley, John S. "Le Commerce de la France de l'Ouest et de la guerre maritime, 1702–12." *Annales du Midi* 65 (1953).

_____. "Decline of Absolute Monarchy, 1683–1774." In *France: Government and Society, an historical survey.* Edited by J. M. Wallace-Hadrill and John McManners. London: Methuen and Co., 1957.

_____. "French Privateering War, 1702–12." In *Historical Essays Presented to David Ogg.* Edited by H. E. Bell and R. L. Ollard. London: Adam and Charles Black, 1964.

Buffet, Henri-François. *Lorient sous Louis XIV.* Rennes: Oberthur, 1937.

Carrière, Charles, and Pillorget, René. *Histoire de Marseille.* Toulouse: Privat, 1973.

Chaussinand-Nogaret, Guy. *Les Finances de Languedoc au 18ᵉ siècle.* Paris: SEVPEN, 1970.

Chauveau, Jean-Pierre. "La Mer et l'imagination des poètes au 17ᵉ siècle." *Dix-Septième Siècle*, no. 86–87 (1970).

Clark, Sir George. "New Social Foundations of States." In *The Ascendancy of France, 1648–88*, edited by F. L. Carsten. Vol. 5, *The New Cambridge Modern History.* Cambridge: At the University Press, 1961.

_____. *The Dutch Alliance and the War against French Trade, 1688–97.* London: Longmans Green, 1923.

Cole, Charles W. *Colbert and a Century of French Mercantilism.* 2 vols. New York: Columbia University Press, 1939.

Corre, A. "Les anciennes corporations brestoises." *Bulletin de la Société archéologique de Finistère* 21 (1894).

_____. "L'Instruction publique et les écoles à Brest avant 1789." *Bulletin de la Société archéologique de Finistère* 22 (1895).

Couturier, Michel. *Structures sociales de Chateaudun, 1525–1789.* Paris: SEVPEN, 1969.

Dainville, François de. *Le langage des géographes.* Paris: A. J. Picard, 1964.

_____. *Les Jésuites et l'éducation de la société française.* Paris: Beauchesne, 1930.

Dardel, Pierre. *Commerce, industrie et navigation à Rouen et au Havre au 18ᵉ siècle.* Rouen: Société libre d'émulation de la Seine-Maritime, 1966.

Daumard, Adeline. "Une référence pour l'étude des sociétés urbaines en France aux 18ᵉ et 19ᵉ siècles, projet de code socioprofessionnel." *Revue d'histoire moderne et contemporaine* 10 (1963).

Delumeau, Jean, ed. *Histoire de la Bretagne.* Toulouse: Privat, 1969.

Dermigny, Louis. "Armement languedocien et trafic du Levant et de Barbarie, 1681–1795." *Provence historique* 5–6 (1955–1956).

———. "Esquisse d'une histoire de Sète. *Sète.* Sète, 1968.

———. "De Montpellier à La Rochelle: route du commerce, route de la médicine au 18ᵉ siècle." *Annales du Midi* 65 (1955).

———. "Négociants bâlois et genevois à Nantes et à Lorient au 18ᵉ siècle." *Mélanges d'histoire économique et sociale en hommage au Prof. Antony Babel.* Vol. 2. Geneva, 1963.

Descartes, René. *Discours de la méthode.* Edited by E. Gilson. Paris: Vrin, 1964.

Dessert, Daniel, and Journet, Jean-Louis. "Le Lobby Colbert: un royaume ou une affaire de famille?" *Annales ESC* 30 (November–December 1975).

Dienne, Comte de. *Histoire du déssèchement des lacs et marais en France avant 1789.* Paris: H. Champion, 1891.

Dupaquier, J. "Problèmes de la codification socioprofessionnelle." In *Histoire sociale: sources et méthodes, colloque de St. Cloud, 1965.* Paris: Presses universitaires de France, 1967.

———. "Problèmes de mesure et de représentation graphique en histoire sociale." In *Actes du 89ᵉ Congrès des sociétés savantes.* Vol. 3. Lyon: 1964.

Durand, R. "Le Commerce en Bretagne au 18ᵉ siècle." *Annales de Bretagne* 32 (1917).

Faille, René. "Les Phares et la signalisation au 17ᵉ siècle." *Dix-Septième Siècle,* no. 86–87 (1970).

Fontaine. "Les Origines de la population [de Rochefort], 1665–1688." In *Mélanges historiques publiés à l'occasion du tricentenaire de la fondation de Rochefort.* Rochefort, 1966.

Fréville, Henri. *L'Intendance de Bretagne, 1689–1790.* Rennes: Plihon, 1953.

Gabory, E. "La Marine et le commerce de Nantes, 1661–1715." *Annales de Bretagne* 17 (1901–1902).

Garden, Maurice. *Lyon et les lyonnais au 18ᵉ siècle.* Paris: Les Belles lettres, 1970.

Giraud, Marcel. "Crise de conscience et d'autorité à la fin du règne de Louis XIV." *Annales ESC* 7 (April–June 1952).

———. "Marins et ouvriers des ports devant la crise à la fin du règne de Louis XIV." In *Hommage à Lucien Febvre: Eventail de l'histoire vivante.* Vol. 2. Paris: Armand Colin, 1953.

———. "Tendances humanitaires à la fin du règne de Louis XIV." *Revue historique* 77 (April–June 1953).

Goubert, Pierre. *Louis XIV et vingt millions de français.* Paris: Arthème Fayard, 1966.

Grodecki, Louis. "Vauban urbaniste." *Dix-Septième Siècle,* no. 36–37 (1957).

Guerlac, Henry. "Vauban: the Impact of Science on War." In *Makers of Modern Strategy.* Edited by Edward Mead Earle. 1941. Reprint. New York: Atheneum, 1967.

Hatton, Ragnhild. "Louis XIV: Recent Gains in Historical Knowledge." *Journal of Modern History* 45 (June 1973).

Hervé, R. "Ingénieur siennois en France au 16ᵉ siècle: G. Bellarmati et la création du Havre." *Etudes normandes* 23 (1961).

Huetz de Lenps, Christian. "Le Commerce maritime des vins d'Aquitaine de 1698 à 1716." *Revue d'histoire de Bordeaux et de la Gironde,* n.s. 14 (January–June 1965).

Jégou, François. *Marine militaire et corsaires sous le règne de Louis XIV, histoire de Lorient, port de guerre (1690–1720).* Vannes: E. Lafolye, 1887.

Konvitz, Josef. "Grandeur in French City Planning under Louis XIV: Rochefort and Marseille." *Journal of Urban History* 2 (November 1975).

Koulischer, Joseph. "Traités de commerce et la clause de la nation la plus favorisée du 16ᵉ au 18ᵉ siècles." *Revue d'histoire moderne* 6 (1931).

Labrousse, Ernest; Léon, Pierre; Goubert, Pierre; Bouvier, Jean; Carrière, Charles; and Harsin, Paul, eds. *Des derniers temps de l'âge seigneurial aux préludes de l'âge industriel (1660–1789).* Vol. 2, *Histoire économique et sociale de la France.* Edited by Fernand Braudel and Ernest Labrousse. Paris: Presses universitaires de France, 1970.

Lagrange, L. *Pierre Puget.* Paris: Didier, 1868.

La Roncière, Charles de. *Histoire de la marine française.* Vol. 5. Paris: Plon, 1920.

Le Gallo, Yves. *Brest et sa bourgeoisie sous la Monarchie de Juillet.* Paris: Presses universitaires de France, 1968.

Le Méné, J.-M. *Histoire archéologique, féodale et religieuse des paroisses du diocèce de Vannes.* Vannes: Galles, 1894.

Le Prouhon, Roger. "La Démographie léonarde de 1600 à 1715." *Bulletin de la Société archéologique de Finistère* 99 (1972/3).

Le Roy Ladurie, Emmanuel. *Histoire de Languedoc.* Paris: Presses universitaires de France, 1967.

Levot, P. *Histoire de la ville et port de Brest.* 2 vols. Brest: Anner, 1864.

Levy, C. F. *Capitalistes et pouvoir au siècle des lumières.* Paris: Mouton, 1969.

Livet, Georges. "Louis XIV et les provinces conquises." *Dix-Septième Siècle* no. 16 (1951).

Mandrou, Robert. *De la culture populaire aux 17ᵉ et 18ᵉ siècles, la bibliothèque bleue de Troyes.* Paris: Stock, 1964.

_____. *Louis XIV en son temps.* Paris: Presses universitaires de France, 1973.

Marion, Marcel. *Dictionnaire des institutions de la France aux 17ᵉ et 18ᵉ siècles.* Paris: Picard, 1923.

Mauclaire, Placide, and Vigoureux, Charles. *Blondel.* Laon: Imprimerie de l'Aisne, 1938.

Mémain, René. *La Marine de guerre sous Louis XIV: Rochefort, arsenal modèle de Colbert.* Paris: Hachette, 1938.

Merrien, Jean. *La Vie quotidienne des marins au temps du roi soleil.* Paris: Hachette, 1964.

Meuvret, Jean. *Etudes d'histoire économique.* Cahiers des Annales, no. 32. Paris: Armand Colin, 1972.

Meyer, Jean. *L'Armement nantais dans la deuxième moitié du dix-huitième siècle.* Paris: SEVPEN, 1966.

Mitard, S. *La Première capitation, 1695–1698.* Rennes: Oberthur, 1934.

Mollat, Michel. "Réflexions sur quelques constantes de l'histoire du Port de Rouen." *Connaître Rouen,* no. 3.

Mousnier, Roland. "L'Evolution des finances publiques en France et en Angleterre pendant les guerres de la ligue d'Augsbourg et de la succession d'Espagne." *Revue historique,* no. 208 (January–March 1951).

_____. *Fureurs paysannes.* Paris: Calmann-Levy, 1967.

_____. "Problèmes de méthode dans l'étude des structures sociales des 16ᵉ, 17ᵉ, et 18ᵉ siècles." *Spiegel der Geschichte: Festgabe fur Max Braubach.* Munster: Aschendorff, 1964.

Olivier-Martin, F. *Histoire du droit français.* Paris: Domat-Montchrestien, 1948.

Parent, Michel, and Verroust, Jacques. *Vauban.* Paris: J. Fréal, 1971.

Parent, P. *L'Architecture civile à Lille au 17ᵉ siècle.* Lille: Raoust, 1925.

Pariset, François-Georges. *Bordeaux au 18ᵉ siècle.* Vol. 5 of *Histoire de Bordeaux.* Edited by Charles Higounet. Bordeaux: Fédération historique du Sud-Ouest, 1968.

Pérouas, Louis. *La Diocèse de La Rochelle de 1648 à 1724.* Paris: SEVPEN, 1964.

Pilgrim, Donald. "The Colbert-Seignelay Naval Reforms and the Beginnings of the War of the League of Augsbourg." *French Historical Studies* 9 (Fall 1975).

Prigent, René. "Les Protestants à Brest après la révocation de l'édit de Nantes." *Mémoire de la Société d'histoire et d'archéologie de Bretagne* 5 (1928).

Rambert, Gaston. *De 1660 à 1789.* Vol. 4 of *Histoire de Commerce de Marseille.* Edited by Gaston Rambert. Paris: Plon, 1954.

Rambert, Gaston. *Marseille, la formation d'une grande cité moderne.* Marseille: S. A. du Sémaphore de Marseille, 1934.

_____. *Nicolas Arnoul, Intendant des galères à Marseille.* Marseille: Provincia, 1931.

Ranum, Orest. *Paris in the Age of Absolutism.* New York: John Wiley and Sons, 1968.

Robin, Régine. *La Société française en 1789: Saumur en Auxois.* Paris: Plon, 1970.

Roger, Paul. "La Vie économique du port de Brest au 18ᵉ siècle." *Revue maritime* 184 (January 1962).

Röthlisberger, Marcel. "Subjects of Claude Gelée's Paintings." *Gazette des Beaux-Arts* (April 1960).

Rothkrug, Lionel. *Opposition to Louis XIV.* Princeton, N.J.: Princeton University Press, 1965.

Rowen, Herbert. "L'Etat c'est à moi: Louis XIV and the State." *French Historical Studies* 2 (Spring 1961).

Rule, John, ed. *Louis XIV and the Craft of Kingship.* Columbus: Ohio State University Press, 1969.

Russo, François. "L'Hydrographie en France aux 17ᵉ et 18ᵉ siècles: écoles et ouvrages d'enseignements." In *Enseignement et diffusion des sciences en France au XVIIIᵉ siècle.* Edited by R. Taton. Paris: Hermann, 1964.

Spengler, Joseph. *French Predecessors of Malthus.* Durham, N.C.: Duke University Press, 1942.

Taillemite, Etienne. "Les Archives et les archivistes de la Marine des origines à 1870." *Bibliothèque de l'Ecole des Chartes* 127 (1969).

―――. "Royal Glories." In *Great Age of Sail.* Edited by Joseph Jobe. New York: Viking Press, 1971.

Tapié, Victor-Louis. "Comment les français voyaient la France: la patrie." *Dix-Septième Siècle,* nos. 25–26 (1955).

Vignols, L. "Le Commerce maritime et les aspects du capitalisme à St. Mâlo, 1680–1792." *Revue d'histoire économique et sociale* 9 (1931).

Vivarès, L. "Le Port de Cette ses origines, sa situation économique, avant et pendant la guerre." *Bulletin de la Société languedocienne de géographie* 40 (1917).

Wallon, H. *Les Phares établis sur les côtes maritimes de la Normandie par la Chambre de Commerce de Rouen et administrées par elle de 1773 à 1791 et leurs transformations au 19ᵉ siècle.* Rouen: Agniard, 1900.

Wolf, John B. *Louis XIV.* New York: W. W. Norton, 1968.

―――. "The Reign of Louis XIV: A Selected Bibliography of Writings since the War of 1914–1918." *Journal of Modern History* 36 (June 1964).

Wolff, Philippe, ed. *Histoire de Languedoc.* Toulouse: Privat, 1967.

Zarb, Mireille. *Les Privilèges de la ville de Marseille.* Paris: Picard, 1961.

Studies in American Urban Development

Bridenbaugh, Carl. *Cities in the Wilderness.* New York: Ronald Press, 1938.

Bureau of Governmental Research. *Plan and Program for the Preservation of the Vieux Carré.* New Orleans, 1968.

Burnham, Daniel H., and Bennett, Edward H. *Plan of Chicago.* Chicago: Commercial Club, 1909.

Committee on Interior and Insular Affiars, United States Senate, "Deepwater Port Policy Issues." Washington, D.C.: U.S. Government Printing Office, Serial no. 93–41 [92–77], 1974.

Condit, Carl. *Chicago, 1910–19.* Chicago: University of Chicago Press, 1973.

Hammer, J. Gordon. "Ocean Installations: State of Technology." In *Coastal Zone Management, Multiple Use with Conservation.* Edited by John F. Brahtz. New York: Wiley-Interscience, 1972.

Lear, John. "Cities on the Sea?" *Saturday Review* (4 December 1971).

Lewis, Emanuel Raymond. *Seacoast Fortifications of the United States.* Washington, D.C.: Smithsonian Institute Press, 1970.

Mann, Marshall; Marcus, Henry S.; Kuypers, John C.; Roberts, Paul O.; and Short, James E. *Federal Port Policy in the United States.* Washington, D.C.: U.S. Department of Transportation DOT–TST–77–41, 1971.

Mann, Roy. *Rivers in the City.* New York: Praeger, 1973.

Marshall, Douglas. "The City in the New World: The Military Contribution." A guide to an exhibition at the William L. Clements Library, University of Michigan. Ann Arbor, 1973.

Nettleton, Arthur. "Cities in the Sea." *Oceans* 5 (March–April 1972).

Price, Jacob. "Economic Function and the Growth of American Port Towns in the Eighteenth Century." In *Perspectives in American History.* Vol. 8. Cambridge, Mass.: Harvard University Press, 1974.

Reps, John. *The Making of Urban America.* Princeton, N.J.: Princeton University Press, 1965.

Saarinen, Eliel. "Project for Lakefront Development of the City of Chicago." *The American Architect* 124, no. 2434 (5 December 1923).

Schonberger, Harold B. *Transportation to the Seaboard.* Westport, Conn.: Greenwood Publishing Co., 1971.

Trachtenberg, Allan; Neill, Peter; and Bunnell, Peter C., eds. *The City: American Experience.* New York: Oxford University Press, 1971.

Warner, Sam Bass, Jr. *The Private City: Philadelphia in Three Periods of Its Growth.* Philadelphia: University of Pennsylvania Press, 1968.

―――. *The Urban Wilderness.* New York: Harper and Row, 1972.

Writers' Program of the Works Project Administration. *A Maritime History of New York.* New York: Doubleday, Doran and Co., 1941.

Index

Library of Congress Cataloging in Publication Data

Konvitz, Josef W
    Cities and the sea.

    Bibliography: p.
    Includes index.
    1. City planning—Europe—History. 2. Harbors—
Europe—History. I. Title.
HT169.E8K66   309.2′62′094   77–12976
ISBN 0–8018–2038–3